ONE MAN PERCHED ON A ROCK

One Man Perched On A Rock

A BIOGRAPHY OF DR. WARREN CARROLL

Laura S. Gossin

Christendom Press
2017

Gossin, Laura S.

One man perched on a rock : a biography of Dr. Warren Carroll / Laura S. Gossin. — Front Royal, VA : Christendom Press, 2017.

pages; cm.

ISBN: 978-0-931888-88-5
Includes bibliographical references and index.

LCSH: Carroll, Warren Hasty. | Catholic historians—Biography. | Catholic intellectuals—Biography. | Christian college teachers—Biography. | Christendom College—History. | Catholic universities and colleges—Virginia—History. | Education, Humanistic—United States. | BISAC: RELIGION / Christianity / Catholic. | RELIGION / Christian Education / General.

BX4705.C3317 G67 2017
282.092

Published in the United States by:
Christendom Press
www.christendom.edu/press

Cover concept by Laura S. Gossin
Cover design by Niall O'Donnell

Manufactured in the United States of America

"What are thirty barbarians perched on a rock? They must inevitably die."

—anonymous Muslim chronicler

The Muslim tide had engulfed the world, and Christendom was dead,
As Pelayo rode on a coal-black horse where another master led,
Along the road to Cordoba, whose towers loomed ahead,
His land all strange and shadowy in silent, nameless dread.

But a Christian hopes in the pit of night, while one star shines on high,
Though the tramp of doom in the dark of the moon be ever drawing nigh,
One shining blade in a last crusade with the Christian battle-cry:
All for Christ and Christ for all in the realm where no men die!

– From Warren H. Carroll's
"The Ballad of the Reconquista"
printed as Appendix IV in
A History of Christendom, vol. 6, *The Crisis of Christendom*

Nobody dies, anywhere, as long as one is left to remember him,
Remember exactly where and how he lived;
What he said
His way of saying it;
What he did;
What he stood for.

— Gladys Hasty Carroll, *Dunnybrook*

To found anything is an awesome thing. To put something into existence that otherwise would never appear is both an act of faith and a rash hope.

— James V. Schall, S.J., regarding Dr. Carroll's founding of Christendom College, made on the occasion of the college's fortieth anniversary

Contents

Prologue

by Warren H. Carroll

FOR YEARS, WHENEVER I was asked if I someday intended to write my autobiography, I said I never would, because I feared it would involve me in the sin of detraction, and because I am not an introspective person. Why have I changed in my old age? I am still not an introspective person, but have reached the age where many memories crowd in upon me. I have finished writing all the books I really want and need to write and so have time for this last one.

My change began one day in early March of 2001, after a predicted foot-plus snowstorm in the Washington area where I live had totally fizzled out, so that I was able to make my twice-weekly trip to the Christendom College campus in Front Royal, Virginia, where I was in my next to last academic year of active teaching. That day I heard superb lectures by Professor Tim Gray, whom I had already tapped to revise the first volume of my history of Christendom, because he is the only real Scripture scholar I had ever known well personally, and by Dr. Jonathan Reyes, to be my successor as head of the Christendom College History Department, on the horrors of the Mexican war for independence, a subject taboo in Mexico, but still Catholic truth in history, which he and I are dedicated to spreading. As I prepared to leave the college that afternoon, I had a conversation with one of my favorite people, Christina Lundborg, the very efficient and lovely personal secretary of my best friend, Dr. Timothy O'Donnell, third president of Christendom College, which I founded and of which I was the first president. Christina was brought up as a Catholic, but fell away from the church for nine years, until she took a trip to Rome with Dr. and Mrs. O'Donnell, who brought her back to the church.

Christina and I were comparing notes on how we had both come to where we were, she as I have just described, I out of a non-Christian background in Maine, brought to the Catholic faith by my dear wife, the daughter of a dry-land farmer who never went to college, who had crossed the prairie from Kansas to Colorado at the age of two on one of the last of the covered wagons. No one would ever have expected that his daughter would marry me and bring me to the Catholic faith to do all that, with God's unfailing help, I have been able to do with it, helping to found educational institutions dedicated to providing a truly Catholic education on three continents—America, Australia, and Europe. So Christina and I marveled together at God's brilliance as a strategist.

Thinking about this some more the next day, I resolved to write my autobiography after all, because I really think this is an extraordinary story of God's deployment of forces against the modernist heresy which almost destroyed his church in the twentieth century, especially its higher education. As He has so often done, God employed and deployed people that the world would never have expected even to be in his service, to do his will and to prove once again that the gates of Hell shall never prevail against the church He founded on the rock of St. Peter (Matthew 16). I hope I can say without immodesty that it put me in mind of the most extraordinary political alliance in history, that God put together to destroy the communist revolution against Him—the alliance of the Polish Pope, the unemployed Polish electrician Lech Walesa, and the Muslim freedom fighters of the mountains of Afghanistan, an alliance which no mortal man could ever have conceived (and which none did conceive), but which God conceived, and which won the victory over godless communism for Him. So I decided that mine was a tale which should be told, and that I should tell it, because God gave me a talent for storytelling.

I pledge at the outset to do all I can to make sure that this book (unlike many autobiographies) is charitable. I will not engage in detraction of anyone in it. Detraction is probably the least known of all the sins, but I know what it is. I will mention the names only of people I wish to praise and in the strongest terms possible I discourage every reader from trying to guess who are the people whose attempts to interfere with my work I describe.

Also at the outset, I want to give all the credit for the good things I have been able to do to God, the sole author of all good—and also a master strategist. I will not be very effective at doing this, because I am not a "spiritual writer," but a hard-headed Yankee from Maine. But I will try.

– Dr. Warren Carroll[1]

Alas, and to the great detriment of us all, Warren Carroll was not able to complete his autobiography. He did, however, complete sketches of certain phases of his life which I will incorporate into the story—his story. Though I have not his family's great gift for "yarning," I will do my best and pledge to carry out his steadfast wish that this story include no detraction.

Laura Gossin
November 22, 2017
Feast of St. Cecilia

---

1. Warren Carroll, "Unpublished Autobiography."

1

The Warren Land Grant

JAMES RAISED HIS HAND to his brow, shading the sun as his eyes scanned up the side of the two-hundred-foot white pine tree in front of him. "Yes, this would do just fine," he thought to himself as he stepped back and hefted his heavy axe high into the air. Heaving it in a downward arc, he felt the contact of the sharp blade with the soft wood reverberate through his strong arms. Again and again, rhythmically he swung, and his mind wandered—back in time, back to another of the King's Pines on the southern Maine coastland. He was much younger then, and he did not fell that pine tree. Rather, he used his skill with an axe to make three precise cuts into the bark in the shape of an arrow. This was the king's mark, and he was serving under the King's Surveyor General of Primeval Forests. This tree, along with any others into which he cut the king's mark, would be used to fashion masts and figureheads for the mighty ships of the English Navy. Eventually, James completed his job, and for his service was given a land grant, the Warren Grant, which would become known as the small hamlet of Dunnybrook in the parish of Berwick, Maine.

Berwick—the name settled into his thoughts as sweat poured down James's forehead and neck, and he stopped swinging his axe long enough to wipe his brow and roll up his sleeves. There was another Berwick—once. Berwick, Scotland, where James had been born. Yet, here he was in the New World, thousands of miles from his homeland. The painful memories flooded his mind, and he resumed his rhythmic swinging. The Battle of Dunbar a mere twenty-eight miles from his home in Scotland, fighting as a royalist for Charles II. The shocking, crushing defeat. Captured as a prisoner of war and marching, marching, marching; all the while men dying of wounds, of disease, of starvation. And then the imprisonment at Durham Cathedral—and more death. But he had survived; one of the lucky ones. Out of the 5,100 or so taken prisoner, he was one of only 1,400 who had survived. Of those survivors, he joined the nine hundred sent as indentured servants to the New World. He was lucky to be blessed with such a strong and rugged constitution.

Whoosh! The breeze whistled through the branches of the tall pine as it crashed to the ground and returned James's thoughts to the present. His own son, also named James, came to his mind, and he leaned on his axe for a rest while a smile tugged at the sides of his weathered mouth. How proud he and his Irish wife, Margaret, were of their James, one of the local selectmen and the youngest of their five children.

* * *

Upon his death in 1702, this same Cavalier James Warren, originally of Berwick, Scotland, would leave all his lands and buildings on the Warren land grant to this son, James, known to their descendants as James the Younger. The Warren family would remain rooted to this piece of land in the southern tip of Maine for many generations. As the years passed, James the Younger had sons and daughters of his own. Homes were passed down and new homes built by the strong hands of fathers and sons. Outsiders became neighbors and neighbors became relatives.

Approximately eighty-three years after the death of Cavalier James Warren, two weary soldiers, one Gilbert Warren and one Joseph Hasty, trudged side by side over the frozen ground on a chill November night, returning to their homes in Dunnybrook from an American victory in her War for Independence.[1] Gilbert was the grandson

---

1. Gladys Hasty Carroll, *Dunnybrook* (Toronto: George J. McLeod Limited, 1943), 17.

of James the Younger, and Joseph was Gilbert's brother-in-law, being married to his sister Abigail. Joseph's father, John Hasty, originally from County Antrim, Ireland, had settled in the neighboring town of York. With the marriage of Joseph to Abigail, the Warrens and the Hastys—once only neighbors—had become united in a family bond. Although this may have been the first entwining of the Warrens and the Hastys, the lines would meet and entangle again in 1865, when Gilbert's great-granddaughter Sarah Jane Brown became the wife of Joseph's great-grandson George Hasty.

Populated by many generations of Warrens and Hastys, the little hamlet of Dunnybrook gathered its inhabitants into the names of its landmarks. Winter after winter, tears were forced out of the eyes of countless Warren and Hasty children by the icy wind as they flew down Warren Hill on their homemade wooden sleds. And in the heat of the summer, splashing in Hasty's Mill Brook or Warren's Pond brought cool relief to these same children—as well as frolicking fun. And if one did not wish to feel the wetness of Warren's Brook upon his person, he simply crossed over it on Warren's Bridge.[2]

As the people formed the land, so the land also formed the people. These were men and women who relied on the land and one another for both livelihood and happiness and, because of these slow and long simmering relationships, had a strong sense of responsibility, goodness, connectedness, and belonging. One Warren ancestor, upon being offered the purchase of a fast horse, reportedly replied, "I don't want no horse, Mr. Wilder. I never had one and I don't want one. But if I did want one, I wouldn't want that one. We don't go nowhere much from where we be; and if we did, we never'd want to go that fast."[3] The type of people to which the Warrens and Hastys belonged might be summed up by one of Berwick's most celebrated authors, Sarah Orne Jewett, whose father, Dr. Jewett, had taken care of all the ills and pains of Sarah Jane Brown, George Hasty, and their children:

---

2. Ibid., 349.

3. Ibid., 86.

> In rustic neighborhoods there will always exist that class
> of country people who preserve the best traditions of cul-
> ture and of manners, from some divine inborn instinct to-
> ward what is simplest and best and purest, who know the
> best because they themselves are kin to it.[4]

This sense of belonging and of passing down to the next generation what one had preserved intact also inspired the grand tradition of
storytelling, especially well cultivated in one Columby Brown, grandson of Gilbert Warren and uncle to Sarah Jane Brown. The tradition
seems to have skipped Sarah's generation, but shown up again strongly
in her son Warren Hasty. One such conversation has been passed down
in the Warren-Hasty family according to this oral tradition and takes
place around the year 1890, between Francis Dow, who eventually
became Warren's wife, and Warren's sister Vinnie. The young Francis
is shyly inquiring about Warren's personality traits:

> "Which one is—your brother like?" Frances asked low.
>
> "A little like both. But more like Uncle Joe than either
> one of them, though I don't think he's especially adventur-
> ous. There's a lot of Uncle Columby in Warren."
>
> "Only Warren's so tall—"
>
> "That's the Hasty of it. . . . Warren's built like the
> Hastys, I guess; but he walks and talks and smiles like the
> Warrens. He's got as good a mind as father's, but he doesn't
> work it so hard. He doesn't care so much about getting a
> lot done as he does about doing what he does exactly right.
> . . . And Warren likes a good time. That may be partly
> his age, but I shouldn't wonder if he always would; and
> father never did, from all I hear. Uncle Joe laughs at father.
> He says he was born with his nose to the grindstone, and
> never weaned—"

---

4. Ibid., 341–342.

"You aren't like that."

"I am a little. I have my best times when I'm really accomplishing something. I can't bear to sit with my hands folded. You saw how I had to bring in my crocheting even while I was listening to you tonight. I could no more stay a whole evening over at Uncle Columby's, just yarning and listening to yarns, the way Warren does—"

"I kind of wonder at your folks letting him go off over there so much—and stay so late. Don't they worry about him? I've heard my grandfather say he wondered what works went on there every night. Something, he says, calls 'em—"

"If we wondered," Vinnie said, almost sharply, "we'd go to see. But we don't wonder. We know what calls 'em."

"It's Uncle Columby. Boys that know him would rather be with him than anywhere else there is to go, by night; and always would. He's like a magnet to them. That's because he's got a boy's heart, and still he is an old man and can tell them things they want to know. He doesn't preach, but he does teach. Night after night, year after year, he holds class over there, under his maples when it's warm enough and in his kitchen when it's cold. Boys learn life fast and learn it easy with Uncle Columby. I don't know of any place we'd rather Warren went."[5]

If it was true that Warren Hasty loved to sit at the feet of old Columby Brown and take in his "yarns," his sister Vinnie was more akin to Uncle Columby than she probably realized, for it had been her dream to attend high school (something most girls from Dunnybrook were not accustomed to doing) and then to become a teacher herself. And by walking the six miles to Salmon Falls High School and home every day, past the Warren graveyard and over Warren's Bridge, she accomplished her dream. She may not have taught boys

5. Ibid., 361–362.

"under the maple" as Columby did, but she nonetheless had the desire to pass on what had been preserved to the next generation. One of Vinnie's oldest students was Frances Dow, a descendant of another of Dunnybrook's old and established families, and because they were not that different in age, they became fast friends. It was these two who had been discussing Uncle Columby Brown's stories and their effect on the young Warren Hasty. Many a happy evening Frances spent at Vinnie's home singing and playing the organ—for there was always music in the Hasty home—and Warren sat quietly by.

Warren Hasty married Frances Dow in 1893, and during the next eleven years, this Hasty home was gladdened by the birth of their two children, Harold and Gladys. Once again was Uncle Columby's presence felt, this time in young Gladys who inherited the gift of storytelling. Through her pen, the family's wealth of oral tradition—including actual conversations handed down from generation to generation—would eventually be put into print. As a young girl, Gladys was always encouraged in this tradition by all living members of her family. When she was seven years old, her Uncle Joe Brown came to live with her immediate family in the house her great-grandfather had built. One day, while walking together amongst the whistling pines and trembling poplars not far from the house, Uncle Joe declared to Gladys,

> I will make a table where you can sit and write your stories; and when they are done, Aunt Louie and I will sit in our cushioned white-birch chairs and listen while you read them to us. And Aunt Louie will say, "Why, Gladie, how do you think up such things?" But I will tell her, "Have you forgot, Louie? This young one is a Warren. They have to yarn. It's in the blood."[6]

Next to Sarah Orne Jewett, Gladys Hasty would become Berwick's second famous author, writing, among her many works, the captivating

---

6. Ibid., 381.

history of the families of her beloved Dunnybrook. In her preparation for this feat, she did something no one else in either line of the family had ever done. Gladys went to college. It is a tribute to the importance the family placed on education that these subsistence-level farmers were willing to make the sacrifices needed for this to happen. Gladys herself recorded this conversation between her Grandfather George and her Aunt Vinnie on the subject:

> George Hasty would come by his first sincere respect for higher education when Vinnie told him, "Gladie was awarded a scholarship of several hundred dollars at her graduation from the Academy today. But it can be used only if she goes to college. Otherwise it will be wasted." ... George would clear his throat and say, "Then we will put enough with what she's got so she can go to college. But mind she wastes none of it."[7]

Even then, with nothing, the family's commitment to developing the mind and creativity was very strong.

In 1922, during Gladys's sophomore year at Bates College (a short train ride from her home), she met Herbert Carroll, seven years her senior. By the end of her sophomore year, they were secretly engaged, and upon Gladys's graduation in 1925, they were married. Herbert Allen Carroll hailed from the state of Massachusetts, where his parents, Charles and Ina, had raised nine children. Ina (a descendant of Ethan Allen) is described as "thin and proper" in contrast to her husband, who had a "big, open smile telling you 'life is good!'"[8] On Charles's side, the family was of Irish descent. His father, Robert, came directly from Ireland and was a Catholic. Robert's wife, however, was a protestant, and when Robert died at the Battle of Cedar Creek during the American Civil War, she chose to raise her children in her own faith.

---

7. Ibid., 384.
8. Caroline Jones, niece of Warren Carroll, interview by author, 9 July 2013.

There is a very interesting story recorded by Gladys in which her great Uncle Joe Brown (the same who in his old age had promised to build her a desk for writing) not only met, but became good friends with, Charles Carroll—the father of her future husband. As a younger man, Joe Brown had gotten a job in a Boston plant that manufactured steam shovels. After working at the plant for nearly a year, he was selected to travel the country to designated locations awaiting the arrival of new steam shovels. It was then his job to choose a crew and train the men in the proper operation of the new equipment. As Gladys tells the story:

> Setting up steam shovels to build the Boston-Fitchburg railroad, Joe Brown met two of the thousands of people he was never to forget and who would never forget him. One was a tall, broad, big-fisted boy, with bright-blue eyes and curly, red-gold hair, known as Charlie to the big crew of Italian laborers of whom he was in charge. Joe never heard his other name. They were Joe and Charlie to each other. Charlie was big-fisted, but he had only one fist. Still in his early twenties, he was supporting a wife and two little children with one arm, a shoulder harness to which a stout steel hook was attached, his inherited Irish wit, and his native American courage. The other arm had been taken off by railroad coaches which it was his job that day to join together by dropping in a coupling pin at the precise instant that they touched.
>
> "For once I was too slow," grinned Charlie. "They pinned me instead of my pinning them. I ought to have been ashamed of myself. And I was."
>
> . . . He was very young to be a boss, Joe thought. But Charlie's head was as old and wise as his heart was young and his tongue was merry; and dark men twice his age who could not understand a word he said, knew what he wanted from his eyes and his voice and his gestures and did what he wanted because they trusted him and loved him. . . . It

was a fine thing to find a man you could really talk to. This pair talked late into every night, for both had much to tell.

Charlie had brought himself up. He had never been to school a year, all told. But before he was eighteen, he had spent months in Michigan as a member of a survey-ing crew and could tell stories of adventure with hos-tile Indians and bears and snakes. Before he was twenty, he had married the daughter of a druggist in Palmer, Massachusetts; she was only sixteen then, a little thing with brown eyes and a pouting mouth; she did not stand nearly to Charlie's shoulder. Ina her name was. Ina was used to a very different life than Charlie's; that Palmer house from which he had taken her had a room where you could not see the walls for books and another room that was painted from floor to ceiling all around with woodland scenes—trees and birds and flowers and run-ning brooks. Ina had a piano there while with Charlie there was only Charlie's fiddle and he could not play even that for her now.[9]

Gladys then marvels at her own history:

That Gladys, at Bates College deep in Maine, would meet Herbert Carroll of Greenfield, Massachusetts, veteran of World War I, and marry him at her Commencement. . . . And that the first time she went home with him she would talk long with her new father-in-law on a porch overlook-ing three states and five counties, and she would tell him of Uncle Joe because she knew these two would have liked each other. . . . And Charles Carroll, [the] big, sandy-haired, merry, blue-eyed man who had lost an arm while working on the railroad when he was young, and wore a hook in his sleeve, would look at her strangely and say, "Why, child, you can't tell me anything about your Uncle

---

9.   Gladys Hasty Carroll, *Dunnybrook*, 345–347.

Joe. I knew him. . . . Ina! Ina! You remember that Joe I used to tell you about, that was setting up steam shovels for us the spring Josie was born? Well, by gorry, he was uncle to Gladys here. His last name was Brown. . . . I always wished I knew Joe's last name."[10]

With such a sense of rootedness and belonging to a particular group of people in a particular area of the country, it is hard to believe that Gladys and Herbert Carroll brought their first child into the world approximately 1,500 miles away, in Minneapolis, Minnesota—but they did; the reason being Herbert's job as a professor of educational psychology at the University of Minnesota. The year was 1932, which was a red-letter year for the Carroll's in two ways, for it was in this year that Gladys completed her first full-length novel, *As The Earth Turns*, and that their first child, a son, was born. They named him Warren Hasty Carroll in honor of his maternal grandfather and promptly christened him Renny.

Gladys was a warm and caring mother from the start and absolutely enveloped her darling Renny in love. She genuinely loved and delighted in being with her child as can be seen in the letters she penned at the time. To a friend, she wrote:

> You know what an effort it has been for me to get up in the morning ever since I was a child, even at eight o' clock or later. But do I ever hustle out of bed with glee at six o'clock these mornings! Why? Because our son is going to smile at me! Wonderful as his smiles are the rest of the day, they are never with quite such sheer delight as the first thing in the morning. I'm never in bed at night before eleven and usually it is nearer twelve, but I guess I don't need as much sleep as I used to for I am always wide awake at six, so happy that it is time to go and see if

---

10. Ibid., 385.

Renny may be awake. If he isn't, I sneak away and wait—
as I am doing now.[11]

In another letter she confesses, "Have I said enough about our
baby? He looms so large in our lives that we hardly notice anything else
even if it does happen!"[12] One can naturally expect of any new mother
such a sense of joy and love for a firstborn, but this devotion towards
her vocation of motherhood evidently did not diminish in any way
throughout Warren's life, for he would later claim that "My mother
was one of the two women who shaped my life."[13] *As The Earth Turns*
became an immediate bestseller, and its author would go on to write
many more such books, but it was her family that would forever remain
at the heart and very center of her life.

Though the young family of Carrolls was devoted to one another
and imbued with a strong sense of goodness, an organized faith played
no role in their lives. In Warren's words,

> My mother did not belong to any church and did not re-
> ally understand Christianity, because in our rural Maine
> community the protestant churches had fought each other
> so ferociously that her father advised my mother to stay
> away from all of them, though she was influenced all her
> life by her admiration for a Baptist minister named Ze-
> bulon Knight, whom I am convinced by everything she
> told me about him was very close to God. So she brought
> me up unchurched and without the benefit of any orga-
> nized Christian doctrine, but always believing in God and
> an afterlife, and knowing that something very important
> happened on the first Christmas day, though I was never
> quite sure what it was. My father was agnostic, though
> thank God he had been baptized as a young man, and I

11. Gladys Hasty Carroll, *Years Away From Home* (Boston: Little, Brown and Com-
    pany, 1971), 284–285.
12. Ibid., 298.
13. Carroll, "Unpublished Autobiography."

do believe (and hope and pray, now) that he always retained some of the grace of the sacrament. Despite his lack
of formal belief, he was one of the most charitable men I
have ever known, who always wanted to help people and
treated hundreds of patients (he always called them cli-
ents) without any charge when he began to practice clini-
cal psychology later.[14]

While being absolutely devoted to their firstborn, both Herbert
and Gladys found time to exercise their gifts for writing. In addition
to teaching his regular classes, Herbert wrote articles and gave lectures on the topic of psychology, which would eventually culminate
in a published textbook on the subject. Gladys, in the meantime, was
negotiating with Warner Brothers over the movie rights to her highly
successful novel. Success, however, was not what the young family
pursued—at least not in the way that the world perceives—and when
young Renny was three years old, they returned to Gladys's beloved
hometown in Maine. Warren stated that his father suffered from an
affliction of his eyes which "meant that for much of his professional
life he could do little reading."[15] He also remembers that

> The last book he [Herbert] ever read all the way through,
> Douglas Southall Freeman's splendid four-volume biogra-
> phy of Robert E. Lee, he gave to me since he could no lon-
> ger read it, which I kept until Christendom College was
> launched, when I donated it along with most of my other
> books to start its library.... He also suffered from excruci-
> ating migraine headaches. Though without any remaining
> religion, he knew the Bible from his youth. I remember
> his saying once, when his suffering became particularly
> acute, "Just call me Job."[16]

14. Carroll, "Unpublished Autobiography."

15. Ibid.

16. Ibid.

God's providential care, which Warren would come to believe in so strongly, was watching over the little family, and Warren describes how Herbert's eye problem played its role:

> The affliction of his eyes forced him to relinquish his teaching position at the University of Minnesota in 1936, three years after my mother's success with her first novel put us in comfortable financial circumstances. This made it possible for us to move back to Maine where her heart had always been and where her parents were still living. She and my father designed and built a home on the site of the Warren Garrison House, originally built by my ancestor Cavalier James Warren. It was on a small hill, surrounded by broad fields belonging to a neighbor named Earle (who gave his name to the little dirt road that ran between my grandparents' home and ours) whom my mother had persuaded reluctantly to sell her the land on top of the hill as a house lot.[17]

That they would return to her beloved home, established so long ago and containing so much history and so many memories, is a thing Gladys too recounts in her touching manner as she marvels on the fact

> That they would come back to Dunnybrook to build on the site of the first Warren Garrison a house of stone and beams and brick collected from all the old cellarholes . . . with doorsteps from the old Hamilton-Brooks house and the old Nason house, doors from the John Brown house, stairway panels from the pews of the Advent Church where Dows had worshipped. . . . That John Brown's pegging awl would come to the beam above their kitchen fireplace, and the gourd which had grown in Jim the Younger and Mary Warren's basket-bottomed chair the last sum-

---

17. Ibid.

mer they lived in the Old Garrison would come again to hang on the brown pine wall, and Columby's iron teakettle would sing on the crane, and Granville Hasty's daughter Ethel and her husband Len would send down from York Road for the back bedroom the fireplace frame which had been in the room where old Joseph Hasty died and where little Emma Chadbourne had proffered in vain her white Scotch rose.... That all the books Sarah Orne Jewett had once given to Judge Doe's wife, affectionately inscribed by the author, would be sent up by Jessie Doe to live on the shelves George Hasty had built for Sarah Jane to keep hers in.... [and] that Herbert Carroll would become professor of psychology at the University of New Hampshire, so near to Dunnybrook that he could drive there from home to meet his classes.[18]

And so, into this tightly-knit town of Dunnybrook, later to be christened South Berwick, with such a solid sense of its own history, entered Warren Hasty Carroll, son of Gladys Hasty and Herbert Carroll.

---

18. Gladys Hasty Carroll, *Dunnybrook*, 386–387.

2

"I Intend to Do Both"

"I HAD BEGUN TO 'write'," says Warren, "by dictating stories to my mother when I was only six years old."[1] Happily, two of these first "stories" have been preserved by the ever-diligent Gladys and are presented below in their original and delightfully child-like form:

MY LIFE

When I was four years old I took a trip to Europe. First I went to London then I went to Kesic and then I went to Windemere. Windemere was very cold. One night I had to go to the bathroom. There were no lights in my room. We lit ourselves into the bathroom with a candle. Next we went to (at last Paris) WE stayed there almost too long. Then we went to the loving place Montrex. Then we went to two other places in Switzerland. Then we went to Vesbarden. Then we went to Lacan. Then we went to Amsterdam Holland There we saw many canals and tug-boats going through them. Then we took a plane to England. Then we took the Queen Mary home. When I was five years old I didn't do anything special all except until autumn in the year 1937 when I had such a lovely time

---

1. Carroll, "Unpublished Autobiography."

saying good-bye to the summer things that I can still see it in my mind.

MY OLD CAR

Long ago Yimminy owned a garage. he sold little thing cars. One day I went into his garage and said, "I would like a car which would last me a long time and I want the brakes to be as right as you have! Yimminy said, "here is a nice one which will last you until you are 22. The brakes are very tight. I think you would like to buy it." I said, "fine! How much is it." Yimminy said. "only 47c I said "I will buy it." Yimminy said, "alright." At that time I was 13 years old. (as I pretendid) then I took my car and drove home. Now I am 16 and a half and I still have that car. an awful lot of people say my old car is a "silly dumpling." I say "it is a lovely old car." I think that you are dumplings too!

END

Written
Nov. 29, 1938

Already we can see in the little Renny sparks that would one day enable him to master the art of making history come alive both in the spoken and in the written word. Although highly concerned with getting the facts straight ("we went here and then we went there"), he had a yearning to yarn ("Yimminy sells little thing cars"). By the time he was eight years old, his rudimentary writing skills had evidently been developed well enough, under the watchful care of his mother, to catch the eye of a radio show host, one A.E. Barnard, who read one of Renny's stories over the airwaves on his program devoted to young artists. Although the story itself is not extant, there is a small excerpt quoted in a letter from Barnard to Gladys which portrays the literary skills of the eight-year-old:

"I don't remember very clearly," said Alley Oop, even more sleepily, "because I didn't have my eyes open when we came away. But I remember what you have told me about it."

"I was just thinking," said Wizard of Oz, stretching. "It was very sad we had to come away, and I wonder if we could ever get back again."

"Oh, we never could, I don't believe," said Alley Oop. "We're very far from Mexico."

"We might try," said Wizard of Oz, wide awake now.[2]

Not only was the story in its entirety a hit with the radio audience, as documented in further correspondence to Gladys from Barnard, but Barnard strongly urged Gladys to pursue the publishing avenue for her budding writer:

> As I told you over the phone, there was considerable comment on the story and all of it favorable. I was tremendously surprised that there was so much discussion, both as to grown-up and child reaction.
>
> Though there are probably few stories by juveniles which should be given publication, I think this is an exception. Its ability to hold a child's interest, its smooth running and enjoyable style, are sufficient reason in my opinion as to why it is worthy of publication strictly on its own merit, even without any reference to the age of its author. I do not profess to be an authority on literature of any type, but I do know from experience in radio storytelling that I have read published juvenile stories by grown-ups which have considerably less merit than this one.[3]

---

2. A. E. Barnard to Mrs. Herbert Carroll, 23 February 1940, Box 7-2B, Folder 2, Archive Collection, Caroline Jones, South Berwick, ME.
3. Ibid., 14 March 1940.

It also seems from the correspondence that Renny was later interviewed on the radio show and possibly narrated another story of his own creation on the program at the close of the interview.

Choosing the characters of the Wizard of Oz and Alley Oop for this particular piece of writing would have come naturally to the young Warren, as he was read to constantly and would have been familiar with Frank L. Baum's *Oz* series, published in the 1900–1920s, as well as the comic strip character of Alley Oop, which ran in newspapers beginning in 1932. Reading was and had been an extremely important part of Warren's heritage for as long as anyone in the family could remember. Although Cavalier James Warren would not have been able to sit on a deck chair perusing a magazine on his trans-Atlantic crossing due, among other things, to the fact that he could not read, his son, James the Younger, brought up in rural Maine in the late 1600s, learned to read—quite an accomplishment given his circumstances. He must have wanted it pretty badly. Tucked away in a corner of the family's attic was an old trunk which passed into the hands of Warren, and from him, to his niece Carrie. It contained a dusty and faded collection of headline newspapers. The top one read "Man Lands on the Moon." The one on the bottom carried the headline "Lincoln Assassinated!" Such a collection, carefully preserved in an attic trunk, illustrates what the family prized.[4] Carrie reports that her grandmother, Gladys, read aloud to her right up until the time she had her own children and, after that, her Uncle Renny read, whenever possible, to her children. It is probably just a slight exaggeration to say that, almost before he could walk, the little Renny was encouraged to "read, read, *read*!" And, following in those footsteps, to "write, write, *write*!"[5]

From Renny's own early writings we have seen that sitting on his mother's lap and listening to a good story was not his only form of exposure to the larger world—at the age of four he was taken on

---

4. Caroline Jones, interview by author.

5. Anne Carroll, wife of Dr. Warren Carroll, interview by author, 15 November 2012.

a European vacation. Warren recalled this trip again, this time as a grown man:

> In the fall of 1936, we went to Europe, our first and only trip there as a family. I was only four years old, and since then my memories of what I actually saw and experienced on it became inextricably entangled with my mother's stories about it, so it is hard for me today to say what in my memory is actual memory and what is hearsay. But let me repeat one story my mother often told, which I must admit I do not remember except from her frequent retellings of it: of my personal encounter with the supreme evil of 1936, Nazism. It was my first brush with history.
>
> As my mother told the story, our family was riding in a train in Germany. Neither my mother nor I spoke any German, my father just a few words. A German riding in the train wanted to entertain me. He was carrying a book or magazine or newspaper full of pictures of soldiers, very popular in militaristic Germany in that year. He kept showing them to me and saying, in one of his few words of English: "Soldier! Soldier! Look, look, soldier!"
>
> Finally I looked him up and down and answered, in no uncertain terms (I have always had a tendency to speak very definitely): "I'm not much interested in soldiers." It was my personal protest against an evil far greater than I could ever have comprehended then. And it began a very important part of my boyhood, following the Second World War from beginning to end, which remained so vivid in my mind that when my teaching career finally came to a close, I chose "Recent American History" (from 1939 to 2000) as one of the last two courses I would teach along with "The Pontificate of John Paul II."
>
> My own actual memories of Europe in 1936 are confined to a few scenes: our trip by plane (our first air travel) across the English Channel from England to France (what I mainly remember is how cold it was, because the heater

didn't work). Many years later, I recalled this memory in a footnote in my book *The Last Crusade* describing the flight of General Franco from the Canary Islands to Morocco to lead the Catholic uprising in Spain in 1936. I have always regretted that I was too young to know anything about this epic of Catholic heroism even though I was actually in Europe when it was going on; my parents paid no attention to it and naturally never thought of taking me to tumultuous and bloody Spain.

Other scenes from Europe in 1936 which I remember were the view of the blue mountains across Lake Geneva from the resort city of Montreux in Switzerland where we were staying (which I actually recognized when I finally went back there in my forties) and our riding in a car through the English lake district and stopping repeatedly to ask directions for Windermere, to which the response always was "Straight on!," the first word being pronounced in the English fashion "strite," which sounded very strange to an American boy.

We returned to Maine by ocean liner (then the only way to go; Lindbergh's history-making flight had happened less than ten years before) at the end of the year. My father was very seasick all the way over and back, but I do not recall being affected by the sea at all. But I was very glad to be home, for I had come to love Maine as my mother always had.[6]

If Warren had an innate sense of evil upon meeting a German soldier at the age of four, he also had a clear idea very early of what constituted a worthwhile education. In 1938, Warren's father got the chance to study with Leta Hollingworth, an eminent psychologist in New York City, and the little family moved. Realizing he had a potentially brilliant son, Herbert enrolled Warren in the liberal and

---

6. Carroll, "Unpublished Autobiography."

progressive Horace Mann School, an experimental school which seemed to have as its motto "let the little darlings do whatever they want." Warren was placed in the second grade. "My experience of this educational anarchy stayed with me always," said Warren. "It was best symbolized the day when my mother asked me, 'What did you learn today?' and I answered, without the slightest feeling I was saying anything unusual or surprising, 'Why, nothing; I've been to school.' The main thing I remember doing at Horace Mann School was 'building' a wooden boat that wouldn't stay upright."[7]

Rather than fooling around with unseaworthy wooden ships, Warren was much more interested in things such as the word "decillion," as manifested in a personal reply to him from the office of the president of the University of New Hampshire. The president, obviously a friend of Herbert's who was teaching there at the time, replied to a question of Warren's:

> As far as I can find out now, the word decillion is a name for a number as large as men seem to care to go in giving a short name to a number.... If you start with a billion, certain large numbers are given the following short names: billion (a thousand millions), trillion (a thousand billions), quadrillion (a thousand trillions), quintillion, sextillion, septillion, octillion, nonillion, decillion. These I have heard you repeat, and so I have added little to what you already know.... If I am able to gather any more facts regarding the last number named, I shall send it on to you.[8]

Not content with simply *reading* such a reply, little Renny's attempt to actually *write* such a number is scrawled across the bottom of the note. The first attempt, begun in the middle of the page, ran out of room for so many zeros, so it is crossed out. The second attempt,

7. Ibid.
8. "Uncle Vritz" to Warren (Renny) Carroll, 5 January 1938, Archive Collection, Caroline Jones.

beginning far to the left of the page, succeeds. So much for progressive education! It seems as though Renny was receiving his true education at home, sparked by his own curiosity and constant stimulation from his parents. How apropos for a man who was to find his life's work in the founding of a college to have a strong sense, *by the age of six*, of what it takes to stir up a desire *to know* in the human heart!

If he had definite ideas of what kind of education he did not like, he also knew and was grateful for real, common sense truths:

> I was delighted when we left this chaos to return to Maine and to be placed in the third grade of South Berwick Central School, where my teacher was as far removed from the types I had known at Horace Mann as could have been imagined: an old Maine "battle-axe," Mrs. Shorey, was known for "giving the ruler" to rowdy students, which meant hitting the palms of their hands hard with a ruler. This would undoubtedly horrify modern Americans, but after a year of Horace Mann anarchy, I thought it was just great. That is how I learned to appreciate the rule of law. For about a year, I rejoiced in being back in Maine, where things made sense. I have always believed common sense to be the most important of all mental qualities. My wife, Anne, possesses it, in spades. I first learned it from my mother and my grandfather—and from Mrs. Shorey.[9]

This quality was evidently deeply ingrained in Warren's father as well, for in the 1960s when college campuses were being turned upside down by radical teenagers and young twenty-somethings, Herbert walked into his classroom, faced down the students, and calmly but firmly stated, "You are going to learn in my class." He gained the upper hand and proceeded to teach them just as he had taught young people for countless years.[10]

---

9. Carroll, "Unpublished Autobiography."
10. Anne Carroll, interview by author, 15 November 2012.

It was about this same time, when the family had moved back to Maine after Herbert's year of study in New York, that an incident occurred which has since proven to be quite prophetic. Again, in Warren's words:

> This involves Dr. Fred Engelhardt, then president of the University of New Hampshire in Durham, who had hired my father to head its psychology department, the two men having been friends since they had been at the University of Minnesota together. Dr. Engelhardt periodically visited us at our home in South Berwick and took a considerable interest in me. Once he asked me: "Do you plan to be a teacher like your father or a writer like your mother?" I responded: "I don't think either one is enough; I intend to do both." And I have.[11]

In 1936, Gladys and Herbert suffered the tragedy of losing their second child at birth. Warren's sister and only other sibling, Sally, was welcomed into the close-knit little family five years later in 1941. By this time, Gladys had become an established author, eventually publishing four works of nonfiction, a collection of short stories, and fourteen works of fiction, along with numerous articles. The rights to make a movie of her first novel, *As the Earth Turns*, had been bought by Warner Brothers. Herbert also was in the business of publishing, having completed a college text in the field of mental hygiene which continued to be used in colleges for years. After founding the psychology department at the University of New Hampshire, he became head of the student counseling service and first president of the New Hampshire Psychological Association. This happy family, devoted to intellectual and creative pursuits, continued to live in the home they had lovingly built just across the lane from Gladys's parents on the old Warren grant. And once there, they stayed put "for nearly twenty years with old pine-paneled walls, four fireplaces, exposed beams,

---

11. Carroll, "Unpublished Autobiography."

open chambers, corner cupboards, kitchen garden, sheep, chickens, dogs, and cats."[12]

Besides being completely devoted to the welfare of her family, and her passion for writing, Gladys's life was driven by the goal of making a contribution to humanity. Shortly after moving back to Maine, she began to direct a local folk play based on her novel in which all the parts were played by local neighbors. Warren himself had a small part in the play and retained vivid memories for his whole life, calling it the "center of his childhood."

> Every summer we presented several performances; they were hailed by drama and literary critics all over the nation. Sinclair Lewis came to one of them and was deeply moved by the powerful though untutored acting of our neighbor Len Hooper as mother's character Mark Shaw in the most dramatically powerful scene in the play, which I always remembered.[13]

Other than meandering amongst the many patrons' cars parked in their field and recording the different license plates, what possibly struck the young boy the most is what his mother did with the money gathered from these neighborhood plays. "The proceeds of these productions restored the neighborhood church and parsonage, bought the deserted district schoolhouse and made it into a community center, brought in electric power, and provided educational, musical, and social advantages as well as such utilities as fire extinguishers for every home."[14] Young Warren was deeply affected by "how often my mother stated that I should make the primary goal of my life to 'make a contribution' to humanity. That had been her goal since college days. She was the lodestar of my early life."[15]

---

12. Gladys Hasty Carroll, *Years Away From Home* (Boston, MA: Little Brown and Company, 1971), 371.
13. Carroll, "Unpublished Autobiography."
14. Gladys Hasty Carroll, *Years Away from Home*, 371
15. Carroll, "Unpublished Autobiography."

Besides the influence of his mother and the Maine rural virtues of common sense, honesty, making your own way, and helping your neighbor, two books in particular had an influence on Warren's developing character and helped to form his worldview. The first of these was *The Song of Bernadette* by Franz Werfel. "I loved it," he says, "though I did not quite know what to make of it. I especially admired St. Bernadette's doughty champion Father Marie-Dominique Peyramale. This was no accident. My mother had no Catholic inclinations, but I am convinced that God wanted me to hear that story when I was young."[16] The other work was C. S. Lewis' space trilogy, of which he read the first two at the age of eleven:

> I loved them passionately. I still have my copy of *Out of the Silent Planet* inscribed in my childish scrawl "QUEEN OF BOOKS." Lewis' strategy, in these books, was to present the Christian universe without saying it is Christian. I had never encountered the Christian universe before and found myself longing to be a part of it. Lewis was published by Macmillan, also my mother's publisher. One of its editors learned from my mother of my devotion to Lewis' books and told him about it. He responded, on March 13, 1944: "I'm delighted to get a *boy* reader for my planet books; only boys really take such stories exactly as they're meant." Alas, when I grew older and finally realized that Lewis was talking about Christianity, I was so prejudiced against it that I decided that I must have been mistaken in liking the books so much. But I never forgot the alluring charm of the worldview he so well presented, and years later, when I began to look into Christianity due to the prayers of my wife, I went first to Lewis, because I remembered him so well, and by then knew that he was a famous Christian apologist.[17]

---

16. Ibid.
17. Ibid.

By this time, Warren was attending South Berwick Central School, an experience which he terms "rather undistinguished."[18] World War II was coming to an end and, upon the victory over Japan, he was able to add an issue of *Time* magazine to the old attic chest with the cover featuring the "rising sun" of Japan with a big black X through it. Warren had been intensely interested in the war and had followed it "with the greatest of care from beginning to end."[19]

Upon entering high school at Berwick Academy, the oldest high school in Maine, Warren would make the acquaintance of the second person to profoundly influence his writing. A Catholic of Irish extraction, Marie Donahue taught English at Berwick Academy. Warren explains her effect upon him: "Up to this point my novelist mother had been my only guide and inspiration for writing. . . . Miss Donahue was very impressed with my writing. She was a very gentle and good person and has remained a lifelong friend. I send her one of the first copies of each of my books as it is published."[20]

Writing was not his only interest, however, for the pursuits of astronomy, biology, and baseball had become high on his list of "loves." In May of 1949, shortly before his high school graduation, he had written a letter to the editor of *Astounding Science Fiction* magazine which he began as follows: "Dear Mr. Campbell: Doubtless you are not surprised to see another letter coming from this hack, yours truly, but I simply have to unload science-fiction on somebody, and you seem to be my only hope. So here goes."[21] Warren first commends the November edition for being "entirely adequate, wonderful in spots and thoroughly satisfactory everywhere," while lamenting that "the endings of some of the stories detracted from their effectiveness."[22] He then proceeds to rate each story from the previous issue. His ratings range

---

18. Ibid.
19. Ibid.
20. Ibid.
21. Warren Carroll, letter to the editor of *Astounding Science Fiction*, edited by John W. Campbell, Jr., Vol. XLIII, No. 3, May 1949, 146, Box 4-9A, Folder 13, Archive Collection, Caroline Jones.
22. Ibid.

from "wonderful, an absorbing, interesting, and thrillingly original piece of work," to "adequate enough," to "averagely good." A few excerpts portray his critiquing skills at this time:

> Instead of a grand organization of intelligent entities fighting and winning their war against the encroachments of tyranny, we have a whole galaxy, with all its worlds, represented as only a pawn on a colossal chessboard, which can be saved only by the sole action of one man. Gosseyn can save the galaxy only with his brain, but this keeps jumping from body to body like a demented jackrabbit. I always thought chess was a rather dull and discouraging business anyway.[23]
>
> "The Love of Heaven:" This was adequate enough, but there was too much time spent on the man and his dog and too little on the mighty story of the intruder. Besides, I have never liked stories of such utter and final failure.[24]

It is interesting that, before coming to any belief in Christianity or even in God, Warren inherently rebelled against an "utter and final failure," an outcome that is the exact opposite of the virtue of Christian hope.

Although not particularly athletically gifted, Warren followed in his father's footsteps as a lover of baseball and an avid Red Sox fan. He also played on the Berwick Academy baseball team for all four years of high school. He got up to bat only twice, but he didn't care. He just loved the game and loved being on the team. Warren believed not in his own glory, but in what was best for the team. He knew there were better players than him, but was confident in himself and in his own gifts. He respected both his own gifts and those of others, and as a result, there was not a jealous bone in his body. He had a great appreciation for the talents of others.[25]

---

23. Ibid., 147.
24. Ibid.
25. Anne Carroll, interview by author, 15 November 2012.

That he had tremendous gifts of his own is well documented in his high school yearbook, where he is described as "representing the brains of the class." According to the yearbook, his main interests at that time were "scientific" and "arguing." Nicknamed "slim," described as "quiet and friendly," and noted for "numerous club presidencies," his accomplishments included class vice president in his sophomore year, member of the student legislature in his senior year, debating club president senior year, member of the science club all four years, and editor-in-chief of the school yearbook. Not limited to the intellectual pursuits (and then there was baseball), Warren garnered a leading role in his senior play, a comedy entitled "Swing Fever" in which he played "the sophisticated dean of men at Strafford College," and was noted for his "amazing talent for acting!" His classmates considered him most likely to succeed in the field of science, while on the page entitled "Sketches," where assorted seniors are described as "going to . . . get married, crack up, the asylum, church, be an old maid" and such, Warren is described as going to be . . . "great."[26]

The crowning achievement, scholastically speaking, of his high school education was most probably his valedictory address entitled "The Promise of Our Times." In this address and in an essay he wrote for the literary section of the yearbook, his central theme was that the greatest danger the world was facing at the time was communism—the greatest threat to democracy and human freedom. Far from recommending a reaction of fear to this threat, Warren stressed hope, for he believed that "it is a profound and unshakable truth, as old as life itself, that a race and a people reach their greatest heights, and advance most rapidly, when facing adversity."[27] "If men and women of the present and of the future resolve to uphold democracy as their beacon," he thundered, "no force on earth can defeat our purpose. The organized might of a people fighting with heart and soul to retain

26. Warren Carroll, "Berwick Academy Quamphegan," editor Warren Carroll, 1949, Box 5-3, Folder 29, Archive Collection, Caroline Jones.

27. Warren Carroll, "The Promise of Our Times," Berwick Academy, South Berwick, ME, 1949.

their way of life has in the overwhelming majority of cases in history proven irresistible even to the most terrible of conquerors."[28] He went on to lay the responsibility for the defense of democracy and the fight against communism squarely on the people of the United States in general and his own generation in particular:

> Classmates, it is our generation, in this country and all over the world, which must bear the tremendous responsibility of continuing the march of freedom during this period of danger to all our institutions. . . . This is more than a question of giving ourselves security from immediate danger; it is a matter of our duty and clear responsibility toward the best of human civilization. We are citizens of the United States, with an obligation to protect and support our country; let us realize that we also have another and even greater obligation to all the human race.[29]

Finally, he spoke of the atomic bomb, which was a great topic of discussion at the time. Recalling this address many years later, he says;

> It was a time when nearly everyone was speculating about the enduring impact of the discovery and use in warfare of the atomic bomb. I decided to take the bull by the horns. The theme of my speech was that it was exceedingly unlikely that anyone would ever use an atomic bomb in warfare again. It was simply too destructive to risk. Most people in 1949 assumed that the atomic bomb would eventually be used by somebody. I remain rather proud that my prediction, as a seventeen-year-old high school graduate, turned out to be true for more than fifty years.[30]

---

28. Carroll, "Berwick Academy Quamphegan."
29. Carroll, "The Promise of Our Times."
30. Carroll, "Unpublished Autobiography."

The title of this chapter, "I Intend to Do Both," is a prophetic line spoken by a very young Warren and fulfilled in a way he could probably never have imagined at the time his little mouth formed the words. Not that many years would pass before he would utter, in this case on paper, more words that would providentially play out in his own life. The words are found in the form of a poem which he wrote and published in his high school yearbook and they read as follows:

The Battle of Châlons[31]

Great walls stand somber in the starlit night
Shadowing black the fields below
Where two great armies lie encamped,
Waiting, in silence, for the coming of dawn.

In the east lie demons in fitful sleep,
Men of the desert, heartless, triumphant;
And, fearsome and frightful, in his own black tent
Attila, the Scourge, dreams of empire to come.
In the west are the hosts of Western Europe,
Soldiers from Germany, from Africa, from Hungary,
Barbarians all. What drew them here,
United and strong, where all was weakness?

On the bank of a river that flows far away
A city lies, whose hallowed name
Still stands through centuries of betrayal and fear
As the symbol of strength and the soul of courage.

---

31. The Battle of Châlons was fought in 451 between Attila and his Huns and an alliance of Romanized barbarians under the Roman general Aetius and the Gauls under King Theodoric, who died heroically on the battlefield. Attila fell back to the Rhine, and Gaul was saved from the Huns. The next year, 452, Pope Leo the Great turned the Huns away from Rome and thus saved the city. Attila died the following year and the Huns left Europe. See Warren Carroll, *A History of Christendom*, vol. 2, *The Building of Christendom* (Front Royal, VA: Christendom Press, 1987), 116.

Rome long ceased to be mighty and strong;
In this day only ghosts live on the Tiber;
Ghosts of men who ruled a continent;
Ghosts who live in the Western capital.

Strike, then, invincible Huns from the steppes;
Charge with your horsemen, in the red light of dawn;
Trample your victims, and shatter the line;
Exult, O Scourge, the day seems yours.

But wait, come there not, from the hill to the north,
New legions of soldiers to the summons of Rome?
The battle still rages, the dead fall fast,
The grass runs red, and the fight goes on.

At last, defeated, the Huns retreat;
Sunset has come, but the day is won;
Attila has fought, and lost his hopes;
The ghosts on the Tiber have triumphed today.

The victors disperse; their work is done;
Europe is saved and civilization preserved;
The future is for the children of Rome;
Romans, now you may die content.

–Warren Carroll,
1949

He could not have known, at the age of seventeen, a high school senior without a thought of God or faith, that his own future was also "of Rome." But God knew—and was leading him there.

3

"I Have Met the Enemy"

IN THE FALL OF 1949, as Warren settled into his freshman year at Bates College, the Soviets exploded their first atomic bomb.[1] Four years earlier, at the Yalta conference in 1945, the Russian communists had seized (or been handed) control over one third of the world.[2] Emerging from the Yalta debacle with a growing clarity, Winston Churchill would eventually proclaim:

> From Stettin in the Baltic to Trieste in the Adriatic, an iron curtain has descended across the continent. Behind that line lie all the capitals of the ancient states of central and eastern Europe. Warsaw, Berlin, Prague, Vienna, Budapest, Belgrade, Bucharest, and Sofia—all these famous cities and the populations around them lie in the Soviet sphere.... The communist parties, which were very small in all these eastern states of Europe, have been raised to pre-eminence and power far beyond their numbers and are seeking everywhere to obtain totalitarian control.[3]

---

1. Warren H. Carroll, *The Rise and Fall of the Communist Revolution* (Front Royal, VA: Christendom Press, 1989), 355.
2. Ibid., 327.
3. Ibid., 352.

In October of 1949, five months after Warren had delivered his valedictory address, China declared herself "The People's Republic of China" and under communist rule. Communist mouths now drooled over neighboring Korea, but the west was awakened to the totalitarian threat. As an avid follower of the war against communism in general and the Korean War in particular, a staunch defender of democracy and freedom, and one who recognized communism as "the greatest threat" free peoples faced at the time, Warren's teeth would have been set on edge by any mention of pacifism or denunciation of patriotism. And it seems that his introduction to the larger intellectual world included both.

Warren's extant writings and letters from his time at Bates give us a clear sense that he backed up the eloquent words of his high school valedictory address with actions. In a letter written home from Bates to his high school English teacher Marie Donahue, he assures her that, while most classes are going well, he is somewhat disgruntled regarding a certain professor. He begins the letter with the same critiquing mind he had for the stories of the science fiction magazine:

> Everyone here is very nice and there are a great many interesting people. So far I have found nothing wrong with the faculty or curriculum and only a very few objectionable students. . . . I have been rather disappointed because Mr. —— possesses strong beliefs diametrically opposed to mine (pacifism, denial of the doctrine of progress, lack of respect for democracy, etc. . . .) which he constantly expresses, often at length. Therefore, we have numerous battles royal—with no hard feelings however.[4]

He seems also to have written about his concern for political indoctrination to his mother, who most likely had some degree of influence

---

4. Warren Carroll to Marie Donahue, 25 October 1949, Maine Women Writers Collection, University of New England, Portland, ME.

with the Bates leadership given her status in the literary world at the time. After traveling to the college herself and sitting in on the particular class in question, she wrote to the president:

> I don't know what you have found to be the fair and feasible attitude to take, administratively, toward political indoctrination in the classroom. I realize it is a knotty problem in these days. But I do deplore it, particularly in a freshman class, and there seems to me to be no question that that is what Mr. —— is working toward, not only openly but dogmatically. He spent the entire period insisting that war is never justified; that young men go to war only because they expect it to be a great adventure; that the United States is and has long been an aggressor nation; that every difference between nations can be and must be settled around a conference table; that patriotism is a manifestation of an emotional disease which makes one race or nation feel itself superior to others, . . . that there is a high degree of masochism in the American people as a whole, and that this has been proven statistically.
>
> The last statement is manifestly absurd. All the others, I think, are the mistaken opinions of a militant pacifist, if not of a fellow-traveler. . . . As an alumnus and as a parent, I regret Stalinesque indoctrination by a member of the Bates faculty, and if I had not reported my observations to you, I should have felt guilty.[5]

Never one to hesitate voicing his own opinion, Warren shot off a letter of his own to the editor of the college newspaper when faced with this same issue coming from a campus group known as the Bates Christian Association. What Warren was objecting to was not the association itself, nor its right to express its beliefs, but the fact that it

---

5. Gladys Hasty Carroll to President Phillips, Bates College, 25 October 1949, Box 5-4, Folder 9, Archive Collection, Caroline Jones.

claimed to represent the entire student body and collected money for its support every semester from every student. Having attended a conference organized by the Bates Christian Association, Warren was appalled at what he heard, stating that the conference "was characterized by a policy of sustained propaganda and indoctrination aimed at the single purpose of getting the complete support, both financial and otherwise, of most of the students present." The main theme of all the speakers was that, even given the grave situation facing the free world, "under no circumstances was war justifiable" and "that the downfall of the United States was inevitable because of our lack of humble and repentant cheek-turning."[6] Protesting vehemently against the aim of the association to turn all Bates students into "little evangelists" for its indoctrination, Warren concluded his letter by declaring:

> We do maintain that the Bates students have a right to know just what the CA is trying to do, how it is utilizing their financial and moral support, and to act in accordance with their convictions. In conclusion, we would like to say that we desire very strongly to resign from the Bates Christian Association unless it shows an immediate change of attitude and approach, and hope that eventually a change in the existing situation will make such action possible. The CA does not represent us![7]

One final anecdote brings a somewhat lighter conclusion to this element of Warren's college experience. It comes in the form of another letter from Gladys, mailed off to the administrative assistant of Bates at the beginning of Warren's sophomore year. After lamenting some of the "personal differences" between students over the past year, she concludes: "For instance, my son would not be happy sharing

---

6. Alan Hakes, John Wadsworth, Warren Carroll, and Richard Breault to editor of the *STUDENT*, "Just What Does the CA Stand For?" Box 5-4, Folder 9, Archive Collection, Caroline Jones.

7. Ibid.

a room with one or more students with leftist tendencies in thinking, nor would they be happy living with him. The division among the men of last year's entering class, in this area, is very marked, and the times are explosive."[8] As always, Warren knew where he stood and although he stood there with charity—he stood firmly.

We now turn again to Warren's own account of his time at Bates where he recalls fine-tuning his skills both as a writer and as a debater:

> In the fall of 1949, I left South Berwick and its venerable Academy to enroll in Bates College at Lewiston, Maine. It had been both my mother's and my father's alma mater; they had met and fallen in love there, and were married in its chapel by Harry Rowe, who was dean of men when I enrolled, a grand old traditional Maine figure who taught me how I should value tradition, a principle I always remembered.
>
> At Bates I was taught by two men who were to join my parents and my future wife as shapers of my life, two men to whom I will always owe an enormous debt of gratitude: Robert Berkelman, professor of English, and Brooks Quimby, professor of speech. They were truly extraordinary men, as I think all their students acknowledged either while they were studying with them, or later. They are still well remembered by those who were students at Bates in their day.
>
> Professor Berkelman was a man of medium height and piercing eye. His creed as a teacher was that you could always do better; you were never doing your very best, at least at first. I had done a lot of writing in my boyhood, and my mother was a famous novelist. I thought I knew how to write; in fact, I thought I wrote fairly well. Professor Berkelman soon set me straight. His slogan, under his

---

8. Gladys Hasty Carroll to Charles H. Sampson, 24 August 1950, Box 5-4, Folder 9, Archive Collection, Caroline Jones.

picture in the college yearbook, was "be meaty, concise, compact, and concrete." I was none of the above, but suffered from that besetting sin of young writers, overwriting and prolixity. One word was never enough where I could think of ten or a dozen.

Professor Berkelman had no patience with this. He gave me the only D I ever received on a paper in four years of college. And he trained me so well that I won the national *Atlantic Monthly* college essay contest with an essay entitled "Thucydides and the Struggle for Democracy." It was almost entirely due to what Professor Berkelman had done for me. I needed to be "brought up short" and have never ceased to bless him for it. If I am a good writer now it is due to him, even more than to Miss Donahue and my mother, who were too kind and charitable to do what Professor Berkelman did. But that is an essential part of good teaching, which I later did my best to incorporate into my own teaching.

Brooks Quimby was then the most famous debate coach in America, the founder of international debating. He was a tall rugged man, whose son was the star center of our basketball team. Brooks Quimby taught me how to speak, which was essential for my later career. He taught me extemporaneous speaking, using 4 x 6 note cards, a method I still use. Just as Professor Berkelman had his slogan in the yearbook, so Professor Quimby had his, just as important, clipped, and to the point: "Let me see your organization!" Every speech for him had to be tightly organized in advance. He trained us debaters by a unique and terrifying method: we had to debate *him*, one on one. He called this the "Quimby Institute." Of course he wiped us out, but we learned from that the key to success in life and every good work: *perseverance*. We had to keep on going no matter how badly we were being beaten, and his formidable presence and arguments called forth the best that was in us to try to contend with him. Brooks Quimby remains

a legend at Bates College, even in an age when intercollegiate debating has descended to the farcical level of seeing
who can say the most in the shortest period of time.

I always remembered one point in particular about
Professor Quimby as a debate coach. When I was at Bates
debating for him, the managers of intercollegiate debate
decided that college teams would henceforth have to debate on both sides of every issue in every debate. Brooks
Quimby would not do it. He said that some debaters might
have objections of conscience to taking a side they strongly
disagreed with. As a forthright old Maine Yankee, he
would never force them to do that. And so we his students
learned from him another vitally important lesson.[9]

It was while he was at Bates that two things occurred which, although not having an immediate effect on Warren's religious beliefs,
at least helped to lay the groundwork for his conversion. The first was
a harrowing incident involving a train and is best told in his words:

I had one very strange experience at college, which I always remembered and often reflected upon, and still do
sometimes. Our core curriculum at Bates included geology, so I was taking a geology course, a subject in which
I had very little interest. One day we took a field trip to
some cliffs along the Androscoggin River which flowed
past Lewiston, the city where Bates College is located. We
were tired and bored. We reached the cliffs from below,
and had climbed up them. At the top we saw, stretching
across the river, a railroad trestle. By crossing it, we could
save ourselves the difficult climb back down the cliffs, and
the long walk back to campus. Our professor was not with
us; we were on our own. Someone proposed that we walk
across the trestle, which we proceeded to do, thoughtless in
the manner of college sophomores. I never thought what I

---

9. Carroll, "Unpublished Autobiography."

would do if a train came. But a train did come. Shouts from the rear warned us of its approach, too late. Those of us on the trestle started to run along it, panting in terror. But we could not outrun a locomotive. Within seconds it was upon us. There was a kind of catwalk along the side of the trestle, which was the only place to go to avoid the approaching train. But the catwalk had no railing. To my right was a sheer drop of at least a hundred feet to the rocky bed of the river. I had no idea whether I could stay on the catwalk as the train passed, and doubted that I could. At the age of eighteen, I faced instant and horrible death.

My mother had always taught me to believe in an after-life, and I had always told myself that, philosophically, I was not afraid of death. But I certainly did not want to fall that hundred feet to those rocks. It never occurred to me at that moment that I was unbaptized; I then had no understanding whatever of the significance of baptism, and had never even considered receiving it. But my mother's teaching that there was life beyond the grave did sustain me and prevent me from giving way to absolute panic, which might have toppled me from that catwalk. I bent over, grasping both sides of the catwalk with my right and left hands. The train passed with a rush and a roar; I was still alive. So I had faced death, and found my belief that it was not the end confirmed in spectacular fashion.

But now, looking back at that moment on the trestle, I really believe that the hand of God, or else my guardian angel (which I never dreamed I had) was holding me on that catwalk, because God had work for me to do in the last half of my life that He wanted done, and wanted me to stay on earth to do it.[10]

The second occurrence was not so much an event as it was a conversation, or a series of conversations, Warren had with another pro-

---

10. Ibid.

fessor at Bates, Dr. Joseph D'Alfonso. Warren's father, Herbert, was a determinist and had passed this belief on to his son. Environment and heredity together controlled who one was, he believed, and one's decisions were pre-determined by these things. But Dr. D'Alfonso, although not a Catholic, believed strongly in free will and was able to show Warren that his determinist beliefs were in fact self-refuting. "If you really think all your beliefs are due to non-rational causes," he challenged Warren, "then that assertion itself cannot be true, since only your psychology is causing you to say that, and truth is unattainable by the human mind."[11] As we have seen, a belief in a truth apart from oneself was already a strong part of Warren's formation, and when presented with D'Alfonso's reasoning as to the effect of determinism on truth, his response was clear: "I would never believe that."[12] Once again, God was placing weapons of intellectual warfare in Warren's arsenal which would enable him to find and fight for the ultimate truth.

While writing, debating, reasoning, and facing trains head-on made up the bulk of Warren's activities at Bates, he also found time to make friends. One of them must not have impressed Warren too much for he says that, as a fallen-away Catholic, this friend "confirmed my prejudiced belief that this religion was only for ignorant people."[13] Two others, Alan Hakes and Jerry Handspicker, became his great friends, and the three of them would eventually attain the highest academic honor bestowed by Bates College: they would all graduate summa cum laude, an honor which had been attained less than a dozen times in the college's history going back at least a century. "Our room was 403 Smith Hall South," Warren tells us, "and wags dubbed that room 4.03, because in our last several semesters we all got all A's (4.0)."[14]

Warren gives an account of his friendships with both of these men, which I quote here in full, as it is revelatory of his character and portrays the "softer side" of such a budding intellectual giant:

---

11. Ibid.
12. Ibid.
13. Ibid.
14. Ibid.

Al Hakes was planning to be a lawyer and had the analytical, incisive mind for it. Though he seemed cold and unemotional, I was close enough to him to know better. He was passionately in love with a Catholic girl who did not return his affection, possibly because (I think now, though I never thought of it then) he had no faith of any kind—none at all. She agreed to go out with him, but only on the understanding that nothing would ever come of it. It was not a good solution, because Al would not stop hoping she would change her mind, and spent a great deal of time with her. I did not know any of this at the time, only that Al was hopelessly in love with her (once he said that he always knew when she was nearby, because it made "vibrations in the atmosphere"). He never married, became a chain-smoker, and died in his early fifties.

My Jewish friend, who is (and remains) very outspoken, and knew more of the story than I did at the time, walked up to this woman at a college reunion shortly after Al's death, after she had long since married somebody else, and asked her how she had felt about Al's death, with the clear implication that her action had had something to do with hastening it, as I believe it did, though my mother once told me this was an absurdly romantic notion (I am, it is true, very much a romantic). After my Jewish friend had told me about saying this, I wrote him that no one else I had ever known would have said anything like that, and I added "and it's about time somebody did!" In a talk at Christendom College many years later, I asked my students to pray for the soul of Al Hakes.

The other man in 4.03, Jerry Handspicker, was and is a liberal protestant. When I first knew him he was a moderate political conservative as I was, but he moved steadily leftward in the years after his graduation from Bates, as I moved just as steadily rightward. He married one of Quimby's debaters, Diane West (known as Dee). She was slender, intelligent, and very attractive, I thought more so than Al Hakes' girlfriend. The interesting fact was that she looked something like my own wife-to-be, who at that time I had never met or heard of. Perhaps in a way Dee West was preparing me for Anne.

I was best man at Dee and Jerry's wedding and honorary uncle to their daughter Amy, who christened me "Uncle Peep-Peep" because I used to read her stories about chickens (which I had raised during the Second World War). For many years Jerry and I kept sporadically in contact. When Dee died, a victim to life-long diabetes, Jerry remarried happily, and I was able to pay a visit to him and his new wife in Bennington, Vermont, in the summer of 2001.[15]

For his part, Jerry recalls his friend, Warren, with glowing words. In the interview this author was able to have with him in 2014, he began by calling Warren a "larger-than-life figure and a good friend." Jerry touched on many of the memories Warren had also recalled, speaking of their times on the debate team (Jerry and Alan were both Quimby debaters as well) and terming Warren a "stupendous debater." "He was an intellectual genius," says Jerry. "He had a wide range of interests and enormous energy in pursuit of his goals. He was a dynamite ping-pong player with a fast serve that dropped on you."

Evidently, Warren had already established his habit of occasionally staying awake far into the night and over-sleeping the next morning. Jerry tells the following story regarding this sleeping trait:

> He found it difficult to get up in the morning—especially since he often was up late working on some project. On the morning senior honors were announced in chapel, his other roommate (Alan Hakes) and I put two alarms under the bunk across the room from his bed (while we went to breakfast). When they went off, Warren got out of bed,

---

15. Ibid.

turned them off, and went back to bed! That was the day it
was announced that he and Alan both had received summa
cum laude—the first time in the history of Bates that two
were given in the same year. Warren heard the news when
he arrived at chapel as we all were coming out.[16]

Mostly, however, Jerry remembers Warren as a man of humility and
integrity. "While he was self-confident (for good reason) he was also
quite humble—an unusual combination, [and] integrity was at his
core." What a beautiful tribute.

The work which was probably chiefly responsible for Warren's
receiving the summa cum laude degree was his senior thesis entitled
"An Investigation of the Causes of the Decline and Fall of Athens During the Peloponnesian War." Totaling 283 pages, it was meticulously
researched (hence his late nights) and, more importantly, drew a completely original conclusion. Warren himself states on page fifteen, "To
the knowledge of the investigator there has not yet appeared in this
field any study dealing specifically with the causes of the decline and
fall of Athens during the Peloponnesian War." He then critiques other
historians who "offer suggestions as to the nature of these causes" but
"fail to deal exclusively with the fall of Athens as an historical problem
of paramount importance. As a result their causal analyses tend to be
superficial and based upon unfounded generalizations."[17]

Here, in this 283-page investigation, we can see the beginnings of
a pursuit that drove the rest of Warren's intellectual career: the study
of historical causalities. He opens his thesis investigation with the following lines:

> The study of historical causality is of supreme impor-
> tance in man's efforts to understand himself and to guide

---

16. Jerry Handspicker, interview by author, 2014.

17. Warren Carroll, "An Investigation of the Causes of the Decline and Fall of Athens during the Peloponnesian War," April 1953, 15, Item 14T-19-10, Archive Collection, Caroline Jones.

the course of cultural development in the direction of a better, safer, and more rational future. In view of the immense significance of understanding the forces which have moulded the past of humanity, there is always a need for more and more thorough investigations into the causal background of the decisive events in the history of man.[18]

Later on, this desire to delve into the causes of the events and streams of history would expand to incorporate the spiritual realm, but at this point his concern was with Athens, its decline, and what that meant not only for the Hellenic world, but for the whole of western civilization. Warren saw very much a parallel between this situation in the ancient world and the situation facing the free world in its struggle against communism at the time:

> In Greece, Athens was the champion of democracy, progress and culture; in the modern world, free Western society has assumed that role. In view of this parallel, it is profoundly disturbing from the standpoint of those who believe in freedom that it was Athens that lost the Peloponnesian War and totalitarian Sparta that won it. This fact stands as a warning to free men of today that the democratic state, despite all its sources of strength, does not always win its wars, even when they are struggles for survival.[19]

The conclusion he draws from his investigation is in keeping with his love of truth and his belief that the intellect has the ability to find it. "Athens failed," he ultimately concluded, "because, though she had progressed so far, she had not progressed far enough—because there still remained in the minds of her people the shadow of an ancient irrationality, expressed in religion, in superstition, and

---

18. Ibid., 1.
19. Ibid., 7.

in anti-intellectualism."[20] He then issued a warning to his present world:

> "It is equally clear what we must avoid. We must avoid, above all things, a permanent divorce between the intellectuals and the people. We must live up to our democratic ideals in practice as well as in theory, and in doing so we must educate all the people so that they will learn to accept and practice reason."[21]

It is interesting to compare his conclusions as a college senior with his conclusions on the same topic as a fifty-year-old professor. The college thesis, although it does not denounce religion per se, cautions strongly against its possible hindering of "progress" and gives it second place (or lower) in the list of essentials needed for a great civilization. "We must be forever on our guard," he says,

> against a successful revival of the indestructible barbaric element in human nature. Specifically, we must oppose with a full realization of the danger they represent all those individuals and organizations, whether or not they claim religious sanction, that threaten the progressive realization of our ideals, that condemn reason and ignore democracy and attack our society because of its adherence to the conviction that man can attain a better world through his own unaided efforts.[22]

In contrast, his assessment of Athens presented in volume one of his *History of Christendom* proposes quite a different reason for Athens' downfall: "The confidence in their capacity to achieve in freedom, which had brought about the superb creative flowering of the Hellenes

---

20. Ibid., 273–274.
21. Ibid.
22. Ibid., 275.

of the golden age, was passing; the cosmic despair which lies at the end of every pagan road, even the most brilliant, drew closer."[23] As a young man, he possibly felt the vitality of youth pulsing through him, as do many young men, and took it as a sign that all was achievable by man. As an older and wiser man, he knew that nothing of great worth, especially freedom, was achievable without God.

After graduating from Bates, and with fellowships of all kinds towards his goal of attaining a doctorate in history, Warren headed to New York City and Columbia University. What he found there was not what he expected:

> It was the beginning of the worst two years of my life. As I often said later, Columbia University was where I "met the enemy." That is where I first encountered established in full power the dragon of modern intellectual endeavor: the denial of the attainability of truth, fundamental skepticism. I can see now that there were a few professors at Bates who had also believed that, but the ones who had most influenced me—Berkelman, Quimby, D'Alfonso— would have scorned it, and I knew it. But at Columbia, I found them all around me.... To be thrust from the warm comradeship and solid foundations of moral principle which had characterized my education at Bates College into this sea of grayness or worse, at Columbia, was an almost traumatic experience. I was desperately lonely, and felt I was fighting a losing battle with no allies.
>
> In my depression, I even thought of looking into Christianity, which I had never seriously considered before. I went to the protestant Riverside Church for several Sundays. The main thing I remember about it was the little man with the booming voice who announced unctuously before the collection: "The Lord loves a cheerful *givah*!" Believe it or not, it never even once occurred to me

---

23. Warren Carroll, *A History of Christendom*, vol. 1, *The Founding of Christendom* (Front Royal, VA: Christendom Press, 1985), 188.

even to step into a Catholic church. After all, one of my good friends at Bates was a fallen-away Catholic; another was a Jew. . . . I had never met a Catholic who could tell me why he was Catholic. They had some silly rules about always kneeling in church. I supposed it might be a good religion for French Canadians, of whom we had a substantial number in South Berwick, but that was their thing and meant nothing to me. Such are the ways prejudice works on the mind, and blinds it.[24]

Added to his critique of Columbia in this autobiographical excerpt were others he would later relate to his wife, Anne. "The rooms were cheerless," he said. "Someone could die in there and no one would notice until it started to smell. No one was interested in the students as persons."[25] He told of the boring lectures with almost no exams (something he would later correct when he started his own college) and little accountability. Choosing German for his language of study, he was required to translate one page using a dictionary to prove proficiency. "I could have passed an exam in Swahili!" he exclaims. He made no lasting friendships at Columbia.[26]

As to his dip into organized religion, the non-interest in the Catholic faith had much to do with his upbringing. In South Berwick, the only Catholics were French Canadians who were mostly lumber jacks. These were considered lower-class people and not intellectually respectable. Being such an intellectual himself, his thought was, "If there was anything to Christianity it surely would not be found with those lumber jacks!"[27]

But all was not lost there at Columbia. Warren had one professor, Garrett Mattingly, whom he christened his "best professor there!" Warren later cited two of Professor Mattingly's books, one on Catherine of

24. Carroll, "Unpublished Autobiography."
25. Anne Carroll, interview by author, 29 November 2012.
26. Ibid.
27. Ibid.

Aragon and one on the Spanish Armada, in his own works on the history of Christendom. Another professor, Richard Morris, compiled a collection of original sources on the American War for Independence. Warren did most of the research for this book and is acknowledged therein for having done so.[28] This work with Professor Morris most likely laid the foundation for his master's thesis entitled "The Stamp Act Congress: Herald of American Union." Warren acknowledges his debt to Morris along with a touch of "I'm ready to be done with school!" in a letter written to Marie Donahue dated March of 1954:

> I am expecting now to have my M.A. thesis completed this spring. My topic is the Stamp Act Congress of 1765, which is not very widely known but which I believe to have been highly significant in the development of a spirit of common nationality in the American colonies and which was responsible for the first statement of the common political aims and principles of Americans. My connection with Dr. Morris should be of great help to me when I go on for my work for the doctorate. I'm not just sure when I'll be doing this, since I may be drafted this summer, but as soon as I can I will try to complete the work for the Ph.D. Then I will at last have finished my nineteen years of education! It's a long stretch, when you look back upon it; and sometimes, however much you welcome learning, you wish it were all over.[29]

It was not a professor, however, who made the greatest impact on Warren during his time at Columbia. No, it was a large, soft-spoken man by the name of Whittaker Chambers—a man who had actually joined the communist party at the same Columbia University thirty years prior to Warren's attending. In 1952, Chambers published his

---

28. Ibid.
29. Warren Carroll to Marie Donahue, 9 March 1954, Maine Women Writers Collection.

autobiography, describing in graphic and agonizing detail his journey out of the communist party and consequent virulent attack from the evil powers that are communism which had penetrated into the upper echelons of America and even deeply into the Roosevelt administration.[30] Reading Chambers's book at Columbia in the summer of 1955, Warren flatly states that it "changed my life . . . I consider Whittaker Chambers's *Witness* to be the greatest book written in the twentieth century," adding that it "has particular significance for me because it made me a firm anti-communist for life."[31] It also had an influence on Warren's later conversion to Christianity, especially as it described Chambers's own conversion experience which enabled him to break with communism. The following passage gives a feel for the type of influence Chambers had on Warren, a passage that Warren deems "the most inspiring and memorable passage in the entire book." It is the final paragraph of Chambers' letter to his children which introduces the story of *Witness*:

> My children, when you were little, we used sometimes to go for walks in our pine woods. In the open fields, you would run along by yourselves. But you used instinctively to give me your hands as we entered those woods, where it was darker, lonelier, and in the stillness our voices sounded loud and frightening. In this book I am again giving you my hands. I am leading you, not through cool pine woods, but up and up a narrow defile between bare and steep rocks from which in shadow things uncoil and slither away. It will be dark. But in the end, if I have led you aright, you will make out three crosses, from two of which hang thieves. I will have brought you to Golgotha—the place of sculls. This is the meaning of the journey. Before you understand, I may not be there, my hands may have slipped from yours.

---

30. Warren Carroll, "*Witness*: Whittaker Chambers" (lecture, Christendom College, Front Royal, VA, December 2, 2009). The lecture may be accessed at http://media.christendom.edu/2009/12/witness-whittaker-chambers/
31. Ibid.

It will not matter. For when you understand what you see, you will no longer be children. You will know that life is pain, that each of us hangs always from the cross of himself. And when you know that this is true of every man, woman, and child on earth, you will be wise.[32]

Of this passage Warren declares:

I maintain that no Christian spiritual writer, anywhere, has ever described conversion to faith in Christ—the road to the Holy Cross—better than that. This passage above all shows why Whittaker Chambers's *Witness* is the finest book written in the accursed twentieth century, and it shows that Jesus Christ can and will always triumph over every one of the evils of that century. And it also, in a single paragraph, sums up the history of our modern age.[33]

Whittaker Chambers emerged into public view during the famous Hiss-Chambers case which began in 1948—Warren's junior year in high school. Six years later in the spring of 1954, Warren's first year at Columbia, another man, similar to Chambers in his fierce opposition to communism, would hold the spotlight in the American political arena. This time the venue was the Army-McCarthy hearings, and the man's name was Joseph McCarthy. Once again the evil that dragged an innocent man into the public view to be ridiculed, denounced and vilified for telling the truth, was the evil of communism. And just as in the case of Whittaker Chambers, Joe McCarthy's only real "crime" was telling the truth. Warren relates his view of the McCarthy hearings while a student at Columbia:

---

32. Whittaker Chambers, *Witness* (Washington, DC: Gateway Editions, 1952), 21–22, quoted in Warren Carroll, *"Witness*: Whittaker Chambers."
33. Carroll, *"Witness*: Whittaker Chambers."

I was at Columbia during the famous televised Army-McCarthy hearings, which I watched in the university's television room, where raucous students booed and hissed Senator McCarthy at his every appearance. In sharp contrast, I was greatly impressed with him, regarding him as an honest and sincere patriot, quite out of his depth in controversy with the intellectuals who were determined to destroy him. Senator McCarthy became a demonic villain to the intellectual establishment, which foisted the blackest picture of him upon the country. Years later I would be asked by young people what it was like to have lived during "the McCarthy years." I would try to tell them that most of what they had been told about Senator McCarthy was false.[34]

It had been a long road and very much of an eye-opener for Warren from the small, warm, close-knit community nestled in the southern tip of Maine to the metropolis of New York City and the cold, impersonal walls of Columbia University. He had indeed "met the enemy," but he had been armed well to face him. He himself states:

> When I encountered the general denial of the attainability of truth ... in graduate study at Columbia University, I had already been armored by Dr. D'Alfonso against this most fundamental error of twentieth-century American intellectuals, which I was eventually to learn as a Catholic is called fundamental skepticism, the heart of the modernist heresy, first denounced by Pope St. Pius X in 1907 in his great encyclical *Pascendi*.[35]

---

34. Carroll, "Unpublished Autobiography."
35. Ibid.

4

First Novels

In the summer of 1955, I shook the dust of Columbia University thankfully off my feet and "volunteered for the draft," which meant that I made myself available for it, under the terms that I would only have to serve in the Army for two years. I wanted an environment as different as possible from the soul-crushing denial of truth and reality that I had found at Columbia, and the vicious sneering hostility to patriotism and anti-communism I had seen among those listening to the televised Army-McCarthy hearings. And I found it.

Mine was an Army still dominated and permeated by veterans of the Second World War, that mighty conflict so well described by Robert Leckie (a veteran of the epic struggle on Guadalcanal) in his great book *Delivered from Evil: The Saga of World War II.* They knew what it meant to fight evil face to face, hand to hand, and they had done it. They had everything to teach me about it, and I knew I had a great deal to learn from them.

I had never done anything really physical before, except "going out for" the baseball team in my high school.

... I had fired a gun only briefly at summer camp. I had never hunted anything more than a fish. So I was not, to put it mildly, good soldier material. But I found a man who made me a soldier.

His name was Luther Richards, and he stands right up with Marie Donahue, Professor Berkelman, and Professor Quimby among the shapers of my life. Luther Richards had been a ranger in World War II. He was a small insignificant looking man with a receding chin, except when he spoke. Then you listened—and obeyed. I have never heard a voice like his—rich and ringing, calling to heroism, thrilling you through and through, telling you that you could be a better man than you were, that nothing was impossible for you. . . . When later I became founding president of Christendom College and faced no less than ten years of wearing, crushing struggle to keep it alive and forging ahead despite the worst the world and the Devil could do, it was the memory of Sergeant Richards that was my chief inspiration. I had no contact with him after I left his platoon with a cracked ankle-bone, and he must be dead now. God rest his soul. He gave me more than he could ever have imagined, because he was a man who knew how to win, and showed you that you could win, and made you believe it.[1]

After recovering in the hospital for two weeks from the broken ankle, and with a letter of recognition from his commander informing him that "your diligence and application have placed you in the top ten percent of your class," Warren was placed in the signal corps and sent to Camp Kokura, Japan, where he worked in a warehouse for roughly the next year and a half.[2] A man with a Ph.D., working in a warehouse! But he loved it. He loved being driven physically to reach

---

1. Carroll, "Unpublished Autobiography."
2. Colonel Otto T. Saar to Pvt. Warren H. Carroll, 2 March 1956, Box 7-2B, Folder 2, Archive Collection, Caroline Jones.

his potential. And the tough, physical reality of life in the Army provided such a contrast to the artificial world he had experienced in academia. Something that struck him during this time was the attitude of his Japanese assistant. Warren came to know this man and to learn that he had had his whole unit wiped out during World War II, but that despite this tragedy, he harbored no animosity whatsoever towards Warren or the United States. Warren also learned that the Japanese, in general, greatly admired General MacArthur because of the dignity with which he had treated all the Japanese he had met.

Camp Kokura proved to be not just a place for learning the colors and patterns of signal flags, however, for Warren was a man driven to write—and write he did—even as a soldier in the U.S. Army stationed in Japan. Much of the free time he had was spent working on his first space novel which, in its draft form, was entitled *Mission to the Stars*. With noticeable influences from the "Queen of Books," Lewis's space trilogy, Warren's novel was intimately connected to his interest at the time in the Puritan faith. In his brief foray into organized religion while at Columbia, he had found nothing which satisfied him. Now, however, he became enamored for a time with the high standards and rigid code of the Puritan tradition, qualities that had also drawn him into the Army. He was thriving on standards that could not be arbitrarily changed.[3] He describes this interest himself in a letter dated October 20, 1957, to his high school English teacher Marie Donahue:

> One of the main consequences of the writing of this novel
> for me in my professional work, which I am sure will not
> come as a surprise to you after reading it, is a consuming
> interest in the entire subject of Puritanism as it developed
> in Europe, Great Britain, and colonial New England. My
> doctoral dissertation and planned complete biography on
> John Adams grows naturally out of this heritage, but I also
> intend to concentrate most of my historical research on

3. Anne Carroll, interview by author, 29 November 2012.

different aspects of this movement and the Puritan people
themselves, hoping eventually to attain sufficient mastery
of it to be able to write the whole story of the Puritan Revolution in the Western World.[4]

The novel itself is a somewhat odd juxtaposition of science fiction, condemnation of Russian communism, beliefs regarding God
and the Puritan faith, and tender, although somewhat naïve, references to the beauty of womanhood and married life, probably illustrative of Warren's own diverse thoughts at the time. Taking place in
the year 2381, it is the story of ten couples, seven Puritan and three
Muslim, and their joint mission to bring God to another solar system.
"If the Oliver Cromwell [the name of the spaceship] could reach its
goal in safety and survive its return journey, it could only mean that
man had at last been judged worthy to serve his Creator on the greatest of all missions—the mission to the stars."[5] Although he does not
explain how, the Puritan and Muslim faiths are in harmony on this
mission and share a joint goal. Just before take-off, the commander of
the mission makes a speech in which he states: "Tomorrow is one of
the supreme days in the history of man. I think I may say without fear
of blasphemy that it is the greatest day since Our Lord ascended into
Heaven and the Prophet recorded the words of the Glorious Koran."[6]
At the start of the story he chooses two passages, one from the Bible
and the other from the Koran, which refer to the stars. The first is
from the Psalms:

> When I behold the heavens, the work of thy fingers;
> The moon and the stars, which thou hast established;
> What is man, that thou visitest him?

4. Warren Carroll to Marie Donahue, 20 October 1957, Maine Women Writers
   Collection.
5. Warren Carroll, *Mission to the Stars*, unpublished novel, Item 14T-19-14, Archive
   Collection, Caroline Jones, 3.
6. Ibid., 7.

> Yet thou hast made him a little lower than the angels,
> And dost crown him with glory and honor.[7]

And the other from the Koran:

> By the heaven and the Morning Star
> Ah, what will tell thee what the Morning Star is!
> The piercing Star!
> No human soul but hath a guardian over it,
> So let man consider from what he is created.[8]

In fact, the first six pages are filled with his thoughts on God and the gravity of man's mission to spread belief in Him.

Much of the novel is told in the form of conversations between members of the crew as they pass the time on the fourteen-month journey that will bring them to the "Beacon System" where they are to look for life. From these conversations, the reader learns that Armageddon has occurred on earth and was the result of the use, by Russian communists, of radioactive cobalt and strontium-90 unleashed on 150 million of their own people "for the supreme crime of demanding a society which would serve God rather than man."[9] Eighty-four percent of Russia is now uninhabitable. He refers to those 150 million Russians as martyrs: "The nineteenth and twentieth centuries glorified heresy and the result was communism; so that when the twenty-first century had to make the Puritan and Moslem Revolutions, the result of those was Armageddon. One hundred fifty million human beings gave their lives to save five billion from perpetual slavery to materialism and human bestiality."[10] There are many, many pages of conversation, much of it somewhat repetitive, detailing the beliefs of those on board the spaceship regarding the fact that they are the chosen ones, they live

---

7. Ibid., 2.
8. Ibid., 5.
9. Ibid., 15.
10. Ibid., 37.

by a creed, and they are comforted by their belief in the doctrine of predestination "as preached by both Puritans and Moslems."[11]

When they are not having theological discussions, they are often gushing over one another in a rather utopian but very sweet manner. Never an argument nor even an unkind word occurs among twenty people, on a voyage in close confinement, lasting upwards of two and one half years. Not very realistic. It must be remembered, however, that Warren had, as his closest example of what a marriage relationship meant, his own parents' strong, faithful, and loving relationship and from them he had grown up with a devotion to and love for the indissolubility of the marriage bond. As an example, the main character Lincoln Adams speaks his thoughts shortly before the mission's departure as he watches his wife, Sarah, take her place among the crew members:

> None of his people feared death, for all knew that it was only a doorway to a greater Beyond. What he did fear, of course, was for Sarah if she should survive while he did not. But Puritan women were strong. Deep love between one man and one woman was almost universal in Puritan (and Moslem) society, and of necessity separations were frequent, yet people survived them. God's will could only be obeyed; and years apart were insignificant compared to the ages together that would follow their eventual reunion. The Puritan Book of Services made only one change in the ancient form of the marriage service—for the old "till death do us part" Lincoln Adams' people read "unto all eternity."
>
> ... I know it's useless to try to be objective, he told himself as he watched her [Sarah], so I might as well come

---

11. Ibid., 9. Both Muslims and Puritans believe in a predestination which denies free will. Perhaps Warren saw their beliefs as divine providence, which is very different. But perhaps not. He may not have understood the full ramifications of predestination. For his thoughts on the issue, see 274–275 of the manuscript.

right out and admit it—she is without a doubt the loveliest woman who will board the Oliver Cromwell. Lanie Crucis may be more spectacular, and Martha Strandom more winsome, and Sherry more vivacious, but Sarah is—well, Sarah. He let his eyes wander for what must be the ten-thousandth time over her lovely, upturned, heart-shaped face, her eyes of that incredible deep, dark, scintillating blue with their perpetual quiet radiance, the ghosts of dimples in her cheeks, her glorious torrent of hair with its bronze and amber and chestnut lights, her perfectly proportioned and symmetrical form. She glanced at him, then at Ireton Edwards, and returned their smiles; and Sarah's smile.... He could not describe it, except that it seemed to concentrate that radiance of hers in a sort of beam reaching out toward whoever or whatever she was smiling at, until both were enveloped in a pure and shimmering glow. It was enough that such beauty existed, without trying to describe it.[12]

Warren's love for and knowledge of astronomy also comes shining through the narrative. The ship is powered by a contraterrene drive, gets sucked into the gravitational field of a black dwarf star, and travels sixty-seven trillion miles at ten times the speed of light:

As the world watched, the vast dead mass of the starship quivered, then seemed to come to life, rising slowly, slowly, then gradually faster on a pillar of the coruscant, unearthly, half-invisible subatomic fire that streamed from contraterrene fusion, wrapping in a shimmering indigo lightning the phosphorescent letters of OLIVER CROMWELL. It seemed to hang below the clouds for an instant, then clove the sky like an avenging angel and was gone into the unknown ocean of the Infinite upon the shores of which Isaac Newton had visualized himself as picking

---

12. Ibid., 19–21.

pebbles while the First Puritan Revolution was dying, so many centuries before.[13]

Further on in the novel, the members of the crew gather around the ship's telescope to observe,

Sirius, the Dog Star, on their left hand and behind them now, nearest of the really bright stars, glowing at a little more than a right angle to their course. Then the twin suns of Altair, whirling at their fantastic speed, only eleven light-years away now, just off the line from Beacon to the star clouds of Cygnus. Farther beyond, in the dark reaches of the abyss, the regal denizens of Sol's section of the great spiral of the Galaxy rushed along their 250-million-year orbits about the invisible center of the whole. Dark orange Aldebaran glinted grimly in the midst of the swarming flock of the Hyades. Fierce Canopus flashed its beams afar. In solemn grandeur the glory of Orion shone from five hundred light-years away and more, a shower of stars caught in the trailing skirts of its Great Nebula, with the Trapezium lodged in the heart of the white mist where stars are born; above it blazed Bellatrix, and below, at exactly equal distances, hung the twin blue infernos of Rigel and Saiph, the pair called in Milton Edwards's famous poem on the Galaxy the Sapphire Gate. Linked upon the illimitable glowed the Pleiades, beautiful and inviting even in the harsh fire-on-night realm of deep space, suggesting in their close clustering and rich radiance a strange friendliness across nearly four hundred light-years. Beyond them all flared the pure white splendor of Deneb, tip of the Northern Cross, brightest start in this whole region of space.[14]

---

13. Ibid., 27.
14. Ibid., 87–88.

We also see Warren's continuing critique of the type of people he encountered at Columbia in contrast to the honesty and warmth of those he grew up with in southern Maine. Given his age and lack of any formal religious training, his penetration into human actions and emotions is astounding:

> "Sophistication is a mask," said Sherry in a clear voice, "a mask of obscurity in ideas and artificiality in emotion that hides a great hollowness inside—a hollowness where the simple, honest, the warm, and the forthright qualities of every healthy personality should be, but in the sophisticate, are not. Its causes are hypocrisy, fear, immorality, loss of faith, and perverted standards of social prestige. Its effects are aimlessness, the cult of unsentimentality, the ridicule of the pure, and a growing decline in the prestige of the educational system, which tends to be the main producer of sophisticates. Societies ruled by a sophisticated culture pattern would require extensive re-education before they could coherently accept even the existence of an advanced religious culture such as our own. What we need to know is whether we can assume that any planet we find in which the Industrial Revolution occurred fairly recently is sure to be ruled by the sophistication pattern, or whether this is merely a tendency and not a law."[15]

Upon reaching their goal (the Beacon System, consisting of seventeen planets and two suns), the twenty crew members of the Oliver Cromwell have the opportunity to put their theories to the test. Reminiscent of Dr. Ransom, the main character in C. S. Lewis's space trilogy (Warren's "Queen of Books!"), the crew of the Cromwell make a landing on assorted planets. On the first, called Tirel, we find a situation much like that at the time between the United States and Russia. Although nine-tenths of its surface is covered in water, Tirel had two

---

15. Ibid., 51–52.

large island continents in its northern hemisphere less than a thousand miles apart, "one with a fringe of islands and archipelagoes, the other a solid granitic block of land rising straight out of the deeps."[16] Upon landing, the crew members discover that the two countries are named Tirand and Talmar, respectively, and consist of very different civilizations. Tirand contained a non-aggressive early industrial type society "at approximately the material level of Europe and North America on Earth about 1925."[17] The second society, on the island of Talmar, is best described by Lincoln Adams's best friend, the Turk Bayazid ibn-Hassan (called Bay for short):

> "We ran into a pure collectivist society; I'm sure of it. Wait 'til you see the pattern of their farms and cities from the air—perfectly geometrical. All planning, no personal inspiration. And their hatchet-men attacked us in such a very regimented and determinedly unimaginative way! They were throwing bullets and shells at us every minute we were there; if we deflected one we deflected a thousand, and by the looks if we'd stayed they'd have kept it up until they exhausted the entire local supply of TNT! Straight militaristic collectivism—no thought, no personality, no sense. We'll have our work cut out for us on that continent!"[18]

They do indeed go on to befriend the Tirandans and help them to secure freedom from Talmarian dictatorship by breaking through their "iron curtain," (Warren's words) incinerating the dictator and his chiefs of staff, and convincing the rest of the Talmarians that they are now free to form a peaceful society.

There occurs one very interesting conversation which is brought up here only to illustrate what Warren would later discover when he entered the Catholic Church: that the human intellect alone, no mat-

---

16. Ibid., 122.

17. Ibid., 127.

18. Ibid., 129.

ter how brilliant, sincere, and open to the truth, cannot be guaranteed to be free from error. The guaranteed infallible magisterial teaching authority of the church is necessary. In deciding how best to help the beings on the planet Tirel, the crew members faced the question of whether or not it was permissible to kill the Talmarian dictator for the sake of the rest of those on the planet. They come to a conclusion:

> The ethical problem which this posed was as old as Moses, who slew an Egyptian in the act of beating an Israelite and then had to flee to the land of Midian. . . . Even the people of the Brotherhood of the Earth in the twenty-fourth century had no final answers to these questions; very likely they are unanswerable by finite minds. History had proved over and over again that there are men who forfeit by their sins their God-given right to live, that there are men whose death would make thousands and even millions happier, and better servants of God. . . . They knew that there *were* greater goods and lesser goods, greater evils and lesser evils, . . . there *were* times when the end justified the means, but only when the end was God's very own, the fruit of His supreme commandment: "Thou shalt love thy neighbor as thyself."[19]

Leaving the now free and spiritually enlightened beings on Tirel, the spaceship makes a landing on three more planets of the Beacon System. The first is a paradise with no intelligent life where the crew rests and takes delight in their surroudings. On the next planet, the planet Lotus, they find intelligent life in the form of beings resembling centaurs but who are under the spell of a drug-like plant which puts them into a trance-like state and hence under the control of something called the Pillars of Death. Again, the crew of the Oliver Cromwell is able to defeat the evil and free the beings, this time only by the brave self-sacrifice of one of the crew member's lives. The last planet, called

---

19. Ibid., 162–164.

Gehenna, is a fiery furnace with beings (if they can be called such) resembling large, slow moving stones. Attempting to discover more about them, two crew members exit the mother ship, which has not been able to make a landing, in smaller, faster ships and try their luck. After a series of explosions and the consequent release of deadly gasses that are capable of melting these smaller ships, the captain speaks via radio to Lincoln Adams who is stuck in one of the ships on Gehenna without a means of escape:

> "We have one recourse left," said Commander Tarn in his iron voice. "And I will not tell you what it is. If there is no change in your situation soon, we shall be forced to employ it; and the result will be in the hands of providence and destiny. I will not mince words with you Adams. You have no better than an even chance of getting out of this alive—if that much. For now, since your fate is in God's hands, I can only advise you, as a brave man and a true Puritan . . . to prepare yourself to meet death as only your kind of man can meet it, and upon the revelation of the will of God."[20]

Although the above passage is taken from Warren's first attempt at a fictional novel, it is illustrative of his core attitude towards life—a conviction, the repercussions of which he may not have been fully aware at this time. "The purpose of one's life," this belief states, "is to live it in the service of goodness, even if this service requires one to die for the sake of goodness." Though Warren here speaks of this conviction in terms of obedience to "providence" and "the will of God," he would put such phrases away for some time, losing interest in pursuing Puritan beliefs, recovering such terms in the fullness of their meaning when he came into the Catholic Church. Writing about real-life heroes, such as Colonel Jose Moscardo who gave advice to his own son remarkably similar to the advice given to Lincoln Adams by Com-

---

20. Ibid., 266.

mander Tarn, Warren would come to revel in such men and women and the lives they led.[21] As the above passage illustrates, it was part of Warren's romantic nature to love heroes, even before he discovered them amongst the pages and pages in the story of the real world.

Having thus completed a first draft of his first novel, Warren gives it his own critique in a letter to Marie Donahue:

> While I have no intention of publishing it in its present form, which is in many ways immature and shows the results of being written for my satisfaction only, as the sharpest possible contrast to the kind of behavior I saw all around me at Camp Kokura in Japan, I do have some idea of someday writing a completely revised version of it when I feel I have enough years, experience and thought behind me to do the theme real justice. . . . But the version I finally do for publication, maybe ten or twenty or even thirty years from now, will be entitled *Song of the Morning Stars*. This of course is taken from the reading from Job.

In the fall of 1957, twenty-five-year-old Warren left signal flags and Japanese warehouses behind him and entered the teaching profession, an arena he had always intended to join. He chose Indiana University by default "because," he says, "it was the only position I could find that would hire sight unseen, which was just what I needed, since I was still in the Army when I applied."[22] While at Indiana University, Warren learned something about the world of academia which would change the lives of hundreds—and possibly thousands—in the future. Of his experience he says, "My year at Indiana was unproductive, except in teaching me the very important truth that the problems I had found at Columbia University were general throughout American higher education. I found little or no more companionship there than I had found at

---

21. For the complete story of Colonel Moscardo and his son, see Warren H. Carroll, *The Last Crusade* (Front Royal, VA: Christendom Press, 1996), 79–86.

22. Carroll, "Unpublished Autobiography."

Columbia."[23] Had he found teaching at Indiana University rewarding, there might never have been a Christendom College.

Divine providence was still in charge, however, and, finding a man totally open to the truth, provided him with yet another formative experience:

> One night in the Indiana University library I had one of the formative experiences of my life. I first read the story of the false monk Rasputin in Russia in December 1916, whom would-be assassins killed eleven times—but he would not die. Clearly supernatural forces had been at work, which I did not then understand because I was not yet a Christian and did not believe in the supernatural; but the survival of Rasputin through eleven deaths could be explained no other way. The historian I was reading could not see it or explain it; but even though without faith, I thought I could. I have since become convinced that Rasputin was possessed by the Devil, whom he had invited into himself in occult rites. As a Catholic historian I was later to teach that history is an arena where God and the Devil contend for the souls of men; I had my first vision of that contention that night at the Indiana University library, and never forgot it.[24]

Later, this story would become, as Warren states, "a gripping passage in my first published book, *1917: Red Banners, White Mantle*."[25] And we see here, in his first work of non-fiction, that same high regard of Warren's for those willing to place themselves in harm's way to accomplish a higher good.

Juxtaposing the Russian revolution with the stories of the Virgin Mary's appearance in the tiny Portuguese village of Fatima and

---

23. Ibid.
24. Warren H. Carroll and Anne Carroll, *A History of Christendom*, vol. 6, *The Crisis of Christendom* (Front Royal, VA: Christendom Press, 2013), 806.
25. Carroll, "Unpublished Autobiography."

the involvement of the family of Czar Nicholas II with the diabolical figure of Gregory Efimovich Rasputin, the book contains a gripping account of Rasputin's death. By a series of events, the Russian Czarina, Alexandra, had succumbed to the quasi-hypnotic influence of Rasputin, eventually dragging her husband in with her. Rasputin's complete deception of Alexandra resulted in her own manipulation of her husband and in the eventual reducing of the government to a state of "virtual chaos."[26] By the end of 1916, a handful of undeceived and undaunted men made a decision: Rasputin had to go. Warren's riveting account continues the story:

> At one o'clock in the morning of December 31, Yusupov arrived at Rasputin's house. He had some difficulty gaining admittance at that hour; then Rasputin took time to comb his beard, for he thought he was going to meet Yusupov's beautiful wife Irina. (Actually she was far away, in the Crimea.) He put on a white silk blouse embroidered with cornflowers, and black velvet pants. His normally foul body odor was masked by a strong smell of cheap soap. After half an hour he was finally ready to go, and at two o'clock in the morning he entered Yusupov's house and was taken immediately to the cellar. Upstairs a primitive "gramophone" played raucously, over and over, the rollicking tune of "Yankee Doodle" as a way of suggesting to Rasputin that the noble ladies he had come to see were diverting themselves with the music.
>
> Yusupov went down into the cellar alone with Rasputin. He offered him the rose cakes filled with cyanide. At first he refused them. Then he ate one, then another.
>
> Nothing happened.
>
> Yusupov gave him an unpoisoned glass of wine, then a poisoned glass. He drank it, sipping. His hand went to his throat, and he stood up.

---

26. Warren H. Carroll, *1917: Red Banners, White Mantel* (Front Royal, VA: Christendom Press, 1981), 24.

"Is anything the matter?" Yusupov asked.

"Nothing much," Rasputin replied. "Just an irritation in throat. . . . That's very good madeira. Give me some more."

Yusupov gave him a second glass of the cyanide-laced wine. This time Rasputin drained it almost in a single gulp.

Nothing happened.

Then, as Yusupov tells us in his harrowing account of that night . . . :

> All of a sudden his expression changed into one of fiendish hatred. Never before had he inspired me with such horror. I felt an indescribable loathing for him, and was ready to throw myself upon him and throttle him.
>
> I felt that he knew why I had brought him there, and what I intended to do with him. A mute and deadly conflict seemed to be taking place between us. I was aghast. Another moment and I should have gone under. I felt that confronted by those satanic eyes, I was beginning to lose my self-control. A strange feeling of numbness took possession of me. My head reeled.

Rasputin's head bent, and fell into his hands. Then he raised his head, and asked Yusupov to play for him on his guitar, and to sing him a song.

It was two-thirty in the morning.

Finally Yusupov made an excuse to leave the cellar room, and hurried upstairs. . . . Taking Dmitri's revolver, he went back down the stairs. Rasputin appeared ill, but quickly improved after another glass of wine. Yusupov held the revolver behind his back.

Atop a richly decorated cupboard hung a seventeenth-century crucifix made of rock crystal and silver.

Yusupov went over to it. He stood beneath it.

'I love this cross,' he said.

Rasputin said the trinkets in the cupboard were more to his fancy.

Yusupov replied: 'Gregory Efimovich, you had better look at the crucifix, and say a prayer before it.'

For a moment, after he spoke these words, the almost paralyzing fear left Yusupov; Rasputin no longer seemed to have the power to impose it. His almost colorless eyes were fixed on the crucifix.

Yusupov brought the revolver into view and fired. The two men were standing face to face.

Rasputin roared like a wild beast. The crash of his falling body resounded through the house. The conspirators came rushing down the stairs. . . . They examined the bullet wound. It was in the region of the heart. Rasputin was not yet dead, for they could hear his breath rasping and rattling. But he was still, and must be dying. . . .

Moved by an impulse he could never explain, Yusupov suddenly shook the body violently. The left eyelid fluttered. The left eye opened, then the right—those hypnotic, gray-green eyes—and fastened upon Yusupov a look "of diabolical hatred."

A moment, suspended in time, the darkest and most ancient horrors which haunt the human soul focused upon Yusupov in that underground room as though by a burning glass—and the body of Rasputin rose up with foaming lips and wild-beast roar, grasping Yusupov by the shoulder in a grip of iron, reaching for his throat, repeating "in a hoarse whisper," over and over, Yusupov's name.

"Felix . . . Felix . . . Felix . . . Felix . . . Felix . . ."

Exerting every ounce of his strength whetted by the utmost extremity of terror, Yusupov tore himself free from the nightmare grip and rushed up the stairs screaming:

"Purishkevich! Shoot! Shoot! He's alive! He's getting away!"

For a moment Purishkevich must have thought Yusupov had gone mad. He could think of no response. Then he heard a scrambling sound on the cellar steps.

Rasputin was climbing up on all fours, roaring. For an instant neither of the two men at the top of the stairs could move. They stood stock still, as though paralyzed, as the shape of Rasputin humped and staggered up the last few stairs, across the hall, through the door, and out into the snowy courtyard, saying, "Felix, Felix, I'll tell it all to the Czarina."

It was between three and four o'clock in the morning, the loneliest hour of the night.

Purishkevich was a crack shot. At last he pulled out his Savage revolver and began firing. His first two bullets missed. This scene from Hell was not in the least like the firing range at the Semyonov Barracks where he regularly practiced. The whiplash echo of the futile shots rang through the silent night.

Rasputin scrambled on. He was nearing the only unlocked gate of the courtyard, which opened directly upon the street. He was escaping.

Purishkevich bit his hand to steady himself. He fired again, and again. The bullets struck Rasputin in the shoulder and in the neck. He collapsed in a deep snowdrift, grinding his teeth in rage.

Purishkevich knew the four shots must have been heard. Two soldiers were in the street. He opened the gate, called them over, and told them: "I've killed Grishka Rasputin, enemy of Russia and the Czar."

The two soldiers embraced and kissed him. "Thank God."

He told them not to tell anyone what they had seen and heard.

"Yes, Excellency," they replied. "We are Russian people. Have no doubts of us."

Then they helped him drag the body back into the house.

Repeating, as though in a trance, Rasputin's "Felix . . . Felix . . . Felix," Yusupov, after being violently sick, came back to the body and gazed upon its now blood-spattered and distorted face.

Then he heard a faint whining sound. He saw an eye open. Leaping upon the body in a renewed frenzy of terror and loathing, he beat it frantically with a two-pound leaded walking stick. Purishkevich dragged him away.

Grand Duke Dmitri, Dr. Lazavert, and Captain Sukhotin had now returned in the car. Yusupov and Dr. Lazavert were unmanned by the night of terror; Purishkevich was now in charge. He, Dmitri, and Sukhotin put the body in the car. It had been wrapped in a blue curtain with a rope bound tightly around both its arms and its legs.

Purishkevich felt the body. It was still warm.

Purishkevich drove to the Petrovsky bridge over the Staraya branch of the Neva River. There was a sentry box on the bridge. The sentry was asleep, but the conspirators did not know that. They stopped the car, turned off the engine and the lights, and hurriedly dumped the body head first over the parapet into a hole in the ice kept open by the swift current of the river. On the way down the tumbling body struck either the bridge abutment, or the ice, or both, breaking its head open. In their hurry the conspirators had forgotten to attach to the body the weights they had brought for this purpose; now they were hastily and loosely attached to Rasputin's coat. One boot was thrown down, but it sailed in the wind and landed on the ice instead of in the water of the hole. The other boot lay forgotten in the car.

It was a little after four o'clock in the morning. The world slept—the great and the simple, the good and the evil, from Petrograd all across Europe. In Vienna, Charles and Zita; in Zurich, Lenin and Krupskaya; in Aljustrel near Fatima, Lucia and Jacinta and Francisco.

The car started up, and drove away from the Petrovsky bridge.

Under the black water at the edge of the ice, the shape of Rasputin bobbed and writhed. The cyanide from three poisoned cakes, and then from two poisoned glasses of wine, had long since passed from its stomach to the inner tissues of its body, where it kills swiftly and unerringly—most surely of all when in a lethal dose prepared by a doctor. Yusupov's bullet lay near its heart, Purishkevich's fourth bullet in its neck—both wounds later pronounced surely mortal by medical examiners. Its head, battered by the blows of Yusupov's lead-weighted stick, was broken open in several places by the impact of the head-first fall from the bridge; blood from the gaping wounds eddied in the water. Gregory, son of Efim, the Dissolute, the dark angel of Russia, had already died at least five times that night. Now came the sixth death—drowning, and freezing. No man, however healthy, could live more than a few minutes in the ice-choked Neva River in Petrograd, at sixty degrees north latitude, at four o'clock in the morning on the last day of the year, in the devouring waters under the polar wind.

The shape moved. It held its breath. It tried to draw breath, and water began to enter its lungs. But its hands were busy—those big, fleshy hands with their log thick fingers. The left hand clenched into a fist, straining against its bonds. The right hand twisted and turned until it had freed itself entirely from the hastily knotted rope, whose grip upon left hand and legs alone was still keeping the body from rising to the surface through the hole in the ice, and swimming to shore.

The fingers tugged at the bonds and the knots. No man saw it. No dog howled. There was only the snow and the stillness, white enveloped by black. It was the eve of 1917, the most fateful year in the history of the world since Christ ascended into Heaven.

The scene fades from our sight. We know no more. Not for our minds and eyes is the last battle in that dark river under the ice, nor may we know from what far realms its ultimate combatants were drawn. The Arctic night closes in, to be followed four hours later by the pale dawn and the pale brief day of the far north in deepest winter. That day Rasputin's boot was found on the ice, and tracks in the snow piled at the edge of the Petrovsky bridge. The authorities began a search on the frozen river the next day, using divers, and policemen traversing the ice. One of the policemen, making a hole in the ice, found Rasputin's fur coat. Two hundred feet from the bridge the body was recovered, entirely encased in ice; but its lungs were full of water, signifying that it had been still alive and trying to breathe underwater, and its right hand was free of the constricting rope, and reaching out.

It was dead at last. But so was Imperial Russia.[27]

It was to be in such historical spell-binding passages as this that God would make use of Warren's inherited gift for "yarning." God would also honor Warren's great desire to teach. But not yet; and not in Indiana.

Remembering that his mother had instilled in him the importance of employing his life in making a contribution to humanity, we can see that he not only took her advice to heart, but that this desire had become paramount in his young life. In letters to Marie Donahue, Warren expresses his determination and his desire—to do more:

I hope you aren't missing [Berwick Academy] too much and are finding real satisfaction in your work at Dover

---

27. Ibid., 35–41.

High, as I am certainly finding here at Indiana with my first experience in college teaching. There is no doubt that teaching provides a tremendous opportunity to influence people in every way toward a higher and more constructive type of thought and even of life, if only one knew exactly how to do it. I feel I am accomplishing something, but wish it was in my power to do more.[28]

I am pleased that you do so strongly recommend it [his manuscript *Mission to the Stars*] for publication, and it is possible that in a couple of years I may do so; but as I hope someday to do a really outstanding epic novel along the same lines I may decide to incorporate it into the fuller project. The same message I am trying to convey in this novel can also be conveyed in many other ways— particularly through straight historical writing . . . and I intend to try all the approaches that I can.[29]

In 1959, having completed his dissertation entitled, "John Adams— Puritan Revolutionist: A Study of His Part in Making the American Revolution," Warren received his Ph.D. from Columbia, whose very ground he despised, and decided that the elitist attitude he had encountered both at Columbia and Indiana University was not for him.

So now I concluded that there was no future for me in the academic world as it then existed in America, though all my life I had expected eventually to become a college or university professor as my father had been. I remembered how vividly my Army service had contrasted with the destructive environment at Columbia and Indiana Universities, and decided therefore to get back into government service.

---

28. Warren Carroll to Marie Donahue, 20 October 1957, Maine Women Writers Collection.
29. Warren Carroll to Marie Donahue, 25 January 1958, Maine Women Writers Collection.

I began by applying for the civil service, full of romantic illusions about it, which were rudely dashed when I was bluntly informed that I was "ineligible" because of my oral interview, in which I had stressed my desire to serve my country, preferably in the Department of Defense. This was evidently not what they wanted. Then I thought of the Central Intelligence Agency, befitting my vehement anti-communism, a legacy of my careful reading of Whittaker Chambers's *Witness*. So I interviewed with them, and was relieved to find at least that they did not turn me down because I wanted to serve my country. But the processing of my application included a lie detector test, which was the basis of my later Tarrant story "The Test of Truth" which explains exactly what I think of lie detectors.[30] The main question I had trouble with was "are you married?" Of course I was not, though I passionately wanted to be, and the passion came through on the lie detector. I wonder if they thought I was a bigamist or something like that.

Despite my problems with the lie detector, I was accepted as a CIA recruit, and hired in 1960 as an analyst of communist propaganda in the Foreign Broadcast Information Service (FBIS). Not only did I learn a lot more about communism there, but I also learned a lot about propaganda, the communists being the world's best propagandists. It would stand me in good stead when I began to write propaganda myself, for political causes I supported. But I soon found out that the CIA was honeycombed with Columbia University-type leftists who scorned and scoffed at the communist menace, despite the steady flow of documents across their desks proving how great that

---

30. Beginning in 1963, Warren began working on a series of stories he later called *The Tarrant Chronicles*, in which he denounces all manner of modern day corruption and injustice. The main characters, Victor and Valerie Tarrant, are depicted a bit like Catholic super-hero detectives, taking on cases and "righting all wrongs." Their three children eventually join them in this family business. Only the first book, *The Book of Victor Tarrant*, was published.

menace was. The woman who was my boss actually re-
joiced when the Soviets placed their missiles in Cuba in
the "Cuban missile crisis" during President Kennedy's
administration, on the grounds that "now we'll know how
they feel when we place missiles near their borders." I do
not exaggerate or "spin" this at all. That is actually what
she said. So I became even more sympathetic with Senator McCarthy, though by then he was dead of cirrhosis of
the liver caused by excessive drinking brought on by his
persecution by the media.

I continued as a CIA propaganda analyst through the
Berlin blockade, at one point attending a high-level brief-
ing in which the participants vied with one another to see
how sophisticated they could sound and how dismissive
of the reality of the communist threat. I will always remember the tone of voice with which one highly regarded
participant in that meeting kept speaking with a smirk of
the "Russkis." So I decided once again to shake the dust of
the CIA office where I had worked off my feet, and to get
into something totally different. I applied to a program for
historians to prepare (and supervise the preparation of)
unit histories for the Strategic Air Command, which later
made several appearances in my Tarrant stories. Eventually I became assistant command historian (civilian) of the
Second Air Force of the Strategic Air Command, based
at Barksdale Air Force Base near Shreveport, Louisiana,
which gave me the Southern background for my Tarrant
story "Every Man's Hand Against Them." As that story
makes clear, I did not like or warm up to the south.

But eventually the lack of intellectual stimulation in
the life of an Air Force historian got to me, and I decided
once again to branch out in a new direction. (By this time
my parents were understandably quite bewildered by where
I would eventually end up.) I decided to launch a career
in law, at the beginning of 1962 looking for a law school I
could enter. Only one of prestige accepted students at mid-

year, though its officials were astonished that someone with
an "earned Ph.D." should be applying for admission. I may
have been the only one they ever had.[31]

Lest it be thought that Warren's life at this time was all novel writing and job hunting, it can be told that it was at this point in his life that he purchased his first new car—and began his passion for traveling, taking what he termed his "far-reaching car trips." Sometimes driving thirteen hours a day, he covered most states over the next three years traveling on weekends and holidays. He loved to see places and take pictures.[32] In a Western Union telegram dated December 20, 1961, sent home to "MRS HERBERT CARROLL—EARLS RD. SOUTH BERWICK ME," he says, "FORGING NORTHWARD. GREAT TIME IN SEBRING. PONCE DE LEON HOTEL STILL HERE, LOOKING FOR FOUNTAIN. REN.[33]

While he may not have found the fountain of youth, he was standing on the threshold of his discovery of the fountain of truth. He was just waiting for Anne.

---

31. Carroll, "Unpublished Autobiography."

32. Anne Carroll, interview by author, 29 November 2012.

33. Western Union Telegram, Box 7-2B, Folder 4, Archive Collection, Caroline Jones.

5

Anne's Five-Dollar Bill

WE COME NOW TO the point of turning in the life of Warren Hasty Carroll. We could almost call it the "incarnational" moment of his personal history, just as the conception of the second person of the Blessed Trinity by the Virgin Mary was and is the incarnational moment in all of human history. Warren, the historian, would later exclaim to anyone who would listen, "Truth exists!" and he would raise his fist in the air, "The Incarnation happened!" and down would slam the fist on his desk as he fixed his eyes on an unsuspecting but rapt individual in an unfaltering, piercing gaze. One felt fire behind both eyes and words—a flame which smoldered and crackled because it fed on the truth of which it had been so long in its ardent search. And just as the Son of Man took on a human nature in the "fullness of time," so also was Warren's moment of fullness approaching—dancing impatiently on the threshold of his soul.

Although the seed had been there all along, and God had been guiding and governing this man who longed for and had dedicated his life to the truth, the immediate springboard was, as he would later point out in the lives of many historical figures, something quite ordinary: the University of Colorado Law School in Denver, where he enrolled in January of 1962. Keeping in mind that Warren was applying mid-year and that the University of Colorado was, as he has stated, the only law school of prestige which accepted students at mid-year, we can begin to watch the unfolding of events. First, in Warren's own words:

> So in 1962 I enrolled in the University of Colorado Law School. ... This decision led me to my first political combat. ... What we did at the University of Colorado was to start a campus newspaper, *The New Conservative*, to challenge the official campus newspaper, the leftist-controlled *Colorado Daily* edited by a young declared Socialist named Gary Althen. This was early in the history of the American "conservative movement" headed politically by Senator Barry Goldwater and inspired by William F. Buckley Jr. and his *National Review*. I had become an enthusiastic supporter of both men, who were clearly arrayed against the enemy I had found at Columbia University. I wrote a column for *The New Conservative* and worked with two very talented and go-getting students, Chuck Adams and Dave Jarrett, who were excellent strategists. For example, Dave got us started, when we had only an idea and no paper yet, by getting permission from the powers that be on campus to distribute it wherever the *Colorado Daily* was distributed. Nobody took us seriously because they didn't think we could possibly do it and wanted to appear as advocates of "free speech." But we raised a considerable sum of money from local businessmen to finance our operation (my first experience in fundraising) and set up a double sponsoring organization, the Conservative Club of the University of Colorado, to be the publisher of record, and the Conservative Club of the University of Colorado, Incorporated, to hold the money and keep it out of the grasp of the student government which was certainly not sympathetic. I am still amazed that so transparent a ruse succeeded, but our opponents were not very smart.
>
> We invited Senator Goldwater to the University of Colorado that fall, and he was greeted with ridicule and hostility, which he quite rightly resented. Several weeks

after his visit, a "hippie" student named Mitcham wrote a long rambling article weirdly entitled "Riding the Whale" against Goldwater in the *Colorado Daily*. It referred to him as "a fool, a mountebank, a murderer, no better than a common criminal." Eagle-eyed Chuck Adams spotted this line and cried, "He can't say that!" Chuck fired off a telegram to Senator Goldwater, who demanded an apology. Gary Althen, the editor, refused to apologize. The university administration headed by President Quigg Newton, supported his refusal. We headlined the whole controversy, knowing it put the university and its leftists in the worst possible light. Then Gary Althen played directly into our hands with a steaming editorial in which he explained that he hated his country, and had learned to hate it at the University of Colorado. This was the simple truth, but not one that people (at least in 1962) wanted to hear.

Now there emerged on our side a true hero, who defended our position and urged us to stick with it. His name was Edward Rozek and he was a professor of political science at the University of Colorado. He was a Polish Catholic and had written a brilliant book (which I later used as a source in my history of communism) on the betrayal of Poland at Yalta and before. Dr. Rozek had been a victim of both the Nazis and the communists, and consequently feared no man. He had courage to burn. He was strongly built and dark, built like a block of wood.

To make a long story short, we were able to parlay Gary Althen's statement that he hated his country and had learned to hate it at the University of Colorado, into one of the chief issues in the fall 1962 election campaign in Colorado. The Regents of the University were elected by the people, and its control changed hands. Quigg Newton was fired, along with Gary Althen. Dr. Rozek brought a suit for civil conspiracy against the University of Colorado to destroy his professional reputation. It was argued by the best trial lawyer in Colorado, who lost the case on a technicality but won in the court of public opinion. I had tasted victory against the enemy I had met at Columbia University, and it was sweet.[1]

While tasting his first political victory, however, Warren had inadvertently also met his future wife. One summer evening in 1962, Gerry, whom Warren had met among his conservative friends at the university, stepped out to a movie with his date, Anne, and afterwards ended up at a local hamburger joint by the name of Gaylord's Cafe. Anne was a rising senior at Loretto Heights College in Denver and working at Bob's Pizzeria for a dollar an hour. Seemingly accidental, Anne and Gerry's first date had taken place because Anne's friend's boyfriend had had car trouble. Gerry had a car but couldn't go as a third wheel, so in desperation a call was placed to Anne who agreed to go as Gerry's date. On this particular evening, Warren was also enjoying a hamburger in Gaylord's Cafe. Gerry introduced them. Political issues were discussed. Eventually, Gerry lost interest in Anne, but Anne and Warren did not lose interest in political issues and a correspondence began.[2]

In the meantime, while not typing political letters to Anne, Warren was banging out 532 typewritten pages which were compiled into his second unpublished novel entitled *Banner in the Sky*. Everything went into this pot! Not only his political theories, but his geographical descriptions of almost the entire United States which he had seen firsthand on all those "far-reaching" car trips, his still lingering attraction to Calvinism, his condemnation of higher education and big government, his experiences both in the Strategic Air Command and at law school, as well as his family genealogy and interest in astronomy, biology, and the current popular music. *And* it was a romance! Hence the 532 pages. Before going briefly into the story line, there is one more observation to be made. The manuscript reads very much like an Ayn Rand novel (minus the inappropriate scenes), which is no

---

1. Carroll, "Unpublished Autobiography."
2. Anne Carroll, interview by author, 13 December 2013.

coincidence, since Warren was at this time a great admirer. Although he would later cringe when thinking of the esteem he had had for "this cold, harsh woman, who made her life by denying her womanhood," he considered her an excellent writer and for a time, embraced her libertarian viewpoints.[3] Like Rand, Warren used the thoughts and conversations of his characters to get these viewpoints across to his reader, but unlike her glorification of selfishness, his stories had real heroes and heroines who made great sacrifices for the good of others.

In *Banner in the Sky*, two such heroes, Camilla Carey (who chooses law school because she sees the "absolute primacy of politics as a determinant of [America's] destiny") and Aquilla Carson, known as "Carse," hold together a plot which begins at the Battle of Dunbar in Scotland and ends on . . . well . . . Mars.[4] At the crux of the plot is Warren's yet unbaptized view of American messianism. The beginning of the chapter entitled simply "America" reads:

> Sing of a land, a promised land, far-flung between Earth's rockcore and the sky. Shaper of Dream, Guidon of Hope, let the sun and the wind dance high, let the infinite beckon her sons, but if we do not cherish her we shall lose her, and America will be a shattered huddle twelve stories down and there will be no glimmerlit harbor through darkness for the last boat from Cairncanom and the doors of night will close over a planet and a starlit angel click the lock and wing her destiny farther up the Milky Way. . . . See a land that looks always toward greater glory, however great may be all that has gone before—a land without barriers and without limits, save only in the minds of its own people.[5]

The problem with America, according to another character, is that it is abandoning justice by "rewarding the wrong and the bad and

---

3. Carroll, "Unpublished Autobiography."
4. Warren Carroll, *Banner in the Sky*, unpublished novel, 148.
5. Ibid., 25–26.

punishing the right and the good, by seeing that the person who deserves the most gets the least."[6] The solution, he says, is for America to learn "once more what her founders knew, that strength and pride are always infinitely better defenses against any threat or horror, any present or imagined disaster, than weakness and self-flagellation."[7]

The destiny of bringing together those few who have the intelligence, drive, and excellence to rescue America from its downward slide falls to one Mark Stornoway, the last descendent of a clan of Scottish Calvinists. Taking up the job of a taxi driver, he travels the highways and byroads of America beginning in the Northeast and ending in Texas, by way of Pennsylvania, Michigan, Illinois, Missouri, Colorado, Oregon, and Louisiana, and mysteriously seeks out and then maneuvers from afar a select group of totally unrelated individuals. Warren had obviously been to all of the places he describes, as we can see from the accuracy and detail of the descriptions. Painting a vivid and poetic picture of the Mississippi River from its small beginnings in Northern Minnesota, he writes:

River.

Beyond the divide which is Mesabi it takes its rise, in the little forest-rimmed pond called Itasca, a quick, bright-flowing northwoods stream like so many others, feeling its way from lake to lake, south to north, west to east, east to west, and then in Crow Wing country near a little town named Manganese it whips around a horseshoe bend and squares away to southward, deepening, quieting, beginning to roll in long surges against its banks as it takes up the mighty destiny of three thousand miles that calls from the gulf. And soon it leaves Ore's wilderness behind, absorbing the muddy gush of the farmland creeks, cutting out and building up the thick loamy bluffs, pulsing with the richness of the soil, mingling East and West and North

---

6. Ibid., 41.
7. Ibid., 411.

and South in its steady arterial flow, lord and maker of half
a continent, whose pull is felt from the green summits of
the Appalachians to the diamond diadems of the Rockies,
whose bounty is whole states of lush waving wheat and
high-tasselled corn, this river, Mississippi, Earth Mother
of Mid-America . . .

One hundred and fifty miles below St. Louis the Mississippi takes the Ohio, and thence through Old Dixie becomes a vast looping, surging freshwater tide, held in check
by lofty levees rising above miles of mud-flats and swamps
and crescent lakes, a giant of its kind, with a majesty and
might equaled only twice over all the earth: where the
Amazon floods through the fantastic luxuriance of equato-
rial jungle, and where the Nile brings life to the seared and
barren desert. But the Mississippi knows neither jungle nor
desert, only that warm peace, that mystic beauty, that mel-
ancholy ghost of pride that is America's Heart of Southland,
that bows in lush green cape and pillared coronet to receive
the last of River's servants: gorge-born, prairie-winding,
Ozark-tumbling Arkansas, boggy Yazoo, inconstant Red;
and then it is steaming, vine-hung bayou country, River's
silty thrust out into waiting gulf, legended Louisiana."[8]

There are other passages similar to this one: of the Rocky Mountains, the Upper Peninsula of Michigan, the city of New Orleans, and
this one—of New York City:

The lights changed, to a winking and arrow-flashing bar-
rage of greens, and soon U.S. Highway Number One had
left Northport behind and with the rolling miles sucked in
an ever-growing stream of vehicles all bound for the city
of New York.

Whirlpool.

8. Ibid., 73–74, 78–79.

> Orbiting obediently in their outflung circles, bending
> tangentially inward in a complex knotted skein of shop-
> ping centers, the little cities and the bigger cities and the
> clustering parkways that were all part of the satellite sys-
> tem of New York spun their flotsam toward the central
> eddy, where an intake of many-mouthed bridges funneled
> it in spurts of disciplined regularity toward the tawdry
> vortex of Times Square.[9]

The novel is peppered with autobiographical elements including one Carl who teaches at a university and is eventually driven to suicide by the cold, impersonal milieu in which he is forced to operate, and another Stanley Morrow, teacher at the University of Colorado, who laments that he could find no one to listen to the truths he had learned. In fact, "evil," states another character, "is not open destruction of goodness and truth, but perversion, twisting."[10] Here again is that love of truth and abhorrence of anything which would mar its beauty.

Surprisingly, or maybe not for those who knew him, Warren's antidote to the evil, injustice, and twisting of truth by those who would destroy America includes very much the idea of laughter, a trait which he would celebrate throughout his life. In the novel, this concept makes its first impish entrance in the person of Camilla Carey who

> enjoyed doing the things she liked, however odd. One of
> the most peculiar lessons a frequently very absurd world
> had taught her was how few people did. Some turned it
> right square round. The only things they claimed to enjoy
> doing were things they didn't like. Consider her mother.
> There was nothing Harriet Carey enjoyed more than en-
> tertaining; she often said so, and certainly did enough of
> it. But at the same time it was perfectly clear that each

---

9. Ibid., 49.
10. Ibid., 42.

social occasion was a harrowing ordeal, dreaded in advance and bemoaned in retrospect. . . . Like the time that
she happened to remember, years ago, when her mother
had returned from seeing off the last of an unusually long
guest list with her hand to her temple, announcing grimly
to her long-suffering husband: "Wasn't it a *wonderful* evening? Now I shall be sick for a week." The suggestion that
the one inevitably led to the other had been too much for
Camilla; she had laughed until tears ran down her cheeks,
stopping only when her mother began actually to scream
with vexation, and she realized with a small but sudden
shock that such a sequence seemed entirely natural and
normal to Harriet Carey. By such experiences Camilla
had learned to save most of her open mirth for the sun
and the moon.[11]

A more complete expression of Warren's thoughts on joy and
laughter is given towards the end of the story when Mark Stornoway
has succeeded in gathering "the remnant" of those capable of living life
to their fullest potential and consequently saving America. This small
group of people has now come together at a ranch in Texas called the
Bar X Star and is busy working, each on his or her own project: founding a new institute for ennobling American education, writing a new
concerto commemorating beauty's immortality, developing a new
theory of the nature of cellular life which will enable man to travel
to and live on other planets, and funding, building, and launching a
rocket ship which would carry them to found the first human colony
on the planet Mars. And while they were accomplishing such tasks,

> They laughed. They laughed a great deal. It is necessary
> to speak often of laughter in a true account of such people,
> living and working together, because for all its frequent
> and bitter perversions laughter is the divinely bestowed

---

11. Ibid., 32–33.

instrument of human joy, and of celebration for human victory.... Like beauty, like any of the few human achievements and capacities which are ends in themselves as well as pathways and guideposts to greater things, joy exists in its moment and in eternity, but only by a fractional reflection, in time. It never grows old; its delight is magical because perpetual and undimmed, its impetus ever renewed fresh and pure and crystal-clear, like the outflow from a mountain spring.[12]

There is one more semi-philosophical passage worth quoting as it gives us a peek into Warren's thought at the time. It occurs in the thoughts of Mark Stornoway as he crossed and re-crossed America. Keeping in mind that this is Warren's "pre-Catholic but in-the-process-of-being-formed" mind, the passage is quite revelatory of his propensity for all things metaphysical:

The spirit lives, and the spirit alone matters. All else is evil and enemy, in a thousand guises and with a thousand methods of attack, in the ancient, cosmic strife of Being with Non-Being, of forthgoing Life with downfalling Death: not simple, as we used to think, God versus Mammon, Soul versus Flesh, the One Known Right versus the Many Ignorant of Willful Wrongs, for the uses of wealth and substance and mind are many, both good and evil, and the strife is not for or against them, but for or against the free life of the soul wherever it lives and however it lives, so long as it does not take upon itself the right to deny free life to another; and yet simple, because Non-being is not really able to disguise itself convincingly as Being if you will only ask, not why Non-being believes that neither you nor it should be, but only whether it is there, hooding the comets of life—and who stands yet forth to fight it, how, and where, and why.[13]

---

12. Ibid., 442.
13. Ibid., 136.

At some point in the middle of writing this all-encompassing novel, Warren laughed his way to Dallas, Texas. We pick him up again in his own narrative where he is wrapping up the story of his political victory at the University of Colorado:

> In the process of winning this victory, however, I had run through almost all the money I had, and could find no prospects for employment in or near Boulder, home of the University of Colorado. So I decided once again to pull up stakes. One of the donors to *The New Conservative* was a wealthy Texan named Al Hill, who owned a resort in Colorado. I knew him to be the son-in-law of fabled Texas oilman Haroldson Lafayette (H. L.) Hunt, then considered the second richest man in America (to J. Paul Getty). H. L. Hunt had been in at the beginning of the East Texas oil strike of the 1930's, the biggest in American history. I knew that Mr. Hunt funded conservative writers, and through Al Hill I had a way to get to him. So I left Boulder and drove south to Dallas, Texas, where Hill and Hunt both lived. It was probably the riskiest act of my life, though of course I knew my parents would never let me starve. But I was thirty-one years old and did not want to live off them. So I went to Dallas, carrying on my person every penny I had. I looked up Al Hill, he got me an interview with H. L. Hunt, and in less than a week I was on Hunt's payroll. Since I had so little money, I had some difficulty getting a place to live, and for several days I lived on sardines (which, as a Maine man, I am particularly fond of, though many people find this odd) until my first paycheck arrived.
>
> H. L. Hunt turned out to be a unique boss. He was very eccentric. He had a conservative radio program called *Life Line* for which I wrote scripts, carefully (at his direction) always calling our opponents "the mistaken." I also ghost-wrote books for him. One of the evenings with H. L. Hunt I remember best is when a group of charlatans

visited him trying to convince him they were in possession of "the secret of the universe." There were limits even to his credulity, and he called me in to tell him if they knew anything important. I patiently explained that they were talking through their hats.

In Dallas I began to work with the Republican Party, which was very well organized there after carrying its county for Nixon by a wide margin in 1960. In fact, I was in the offices of the Dallas Republican Party newsletter on the day that President Kennedy was shot in Dallas, having written three of its articles (under three different names). I was an alternate delegate from Texas (Dallas County) to the Republican national convention at the Cow Palace San Francisco, and actually got to attend on the day Goldwater was nominated and gave his famous acceptance speech in which he said "extremism in defense of liberty is no vice; moderation in pursuit of justice is no virtue." I agreed (and still agree) totally with that sentiment.

I believed passionately in Senator Goldwater's call for a major cutback in the size of government, being emphatically convinced that, in the words of his campaign slogan, "in your heart, you know he's right." Though in later years I lost most of my personal enthusiasm for Senator Goldwater, who was influenced by his wife to be "soft" on abortion, in 1964 Goldwater was for me a real crusading leader.

I helped organize and campaign for Goldwater in Dallas County, serving as his coordinator or captain in ten precincts. Our workers and I went door-to-door for him, finding much support, though we later learned that the majority of our apparent supporters had been convinced by the media that the whole city of Dallas was somehow collectively guilty of the assassination of President Kennedy there in the previous year. That election night of 1964 was the saddest political moment I ever remember. We were wiped out. Not only did Johnson carry Dallas County against Goldwater by a considerable margin, but we lost all our incumbent office-holders who were pledged to Goldwater: our U.S. congressman, our state senator, and our whole delegation to the lower house of the Texas legislature. Everybody lost; everybody was politically annihilated. All over the room, people were sobbing and crying.

But I was young and resilient and I had learned from my Maine heritage never to give up . . . so I looked around the country to find a place where Goldwater had triumphed decisively. Found it, and pulled up stakes and went there to live. I had already made a solitary car trip to Orange County, California, where several people lived with whom I had struck up a friendship by correspondence. So I decided that my future lay there rather than at Dallas.[14]

We should now pick up the threads that began in the hamburger joint called Gaylord's Cafe and concerned a young lady by the name of Anne. In order to do this, we must backtrack slightly in Warren's narrative.

While I was in Dallas, I had launched a unique little publication which I called *Freedom's Way*. It was based on the commitment I had made to the fiery novelist Ayn Rand and her libertarian gospel. . . . During the years I had been in Dallas I had contacted other Ayn Rand admirers, notably a group in Orange County, California (the people there with whom I had been corresponding). *Freedom's Way* was intended as a forum for political discussion among admirers of Ayn Rand's novels, particularly *Atlas Shrugged*. I got about fifty subscribers, who periodically wrote me their thoughts, which I then shared with them all, with my commentary. . . . One of my subscribers was Anne Westhoff.[15]

---

14. Carroll, "Unpublished Autobiography."
15. Ibid.

Anne, too, remembers *Freedom's Way*. Living in New York and at-tending New York University at the time, she was understandably frugal with her funds. And Warren charged a subscription fee of five dollars. Anne thought seriously about not subscribing. Warren later said that if she hadn't subscribed, he would have crossed her off his list and that would have been that. The whole of Warren's future, the existence of Christendom College and, we could even say, the lives of the innumerable children born to the parents who met there, hung on Anne's five-dollar-bill! But she did subscribe. One five-dollar-bill *can* make a difference![16]

The oldest of eight children and the daughter of a German Catho-lic father and a mother of French heritage, Anne grew up on a farm near the town of Wiggins, Colorado, attending a two-room school-house in the middle of nowhere. Her father, Vernon Westhoff, had crossed the prairie from Kansas to Colorado at the age of two in one of the last of the covered wagons, and later had acquired farmland for almost nothing during the depression. Warren remembers him as "rugged, weather-beaten, afflicted with a bad limp later in his life. When he died at almost ninety, it was said of him, 'he was tough as leather, and as soft as leather.'"[17] Anne's mother was of the same cali-ber, being born with only one complete hand but determined not to acknowledge or even mention it. Warren's first impressions of Anne as he got to know her by way of hamburgers and correspondence were of a "slender and beautiful [girl] with a broad and infectious smile," her most distinctive qualities being common sense, an intensely practical intelligence, and a brilliant mind.[18]

Before heading to Orange County, California, in that summer of 1965, Warren made a trip to Maine to see his parents. He stopped in New York City on the way. Anne, who never bought new clothes (if five dollars for a newsletter was a tough decision, new clothes were out of the question), bought a new dress. She had her hair done. Warren

---

16. Anne Carroll, interview by author, 29 November 2012.

17. Carroll, "Unpublished Autobiography."

18. Ibid.

and Anne had only met face to face one time, yes, at the hamburger joint, but this time it was the Top of the Sixes, a ritzy downtown restaurant for them. After that, the letters became more interesting. Warren recalls that "after that evening I knew that someone very special had come into my life."[19] He went back to visit for Christmas and the following summer brought Anne to meet his parents. In June, he proposed. Being quite a sentimentalist, the place he chose for his offer was the playhouse in his hometown where his mother's play had been produced every summer and where he had had his own "bit part" as a schoolboy. In July of the following year, 1967, his "bit part" was recast as a duo and he and Anne were married.

Anne's younger brother Pete was in the fourth grade when Warren first visited her family's farm in Colorado. "It wasn't your typical visit," he laughs.

> Warren took the almanac that we had and started going through the presidents of the United States, listing the good and bad qualities of each while my sister, Kath, and I sat politely on the couch. I also remember that Anne was grading papers and I wanted somebody to flunk. But Warren would read the papers and say, "Well, no, this has something good about it." He was more merciful and wanted everyone to pass. He kept encouraging her to give higher grades.
>
> They would come out every other Christmas after they got married—the other one they would spend in Maine. Sometimes they came out in the summer. The thing we did together the most was play ping-pong. He was a college champion. We had our table in a small room in the basement so it was confining. My brother had built the table and it was not the right height and narrower than a regular table. I would play all day long with the table pushed up against the wall so I got really good at de-

---

19. Ibid.

fense. We had also built our own paddles—they were not normal. One we called the stop sign because it was enormously big! We did have real balls. We didn't even know the rules—we just hit real hard. So Warren would come and play and he knew all these slams and was moving all over the place trying to maneuver and I would just stand as far back as I could and return the ball until he made a mistake. He never beat me. But he was just so happy to be playing and never got tired of it. We did this for hours every day. Eventually we got real paddles—for Warren.[20]

In the meantime, Warren's typewriter, now in Orange County, had not been idle. While still accruing his only income from writing *Life Line* scripts for H. L. Hunt, Warren was working on a broad theory in which he systematized all of human history! Carefully scrutinizing all of the great empires, he perceived certain similarities and came up with twenty-five points which he found to recur in many major civilizations. One of these points was that a great leader would be assassinated, and so he viewed the assassination of John F. Kennedy in 1963 as a sign of trepidation for America. His system took no account, however, of the church or of human frailties and he would later call it utter nonsense. He delineated his theories in a book entitled *The Last Crossroads: The Historical Position of America Today*, but never published it. A shorter article eventually appeared in a publication called *Freedom* in which he stated that, based on his point system, the end of our own civilization would be expected around the year 2200. The article concludes:

> That is why we stand at the last crossroads, and if enough decided to do so, the United States of America as a nation could still take the road away from tyranny toward liberty. That road would require us to re-evaluate our whole view of government—to recognize that the only proper

---

20. Peter Westhoff, interview by author, 6 March 2015.

and rightful functions of government are to protect the life, liberty and property of individuals through impartial courts practicing objective law. That road would require us first to halt the growth, then to begin the rollback of all laws and activities of government which regulate production, restrict trade, and redistribute wealth through taxation. History never stands still; and the giant government in our country today certainly will not stand still. It must either grow or shrink. Its continued growth will bring about a total state in a few more years. Its rollback, if begun now or in the next few years, could preserve our freedom and with it, Western civilization.[21]

While his theory in its specifics he later called absurd, he was certainly correct in many of his conclusions.

The true providential value of his theory was that it landed him on a television show which was viewed, on the particular evening of Warren's appearance, by the wife of one John Schmitz. The story of that show and the effect of Warren's words on Mr. and Mrs. Schmitz has made it to Anne, who relates John's words like this: "It was Saturday night and I was taking a bath. My wife called to me and said, 'You've *got* to come listen to this guy!'"[22] Warren's words are a little more eloquent:

It would seem that nothing would be less likely than that my appearance on the *Lomax Show* with this totally contrived theory would accomplish anything significant. But God used it in his deployment of forces. He saw to it that this show was watched by a young man, just two years older than me, who had been elected to the State Senate of California against the Johnson tide in 1964. His name was John George Schmitz. He came originally from

---

21. Warren H. Carroll, "Cycles of Liberty," *Freedom* Vol. 13, No. 5, (1968), 18, Box 5-17, Folder 37, Archive Collection, Caroline Jones.

22. Anne Carroll, interview by author, 13 December 2013.

Wisconsin and was a great admirer of Senator McCarthy. Most important, he was a convinced Catholic and was to become my godfather. I was to work for him for several years, in both Sacramento and in Washington, and he was to play a pivotal role in my life.[23]

To relate the story of Warren's conversion we will flip-flop between the charm of Anne's memories and the intensity of Warren's words in his short autobiographical excerpt. Warren begins:

> When we were married, I was still unbaptized, not a Christian at all. Thanks to my mother, I had always believed in God and an after-life. But she had taught me to avoid all "organized religion." I had no idea (because she did not) who Christ is. The idea that He was god had never entered my consciousness. So I had never faced the issue of His true identity. The only Catholics I had ever known had either rejected their faith or could not tell me (and did not even attempt to try) why they were Catholic. The one great exception, my boss Senator John Schmitz had never discussed his religion with me either, before I was married. So the thought that I might become Catholic had never entered my mind, any more than the question of who Christ is. That so strong a Catholic as Anne was willing to marry me under these circumstances is the greatest miracle of my life. I am not sure that even now she understands how she could have done it. But God was calling me, through her. He had formed her for me, as He formed Eve for Adam. And Anne was a woman of the new Eve, the Blessed Virgin Mary.
>
> She has told me since that when we were married, she thought it would take her ten years to pray me into the church. But because God wanted me in it (He had a job for me to do!) it took her only one year. Prayer is the

---

23. Carroll, "Unpublished Autobiography."

key to almost all conversions, as St. Monica found with St. Augustine. Before we were married, I was introduced to the requirements of the Catholic faith by Father Brady in Sacramento, who explained to me the duties of a non-Catholic in a mixed marriage. He was very wise and understanding, and I had no problems because I respected Anne so deeply and had never even thought of trying to change her religious convictions.

Anne and I never argued about religion. Amazing as it seems in retrospect, especially in view of the absolutely central place of the Catholic faith in Anne's life, we never even discussed it. She said later that she knew she could not beat me in an argument (after all, I was a Brooks Quimby debater) so she decided not to try, especially after I had dismissed several of her Catholic arguments with "oh, that's so irrational."[24]

For her part, Anne went faithfully to Mass every Sunday. Warren dropped her at the church door and then scooted off to the local doughnut shop for coffee, doughnuts, and the Sunday paper. When Christmas rolled around, however, and Warren told his sister, Sally, that he would be dropping Anne off at midnight Mass, she exclaimed in exasperation, "Well, aren't you going to go *with* her?" Caught off guard, Warren replied, "Well, yes, I guess I will!" At his first exposure to the Catholic Mass, Anne remembers that Warren was most impressed by the history of the martyrs which was read aloud. Anne's account continues:

> I never felt comfortable arguing apologetics with Warren because he was so much smarter than I was. He respected my commitment to the Catholic Church, though I think he was somewhat bemused by it at first. (How can this woman, who appears to be rational most of the time,

---

24. Ibid.

go in for this supernatural stuff?) He was a "pagan Deist" as he later described himself, but had always believed in a Creator and in personal immortality. (He probably believed that he would spend the afterlife doing historical research.) But the first Christmas of our marriage, his mother (providentially) gave me a book on St. Peter's Basilica. It was a lovely book, but it would have a greater impact than just inspiring admiration for the architecture. Sometime in the summer of 1968, Warren directly asked me why I believed in Christianity. Being unprepared with the extensive arguments that my seniors now learn, I simply said, "Because of the historical evidence for the Resurrection." He said something to the effect that the Gospel accounts were not historically reliable because they had been written long after the events. I said that's not true, and pulled out the St. Peter's book to prove it. Early in the book, the author discussed the Gospels, and on one page was a picture of the Ryland's papyrus fragment, which confirms a first century dating for John's Gospel, the one most widely debunked in liberal arguments, all of which Warren had heard in college and believed. He looked at that and instantly (almost) decided he had to investigate Christianity more thoroughly. Owning that book was providential, remembering that particular page was providential, but the situation was primarily providential because, I believe, God was no longer going to wait for me to argue Warren into the church, but instead gave Warren the grace to turn toward Christianity on the basis of a small piece of evidence (literally—the Ryland's fragment is just a few square inches).[25]

All of a sudden, this giant of a thinker was presented with historical evidence which his love of truth would not permit him to ignore. "I have to rethink things!" was his response, and in typical Warren

---

25. Anne Carroll, "What You Always Wanted To Know" (unpublished paper, Manassas, VA, July 25, 2011).

fashion, he bounded off to the library for books. Usually he walked to the library. This time he drove. Remembering the author of his boyhood "Queen of Books" (the C. S. Lewis space trilogy), and knowing now that Lewis was a famous Christian apologist, he went straight to "L" in the library catalogue and promptly checked out *Mere Christianity, Miracles,* and *The Problem of Pain.*[26] Walking out of the library, most likely with his nose already buried in a Lewis book, Warren forgot that he had driven and kept walking until he reached home. "I plunged into them [the books]," he tells us, "and could not put them down. For two full days I read them, every waking hour. I was taken right out of the world, so much so that I forgot I had parked my car at a parking meter in downtown Sacramento, California, and as a result accumulated a mass of parking tickets!"[27] He continues:

> Lewis, a relentless logician, forces his reader to face the issue I had never faced: *Who is this Man?* He shows you that you must recognize Jesus as God, or conclude that He was insane. And as the great G. K. Chesterton (to whom Lewis handsomely gives credit for this clinching argument) points out in *The Everlasting Man,* "No atheist or blasphemer believes that the author of the parable of the prodigal son was a monster with one mad idea, like Cyclops with one eye." I certainly was not going to believe that, and did not. Therefore I had to face the fact that Jesus is God.
>
> The effect on me was overwhelming. I had literally never even considered the possibility of the Incarnation, never even heard the word (like so many others in my pathetically ill-instructed generation). But I could not escape the pile-driver impact of this logic. I now realize that most people are not so impressed by logical argument as I, a Quimby debater—that there are other roads to conver-

---

26. All three of these works were required reading when this author attended Christendom College.
27. Carroll, "Unpublished Autobiography."

sion than this one. But this was the one that worked best for me; in fact, I doubt that any other road would have taken me to my God and savior.

I emerged like a diver from my plunge into this new world, still hardly able to believe what I was seeing. I began attending Mass with Anne. Since I had never been a protestant, I had no problem rejecting protestantism. In fact, I knew more than enough history to see how utterly unlikely it was that the Lord of the universe would have founded His church and then gone away and left it to go bad for 1,500 years (I still think this is far and away the most powerful single argument against protestantism, though it doesn't resonate with people who have no sense of history, who cannot really imagine how long 1,500 years is).

Not coincidentally, it was the same month when this cosmic insight came to me that I saw John Schmitz taking his heroic stand on the floor of the California legislature against Governor Regan's tax bill . . . and it began to dawn on me that only because he was truly Catholic was he able to do it.

John Schmitz made his stand on the last day of the California legislature's 1968 session, which was artificially prolonged by the absurd method of literally "stopping the clocks" in the halls of the legislature, until the prolonged debate on the tax bill was over and John Schmitz had NOT surrendered. The next day, in midsummer, we went south to Orange County where Schmitz's district was, where we lived during the second half of every year when the legislature was not in session. As soon as possible after we got there, I went to see the pastor of our parish church in Santa Ana, Monsignor Harry Trower. He later told me, "I knew you had the faith when you walked through my door."[28]

---

28. Carroll, "Unpublished Autobiography."

At long last, Warren heartily drank directly from the fountain of truth and it became a reconciling, so to speak, of the different streams which had weaved themselves into the fabric of his adult life, baptizing them with a logic and fullness of understanding. These streams included his in-depth study of historical cycles and desperate desire to place his hopes in America as the only answer for the future, his involvement with Ayn Rand, her libertarian philosophy, and her followers, a plan that was currently on his back burner for emigrating to Australia, and a number of projects he and Anne were working on. Much of the change in his thought process is captured in a few letters which he sent home during this crucial time in his life. In a letter to his parents dated August 28, 1968, he states the following:

> Once again I have come to a major turning point in my life. Sometimes it must seem to you that there have been an unconscionable number of these—you must be wondering why I don't at long last settle down and stay put, intellectually if not geographically. Well, whether it's due to my own errors or the mess the world is in—or, more likely, to a combination of both—so far each new turning I have taken has led to the dead end of a lost cause. So I have to keep searching for another road. This time I think I have found one which has no end. Almost exactly nine years ago, I wrote you from Washington: "I have found my answer"—meaning the answer to the world crisis for which I had been searching ever since I first realized its full dimensions while at Columbia. That answer—Ayn Rand's objectivism—has proved inadequate.... [While] it provides an internally consistent and logical basis for recognizing and dealing with the world of objective reality, ... her doctrine of "the virtue of selfishness" is wrong ... and has led some of her disciples to the acts of outright evil which Sally and I both witnessed repeatedly while working with them. No philosophy which refuses to recognize the evil of which men are capable ... can be a complete answer....

Ours is the first civilization committed to God during its rise; that commitment, if kept, might have broken the cycle; but it was lost, and the result was to keep us in the cycle. . . . I wanted to break the historic cycle, or at least escape its worst effects. The Catholic Church has already done so. In all the earth, only the people of the Old Testament and those in direct succession from the apostles of the New Testament have remained outside that cycle and essentially untouched by it. Only the papacy, of all human lines, has retained its succession unbroken for two thousand years. The Catholic Church has already conquered history. Mankind will conquer it only when his culture-makers follow their example. I wanted a cause to serve which would not fail. This is a cause which cannot fail. We have Christ's own promise that "the gates of hell shall not prevail against it."[29]

An idea that had begun while Warren was involved with his Ayn Rand group of friends was that America was headed towards a dictatorship and they must leave the country in order to live in freedom. "The thought of moving was much on my mind in those days," he admits. "I was toying with the idea of leaving the country altogether, trying to flee physically the encroaching evils I could see and feel, even without yet having the benefit of the faith (and so being without the inspiration the faith gives to stand and fight for right and truth, rather than run away)."[30] Australia was their chosen destination and hence, Anne and Warren learned to sail. In November of 1968, their anticipated trip to Australia materialized and Warren describes his plans to his parents in a letter dated the third of that month:

Our Australian itinerary is enclosed; it will enable you to follow us along the way. . . . Not only do we have a

---

29. Warren Carroll to Gladys and Herbert Carroll, 28 August 1968, Box 7-2B, Folder 4, Archive Collection, Caroline Jones.
30. Carroll, "Unpublished Autobiography."

number of people lined up to meet as a result of Senator Schmitz's trip in September, but an American who has just emigrated to Australia, Bill Place (originally a New Englander, by the way), whom we met last June, will probably be meeting us in Melbourne. . . . This ties in rather closely with some characteristics of the people interested in our Foundation project of which we have become increasingly aware.[31] With few if any exceptions, those who come to libertarian views through objectivism have little interest in establishing any cornerstones for a building which will outlast their own life. Those without children have, in view of their philosophy, nothing at all to link them with the future and give meaning to an outcome beyond their life-time. Even those with children seem principally interested in protecting them from collectivism during the years when they are too young to fight it, and believe they can do that even in the present environment through good home training. Their interest in emigration and a colony is primarily if not solely to rid themselves of present or anticipated future restrictions on their economic activity, or to remove them from the unpleasant personal consequences of immersion in a collectivist society. These are not inconsiderable motives; they are strong enough so that I believe many of these people will eventually emigrate. But they are not really looking for a colony such as we have been talking about setting up in Tasmania. . . . We now see our trip as a means of helping to determine just how hospitable Australia and Tasmania would be [and] . . . how secure a refuge could be established there if conditions in this country became intolerable. We can still see circumstances in which we ourselves would need such a refuge though we are by no means as sure as we were in the winter and spring that these circumstances will arise. . . .

---

31. Warren took this idea of a "foundation" from science fiction writer Isaac Asimov's *Foundation* series about a group of people preserving civilization in the face of totalitarianism.

Senator Schmitz, incidentally, seems so "sold" on Australia that it now seems more likely he will go there to stay than we will.[32]

It is at this point, here, in this letter, that one finds in writing the first inkling of what was to become Warren's life-work (along with his historical writing)—the founding of Christendom College:

Our primary interest has become, what was always a vital element in the foundation project, a school of some kind, fixed or mobile as the case may be. . . . We have been giving a great deal of thought to the best means of carrying on our educational work, in teaching fundamental truths and values in religion, history, economics, politics, philosophy and literature, and believe we can develop a new concept which will offer people in the United States and Canada—and Australia, if necessary—what in these years, and even more in the years to come, they will so conspicuously lack and so desperately need.

Msgr. Trower must have discussed Warren's plans with him to some extent while instructing him in the faith, and hence, handed him his marching orders:

Monsignor Trower pulled no punches. His own faith was rock solid, and he wanted me to know that, presuming mine was equally solid, I would face a major battle for it. Ever since, people have been amazed that I came into the church at such a time. But I gloried in it. It seemed to me that God was calling for reinforcements to His embattled legions. I am a very combative person, and was especially so then, at thirty-five. . . . I was baptized in December, and

---

32. Warren Carroll to Gladys and Herbert Carroll, 3 November 1968, Box 7-2B, Folder 4, Archive Collection, Caroline Jones.

came down from Sacramento to be confirmed by the great Cardinal Manning (from Ireland originally) the next fall. My baptism made our marriage instantly sacramental, which I now understood well enough to rejoice in.[33]

Just as Jesus' Incarnation was a point of turning in the history of the world, so too was His coming, sacramentally, into the soul of Warren Carroll who described it to his mother as "opening up a whole new world."[34] "I was ready to take on the world," he proclaimed, "and soon learned that this is exactly what God had in mind for me."[35]

33. Carroll, "Unpublished Autobiography."

34. Warren Carroll to Gladys and Herbert Carroll, 28 August 1968, Box 7-2B, Folder 4, Archive Collection, Caroline Jones.

35. Carroll, "Unpublished Autobiography."

6

Schmitz for President!

SO WHAT DOES WARREN Carroll do when he decides to take on a whole new faith and world view? He writes a book, of course! And being Warren, this will not be a small book elucidating a few of his thoughts on Catholicism. Oh no, he is going to write the *entire history of the world*—from a Catholic point of view.[1] But before his impatient fingers can hit the typewriter keys, he must garner information. And that he does:

> I found a book called *A Summary of Catholic History* by Father Newman G. Eberhardt, in two volumes, which I later used as my text in teaching Catholic history at Christendom College. It acquainted me with several events of Catholic history of which I had never heard, and whose enormous significance was immediately apparent to me....
> My Catholic reading continued with the many volumes of Henri Daniel-Rops's great (though unfortunately undocumented) history of the church, then recently published in

---

1. He did indeed accomplish this goal, publishing the first of his six-volume history, *The Founding of Christendom*, in 1985. The final volume, *The Crisis of Christendom*, was written jointly by both Warren and Anne and published posthumously in 2013.

paperback by Doubleday Image Books, and the Jesuit histories of James Brodrick. I was fascinated by St. Ignatius of Loyola and his absolute invulnerability. When falsely imprisoned by the inquisition and told he was now free to leave, he responded with a request to remain in his cell for a while longer so that he could do more prayer and penance there. Nothing could deter or even touch such a man![2]

One of these extraordinary stories Warren discovered in Fr. Eberhardt's book was that of Pope Vigilius, which affected him so much that he, in his own words, "told and retold [it] all over the country. . . . I thought, and still think, that this is the most spectacular example in Catholic history of the direct intervention of the Holy Spirit to prevent a pope from betraying the church."[3] This story, which culminates in the year 538 or 539, centers around the Byzantine Emperor Justinian, his wife, Theodora, and the Monophysite heresy. It is also embroiled in the muddle of papal elections occurring at the time.

The Empress Theodora, having been highly influenced by some Egyptian monks in favor of Monophysite doctrines (which claimed that Christ had only one nature and was not truly human), was intent on spreading this heresy, and had set her sights on controlling the four major sees at the time, i.e., Constantinople, Antioch, Alexandria, and Rome. By the year 536, with the help of Theodora, three of these sees were held by Monophysite patriarchs and the sole see holding back the deluge was Rome. As Warren was later to write in Volume II of his *History of Christendom:*

> Meanwhile the church and the pope, as always in the world while not of it, were beset on every side by dangers as great as any they have experienced in all the two thousand years of the church's history. In the heart of the age of Justinian, for twenty-four long years—531 to 555—

---

2. Carroll, "Unpublished Autobiography."

3. Ibid.

one man stands at center stage of a drama ranging from Heaven to Earth: Vigilius.

Probably ordained deacon by Pope Felix III when quite young, he came from a family prominent in Roman government service; his father had been praetorian prefect and his brother prefect of the city of Rome. He and his family had influence both at the gothic court and with the old roman senatorial aristocracy. Vigilius was intensely ambitious, eager for office and for gold. He was tall and distinguished in appearance, but with the passing years he grew fat. From all we hear and know and can imagine of him, he resembled no type familiar in our experience quite so much as the successful lobbyist and influence peddler, caricatured with paunch and cigar, who knows every man's weaknesses and uses that knowledge to get his way, who would deal with any man, however evil or untrustworthy, for a favor for himself or for his client.

This was the man who, pope for seventeen years and prisoner for ten of them, saved the church of Christ in his time.[4]

Amidst a series of tumultuous papal elections, Vigilius rose to the top of the list of contenders. When the reigning pope, Agapitus, died suddenly, the stage was set. Vigilius, then in Constantinople, solidified his connections with Theodora:

Before Vigilius left Constantinople, Theodora called him to her in secret. She asked him to make her a promise of what he would do if, by her help, he achieved his great ambition of becoming pope. Under her prodding, he promised to abrogate the Council of Chalcedon and approve the Monophysite belief of Patriarchs Theodosius, Anthimus, and Severus. She then promised in her turn to or-

---

4. Carroll, *A History of Christendom*, vol.2, *The Building of Christendom*, 163–164.

der Belisarius [the Emperor's top general], when he took Rome, to make Vigilius pope—and to give Vigilius seven hundred pounds of gold. "With pleasure Vigilius made the promise," we are told, "for love of episcopacy and gold; and after making the promise, he set out for Rome."[5]

It was not Vigilius, however, but Silverius who was installed as pope, upon which Theodora wrote to the new pontiff urging him to restore Anthimus, the Monophysite Patriarch of Constantinople who had been removed from office by Pope Agapetus for his heretical stance. Silverius refused:

> "Never will I do such a thing as restore a heretic who has been condemned in his wickedness." Thereupon Theodora wrote Belisarius: "Find some occasion against Silverius and depose him, or at least send him to us. Herewith you have our most dear deacon Vigilius, who has promised to recall the Patriarch Anthimus."[6]

Belisarius, though an honorable man, was pressured by his wife, a close friend of Theodora's, and within the year had Silverius denounced:

> His pallium (the symbol of episcopal office in those times) was ripped off; he was dressed as a monk and hurried to a ship bound for the isolated, rocky coast of Lycia in Asia Minor. . . . In the room of the degradation, Vigilius sat watching. Eight days later a subservient clergy in besieged Rome proclaimed him pope, under the pressure of Belisarius. Not all agreed with this action. . . . On June 20, 538, Pope Silverius, dead of starvation, was buried on the island of Palmaria, where his mortal remains still lie. It is his feast day, as a saint and martyr of the universal church.

---

5. Ibid., 168.
6. Ibid., 169.

Few saints and martyrs have more richly deserved such honor. Alone, abandoned, forgotten, on an island twenty miles out from the coast of Italy, so small as to be a mere dot on the map, this Vicar of Christ was done to death most probably by the man who would become, after him, the head of the church of Christ on earth, under the authority of the Christian emperor, who could not be troubled to investigate his fate. Slow starvation is one of the cruelest of deaths; the victim, at the end, is but a twisted shadow of the image of God in which he was made. That Silverius prayed, toward the end without ceasing, for Vigilius we may be morally certain, for he knew better than any other man the peril in which the church now stood, and that when he died Vigilius, however unworthy, would almost certainly become the true pope. The impact of his prayers on the future of Vigilius, of the church, and of Christendom, we shall soon see.

There is no record or suggestion that Silverius ever resigned the papacy.... As for Vigilius, he was not and could not be pope until Silverius resigned or died; the church has only one pope at a time. But either in November 537 (if Silverius resigned then) or in June 538 (when he died) the See of Peter became vacant—and who but Vigilius could fill it? The example of Silverius and his fate stood starkly clear; any new papal election advancing anyone other than Vigilius would mark the man elected for death. There was no choice and no escape. The clergy of Rome, the faithful of the church, must accept as pope this man who had in all probability martyred his predecessor, who had promised to embrace heresy to gain the papacy—and collected seven hundred pounds of gold in the bargain. Even if few then knew this last, something of the kind must have been suspected. In all the history of the See of Peter there is no darker moment than this, the year of Our Lord 538, with Rome in the hands of Theodora's minions while she waited in Constantinople for the fulfillment of the remainder of the promise of "our most dear deacon Vigilius."

She waited. And she waited. Silverius lay in his forgotten grave. There were whispers against Vigilius, but
no voice raised openly against recognizing him as pope.
. . . Finally Theodora, growing impatient, got in touch
with him. What about his promise? When was he going
to restore Anthimus?

Vigilius had to reply. The hour of decision was upon
him. The papacy had been captured by its enemies. He
had bought it from the heretics, collecting seven hundred
pounds of gold and paying with the life of his predecessor.
It has been said that he could not have taken the western
church with him into Monophysitism. Would St. Atha-
nasius have thought that his successor patriarch of Alexandria could take his heroic and loyal Christian people
with them into heresy, against the Holy See? But they did.
Would St. Ignatius of Antioch have thought that his successor patriarchs of Antioch could take his heroic Christian people with them into heresy, against the Holy See?
But they did. Five thousand years of history show that,
hard as it is to lead men to truth, few things are easier than
to lead men into error.

The Holy Spirit hovered close, on wings of fire.
Memories of his two predecessors, whom he had known
so well, crowded upon Pope Vigilius. Agapitus before Justinian, saying "I, sinner that I am, desired to see the most
Christian Emperor Justinian, and I find Diocletian," with
Vigilius watching; Silverius before Belisarius and Anto-
nina, the pallium being ripped from his shoulders, and
Vigilius watching. He was probably responsible for the
murder of Silverius. He may have been the murderer of
Agapitus. Did he ask then for martyrdom, knowing how
many sins are washed away when a man sheds his blood
for Christ? Vigilius took pen in hand, and wrote the [fol-
lowing] words:

> "Far be this from me, Lady Augusta; formerly
> I spoke wrongly and foolishly, but now I assuredly

> refuse to restore a man who is a heretic and under
> anathema. Though unworthy, I am vicar of Blessed
> Peter the Apostle, as were my predecessors, the
> most holy Agapitus and Silverius, who condemned
> him."
>
> The papacy cannot be captured by the enemies of the
> faith.[7]

For his continued opposition to Justinian and Theodora, Pope Vigilius was eventually arrested in 545 and spent the next ten years as a virtual prisoner of Justinian (Theodora had died of cancer in 548). When finally released in 555, he died on the way back to Rome in Sicily on June 7.[8]

If Vigilius took his place on the throne of heroes in Warren's eyes, so too did his boss at the time, California State Senator John Schmitz. Although at the time of their meeting Warren did not share John's Catholic faith, they immediately saw eye to eye on all things political, both being proponents of limited government and low taxes as well as staunchly anti-communist. Born in 1930 in Milwaukee, Wisconsin, into a family of daily Mass Catholics, John had spent eight years as a pilot in the Marine Corps attaining the rank of lieutenant-colonel. Joining the faculty of Santa Anna College in California in 1960, he taught political science, American history, philosophy, and logic. A huge history buff and a recognized expert on communism, he taught an anti-communism course as training director of the Marine Corps Leadership School. This, in turn, led to popular support for him in a bid for the state senate from Orange County, California, in 1964, in which he was successful, going on to re-election for a second term in 1966.[9] Then, one night while taking a bath, he heard a call from Mary, his wife, who was watching the *Lomax* television show: "John,

---

7. Ibid., 169–172.
8. Ibid., 178.
9. Brochure, "Elect John Schmitz to Congress", Box 5-17, Folder 38, Archive Collection, Caroline Jones.

come here, you have to *see* this guy!" Rushing down (wrapped in his towel maybe?), John joined Mary and by the end of the show they both exclaimed, "This guy has everything we want!"[10] "This guy" was, of course, Warren, and thus, as we have already related, was established a partnership of two incredibly strong, courageous, and, by 1968, devoutly Catholic men.

Warren became John's legislative assistant and, according to Mary, a match was made in heaven. Here was someone "who was knowledgeable enough to help John research legislation and put into words what John believed. Having Warren," relates Mary, "was the best thing that ever happened to John!"[11] And Warren loved it! Although the major issues for them both were to preserve a limited government, oppose tax increases, fight communist aggression, and protect the lives of the unborn,[12] the scope of John's political abilities and Warren's extensive research covered such topics as social security, the trouble with America's schools, the reason for Sweden's high suicide rate, the use of heroin in schools, the war in Vietnam, the gas shortage, fallout from the 1960s college rebellion, Watergate, terrorist kidnappers, inflation, Spain under General Franco, Portugal's fight for freedom, banning the sale of wheat to Russia, and the list goes on. Doing most of the research and all of the writing, Warren pounded out John Schmitz's monthly newsletters.

Under one heading, "The Iron Curtain Stands," Warren wrote:

> We don't hear the phrase "Iron Curtain" much these days, vivid and descriptive as it always was of the prison walls which the communist world builds around itself. It is not considered quite nice any more, not in keeping with the spirit of "détente." But the Iron Curtain still stands, becoming more impenetrable with each passing year. Nowhere is

---

10. Mary Schmitz, interview by author, 3 February 2014.

11. Ibid.

12. According to Anne, Warren had never thought about abortion before. But once he did, he said, "Of course abortion is wrong, it is taking a life."

this clearer than in Germany, the land of the Berlin Wall. . . . All of it is fenced and guarded by border police and savage dogs. Along more than half of it, no less than two and a quarter million mines have been laid. Recently, at a cost of more than half a million dollars a mile, booby traps have been planted which will tear the body of any border crosser with shrapnel. Ditches are being dug and lined with concrete to prevent escapees from crashing through the border fence in automobiles. . . . Anyone can go to Germany and see this monument to the utter inhumanity and ruthlessness of communism, just as anyone can go to Berlin and see the Wall. And surely any honest person who has done so will not think that the Iron Curtain is a figure of the past. It stands and is growing thicker and heavier.[13]

And under "The Captive Nations—Ghosts At The Banquet":

With the coming of so-called "peace" in Vietnam, with the return of our prisoners of war from that embattled land, our relations with communist governments have reached a stage of cordiality which would have been almost inconceivable as little as two years ago. The whole gigantic effort America made to combat the communist advance, to offer hope to the peoples they had enslaved and protection to the likely next victims of their aggression—an effort that encompassed two major shooting wars and a quarter of a century of "cold war" struggle—has faded away, almost as though it had never been. All now is "sweetness and light," reveling and feasting with the undefeated, unrepentant and never more dangerous communist powers. Yet, as in Shakespeare's *Macbeth*, there are ghosts at the banquet.[14]

---

13. John G. Schmitz, "Schmitz Newsletter," vol. 2, no. 13, July 15, 1974, Box 5-17, Folder 41, Archive Collection, Caroline Jones.

14. Schmitz, "Schmitz Newsletter," vol. 1, no. 7, May 21, 1973, Box 5-17, Folder 40, Archive Collection, Caroline Jones.

In Warren's opinion, however,

the best story illustrating John Schmitz's courage comes from the third year of his service in the California State Senate, in 1967. Future president Ronald Reagan had just been elected governor of California on the strength of his great speech in the Goldwater campaign of 1964 urging that social security be made voluntary. Ronald Reagan was, as the country and the world now rightly knows him, a "great communicator," who had run his eloquent campaign to win the governorship on the theme of cutting down the size and cost of government. But he was a complete political novice, and allowed himself to be persuaded that the state must have a large budget increase in his first year in office, though he had pledged the exact opposite in his campaign, along with all the other Republican candidates including John Schmitz. Reagan was prevailed upon to break that promise. John Schmitz would not break it. John Schmitz did not break campaign promises. His best slogan was "keep the man who keeps his word."

Jesse "Big Daddy" Unruh was then boss of the lower house of the California state legislature, the assembly, a political genius if not a charismatic leader. Unruh decided to discredit the highly popular Reagan at the outset of his career, and his whole party with him, by inducing them all to break their promise in this spectacular fashion. So by the day of the vote on the budget, Unruh and his allies had persuaded every Republican in the entire state legislature to support the Reagan budget increase—except John Schmitz.

For hours the floor managers in the senate held up the vote on the budget increase while they worked on John Schmitz to make Big Daddy's triumph complete by gaining the support of every single Republican for the huge budget increase. They worked on him in relays, using every imaginable form of pressure. I have never

seen a man so hard beset. But John Schmitz had iron
in his soul. He would not yield an inch. At one point
in that terrible afternoon, he said to one of the other
Republican state senators, "they've done everything but
threaten my wife and kids." The senator replied (let us
hope that it was only a singularly ill-timed jest), "Have
you called home lately?" This man was unbreakable.
Now I know that one of the main reasons was that he
was a *real* Catholic.[15]

John Schmitz did not cave under pressure. In fact, pressure seemed
to simply solidify his resolve. The situation ended with Reagan inviting John to a personal meeting in his own offices. On his way to this
meeting, John walked through a long corridor lined with reporters.
Emerging from the meeting with convictions unchanged and resolution intact, John gave these reporters something to print: "Well, I'll
tell you," he spouted off to them, "the next time I have a meeting with
that actor I'm taking a bag of popcorn!"[16]

Being very much a part of John's battles, Warren's recollections
continue:

This was also the year that Governor Reagan took the one
action in his political life that he ever apologized publicly
for: signing California's infamous bill permitting abortion (only the second to be passed by any state in the nation, and before Roe versus Wade) into law. John Schmitz
warned Reagan, before he signed the bill, that its clause
allowing abortions for the supposed sake of the "mental
health" of the mother was a loophole that the pro-abortion
activists could drive a truck through. Governor Reagan,
still politically naïve, responded in a shocked tone, "oh,
the doctors of California would never do that!" But of
course they did do it, and that is why Reagan later apolo-

---

15. Carroll, "Unpublished Autobiography."
16. Mary Schmitz, interview by author.

gized publicly for signing the law, which could never have been passed over his veto.[17]

Warren goes on to describe, in his riveting manner, what he considers to be their two greatest legislative victories, both concerning the public school system.

> Our greatest legislative victory in California was won with the assistance of Governor Reagan, who had finally learned to trust John Schmitz. This was passage of the "Schmitz Act," which I drafted, which guaranteed to the parents of California the right (which the public schools had denied them, and still deny them in many states) to inspect the sex education materials to which their children were to be exposed. We carried that bill through the legislature in the teeth of fierce opposition. Governor Reagan signed it into law, and for the rest of his time in office as governor, he resolutely vetoed every attempt to repeal it.
>
> Our other great victory was in frustrating a brilliant legislative coup by which Unruh had repealed all limits on school taxes in the state of California, not effective until several years in the future, hoping no one would notice the change and therefore not blame him for it. But we noticed, and we pushed through a bill restoring the limits. I cherish the memory of Big Daddy standing up to declare to the assembly about our bill: "anything I said about this would probably be the wrong thing," and then sitting down again. After the debate was over, he had all of it expunged from the record. But the memory remains in the minds of those who defeated him that day, and that record no man can expunge.[18]

---

17. Carroll, "Unpublished Autobiography."
18. Ibid.

Warren became a frequent visitor at the Schmitz household. He loved children, and the Schmitz children, especially the two older boys, have fond memories of him. Terri, the Schmitz's second daughter (now Terri Manion), tells of one particular time that Warren came to their house. They were all inside when the horn on the family's Buick station wagon began to sound for no apparent reason. John was not at home and Warren, being the only man present, felt responsible so he went outside with the two girls. But Warren had no knack at all for things mechanical, and here was this big car with the horn blaring like crazy. He looked at the car. He looked at the horn. Then he turned to the girls with an expression that said, "I have absolutely no idea what to do." Terri says she will never forget that expression of bewilderment on Warren's face and can't keep a straight face to this day when she recalls the incident.[19]

In addition to spending time with the Schmitz children, Warren adored his own niece and nephew, the children of his sister, Sally, who had married Hazen Watson in 1963. They had met while working for the Barry Goldwater campaign, on which Warren had also worked in Dallas. By 1966, Sally and Hazen had two children, Caroline (Carrie) and Jamie. Carrie took particular delight in her Uncle Renny, as she called him. Living still in the old Hasty house in South Berwick, Maine, Carrie recalls something they termed "parlor floor games."

> My grandfather [Herbert] used to come in here in the parlor, and he had his special chair. And he had this ceramic duck and a little metal chicken that you wind up, very old. He would sit with the duck on his knee, and the duck had magical powers—the duck would take us to the land of Chief Geronimo. And we would have this adventure and the duck was this sage, wise duck, and the chicken was his sidekick—the comic relief.[20]

---

19. Mary Schmitz, interview by author.
20. Caroline Jones, interview by author.

She goes on to describe the adventures she played out, there on the parlor floor, with her grandfather supplying the historical background and she acting out, in imaginative play, the scene: "You're in the desert," he would describe to her, "and there are buttes off to the side, and in front of you is the cavalry ,and the sunlight is flashing off their swords!" Carrie believes that her grandparents, Gladys and Herbert, must have played the same way with their own children, Warren and Sally. Whatever the case, games continued to play an integral part of the family's celebrations, especially at Christmas time. Carrie remembers:

> We also had a new Christmas board game each year which we all would play. I still have some of them. One year it was a *Lord of the Rings* role-playing game that was so complicated my mother had to type up cheat sheets. It needed lots of players and took several hours. My parents only had the patience to play it once, but Ren and Anne played it several times with us during their week-long stay that year.[21]

That these Christmas traditions were very dear to Warren we know from his own letters as well as from the memories of Carrie and Anne. In a letter home, Warren states, "I was delighted to learn of the new arrangement for our use of the house on the hill—couldn't have asked for anything better! This will really be a great Christmas. I am prepared to make as much use of the Hasty place as the Watson family may want, just so long as we can have the stockings and the tree in their old locations in the house on the hill."[22] Indeed, Carrie dubs her uncle the "keeper of the Christmas tradition" and describes a strong and structured sense of family and tradition. "In my family, *every* tradition is exactly the same every year! And Uncle Renny was the guardian of 'It's gotta be the same. We don't do it that way. We didn't

---

21. Ibid.
22. Warren Carroll to Gladys and Herbert Carroll, 14 November 1966, Box 7-2B, Folder 4, Archive Collection, Caroline Jones.

do it that way last year, and it's not gonna be different this year.' The ornaments on the tree had to be the same and in the same place."[23] She also remembers helping Uncle Renny wrap his Christmas gifts:

> For some reason, he just couldn't (or wouldn't?) figure out how to wrap gifts. He stressed out so much with the wrapping, but he dearly loved giving them. He had special paper with white glitter saved from his childhood that we carefully recycled every year. As the pieces got smaller and smaller with wear, less and less people could have gifts from him wrapped in his special paper. It upset him so! Eventually, his mother was the only one with a present wrapped in this paper. Anne usually helped him wrap the gifts. As I got a bit older, I loved being chosen to help him wrap Anne's gift, so she would be surprised. We also have a tradition of writing clues on the gifts. If a gift has a clue, the receiver is required to guess what the gift is *before* unwrapping.[24]

For many men, the realities of adult life change or even supplant their childhood thoughts of home and family—but not for Warren. It was most likely with the births of his niece and nephew and his simultaneous courtship with Anne on his mind that he laid out his financial situation to his parents in detail in the same letter home in November of 1966, closing with his hopes: "so you can see that all told I will be making very good money—might even say, enough to support a family!" There was something still quite childlike and trusting, though also idealistic and naïve, in his views of home, family, and children. Although those who knew him as an adult would hardly call him a romantic, he refers to himself on several occasions as such. Even more tellingly, he uses romance, deep, pure, and idealistic love, and the secure warmth of the family as the backdrops for his non-historical writing. This may have been expressed in its most polished form be-

---

23. Caroline Jones, interview by author.
24. Ibid.

ginning in 1963 with his launching of what he later christened "The Tarrant Chronicles."

"The Tarrant Chronicles" were a series of stories individually named for the members of the Tarrant family, beginning with Victor Tarrant, a very determined boy orphaned at the age of fourteen. Set in Chicago in the 1930s, *The Book of Victor Tarrant* tells the story of this young boy as he fights poverty and homelessness to fulfill his dream of finding true joy and sharing that joy with others. Much of this narrative is taken up attacking the idea that people should put their hopes in big government. Having grown up in a slum himself, Victor is able to state that "my hope is in people, not in structures. When people need help—really need help, and a lot of them do, lots of times—the only kind of help that counts comes from another *person*. . . . Slums are produced by people. They are maintained by people. They can only be removed by people. And I mean one-on-one people, not committees, programs, and brochures."[25] "I know *what* society is," Victor declares to his college roommate Ken during a discussion on the problem of poverty and the poor. "I asked you *who* society is. Because only a *who* can cast out. Society can't cast anybody out. It hasn't got hands or feet or a voice. It's only a word."[26] He also casts some blame for their condition on the poor themselves when he states that the larger number of them "had the capability, but never found the desire or the initiative, to get out of the slums; they made a moral slum in their minds and hearts. Nobody can take those people out of the slums unless and until they are willing to make an effort on their own to go."[27] This attitude of viewing government as the answer to all social ills leads to a loss of freedom, argues Victor, ending in the elimination of all who do not have social utility and the extinction of freedom.

Victor's pursuit of an education fit to properly defend those in need is interrupted by the bombing of Pearl Harbor on December 7, 1941.

---

25. Warren H. Carroll, *The Tarrant Chronicles: The Book of Victor Tarrant* (Front Royal, VA: Tarrant Books, 2002), 42–43.

26. Ibid., 38.

27. Ibid., 43.

Probably living vicariously, Warren has his hero spend the night on the sidewalk outside of the recruiting office so that he can be the first in line to enlist in the morning. Eventually fighting in the Pacific as one of Edson's Raders and later in the Fourth Marine Division, Victor is portrayed as the epitome of a courageous and fearless soldier as Warren gives an account of Guadalcanal's Battle of Bloody Ridge, sliding into what will become his written forte of gripping historical narrative.

In the second Tarrant Chronicle, *The Book of Victor and Valerie Tarrant*, Warren again presents us with a whirlwind courtship and an idealistic romance between what are arguably the two most intelligent people in the city of Chicago, quite reminiscent of his hero and heroine of *Banner in the Sky*, Carse and Camilla. To find his perfect soulmate, Victor decides to spend three hours a day scanning the face of every person walking through the arrival gates at Chicago's O'Hare Airport—for six weeks! His motivation for such odd behavior is that he has attained both a law degree and a degree in psychology and is now ready to undertake his long-planned unique professional life. And he did not intend to do it alone—but how to find his perfect partner?

> So here he was at O'Hare Airport, having concluded that what he required would never, in all reasonable mathematical possibility, be discovered by mere casual chance meeting. He had calculated the odds quite precisely [one remembers Warren's calculation of the number decillion]. They came to something like ten thousand to one. Where else would ten thousand people more quickly pass before his eyes, in a situation where he could plausibly intercept any one of them, if he chose?[28]

It is worth giving Warren's description of the meeting of these two unique individuals as it conveys a romanticism which even most who knew him may not have guessed:

---

28. Warren H. Carroll, *The Tarrant Chronicles: The Book of Victor and Valerie Tarrant* (Front Royal, VA: Tarrant Books, 2002), 10–11.

A Braniff flight from Texas came in. Among its load of passengers was a full-bodied Texan with the traditional bronzed features and big hat, a man of perhaps fifty— but his fifty was not the fifty of Chicago. With him was a young woman in her twenties of medium height with an electric swirl of bronze-colored hair, a trim supple figure, regular features, and gray eyes calm as the still sea under the moon. Her lips were slightly curved in the beginnings of a reflective, almost Mona Lisa smile. She walked with a peculiar definiteness of step, each light heel-and-toe placed with a sort of dashing precision in its chosen place. She seemed to radiate indomitability and invulnerability, but quietly, almost effortlessly—not as though she were imposing herself on the world, but as though she would never let the world impose itself on her. She looked as competent as he. And she wore no ring.

She felt Tarrant's eyes boring into her, and flashed him a glance not puzzled but admonitory, as though willing him to take his eyes away. They did not even flicker. Flinty green eyes locked with steady gray. Neither would yield.

Then suddenly he grinned. The effect on that wrought-iron countenance was almost shocking. The green eyes lost their cold glitter and began to dance. The hidden warmth of his mouth, suddenly revealed, was like the sun that follows a snow-storm. It was still far from a handsome face, still not "likeable" in any conventional sense. But now it conveyed a sense of reckless happiness, in a transformation more quick and complete than any ordinary face could have encompassed except under the greatest stimulus or stress.[29]

Within twenty-four hours, this airport romance balloons into an engagement and the Tarrant partnership is begun. Valerie becomes a

---

29. Ibid., 11–12.

girl Friday to her new husband who advertises his services as a lawyer/psychologist/detective and they begin to take on cases. Defending those oppressed by anyone from a labor union executive with a psychotic urge to dominate, to a band of ransom-hungry kidnappers, the Tarrants prosper adding their own three children, not only to the family but to the family business as well. At the age of seven, their oldest daughter, Star, is made a junior partner and the two boys, Rex and Dan, soon follow suit. Reading at times like something out of an old Marvel comic book, this super-hero family of five is often doubled over in peals of laughter owing to some private joke and *always* enjoying themselves immensely, unless, that is, the children are having to go through one of the "nine long months of every exciting year at that unmitigated farce which is a modern grade school."[30]

Once, while taking a lie detector test for the purpose of proving it to be invalid, Victor concentrates on the "truest things he knows":

> On the deep-felt, intensely personal joy in the sound of Valerie's low rich laughter, when something he had said or done had especially pleased her, and the quality of his own joy when he heard it; on the uninhibited, reckless abandon of affection his children poured out upon this hard man when the Tarrants were alone; on the bright light of happiness restored in the faces of the many he had saved from so many varieties of personal destruction; on the invulnerable self-confidence and the capacity for instant, fearless decision for which he was loved or hated, respected or feared by all who knew him; on the bright sky above and the solid earth beneath, between which he lived and moved and had his being, in touch with both, knowing both to be real and knowable through the truth men can learn and keep because they are men and not machines, the truth for which there is no test but itself.[31]

---

30. Ibid., 129.
31. Ibid., 120–121.

I don't think it a stretch to say that these things, also, were the truest things Warren desired and possibly envisioned for himself at the time. Anne later stated that he wrote "The Tarrant Chronicles" really to entertain himself. He hoped other people would read them, but, in the same vein of the Inklings, he just really wanted to read fiction with positive heroes like the ones he wrote about, so he wrote it himself. He wrote about people he wished he had known. Being a natural optimist himself, he always thought the best of people and looked for the best in them. This would lead to disappointments when he felt betrayed by those for whom he had such high hopes, but he was resilient and his natural joy and happiness were augmented with spiritual joy and happiness after his conversion.

In 1970, U.S. Congressman James B. Utt, holding the seat from John's California district, died suddenly, and John decided to run for the now-vacant seat. It was an exciting election, flip-flopping twice over the course of the vote-tallying in the days following the election and finally resulting in a runoff election on the 30 of June with John emerging victorious. This meant not only a move from one coast to the other for the Schmitz family, but for Warren and Anne as well. By July 5, they had arrived at their new home, a rented apartment in Arlington, Virginia, having packed all of their earthly belongings into a tan rambler and traversed the country. Making it into a mini-vacation, they stopped in Minneapolis to attend the *Wanderer* Forum, drove from there along the North shore of Lake Superior so that Anne could get a taste of some of the country Warren had seen on his earlier extended car travels, and visited a former student of Anne's in Detroit.[32] They also made their journey into a sort of pilgrimage, stopping at many shrines along the way, their favorite being the Grotto of the Redemption in West Bend, Iowa, at which an old priest had collected beautiful stones and built replicas of saints' grottos from all over the world.[33]

---

32. *The Wanderer* is a Catholic newspaper founded in 1867 to strengthen the faith of German immigrants. Originally published in German, the first English edition came out in 1931.

33. Warren Carroll to Gladys and Herbert Carroll, 17 May 1970, Box 7-2B, Folder 4, Archive Collection, Caroline Jones; and Anne Carroll, interview by author, 10

Settling into their new surroundings, Anne decided to do volunteer work for the Catholic magazine *Triumph*. Making its debut in September of 1966, *Triumph* was the brainchild of L. Brent Bozell II, a Catholic convert from Omaha, Nebraska, and was founded upon the viewpoint "that every nation is shaped by its religion (or lack thereof); that a religion that has nothing to say in the public arena is not worthy of the name, and that what it has to say must be first of all religious."[34] Stated more forcefully by Brent, "Our goal is the resurrection of Christian civilization, the triumph of God's church, the future: Christ Himself."[35] Anne had been reading *Triumph* since its inception and Warren began reading it shortly after his conversion. Interestingly, Warren's mother, Gladys, was also a subscriber but began having concerns as *Triumph* unabashedly placed Catholicism ahead of conservative American thought. In a letter home, Warren sympathizes with her saying that although he and Anne follow the magazine with great interest, "I can understand how its hostility to many traditional American ideas disturbed you."[36]

In the same letter, dated May 17, 1970, Warren laments the state of higher education in the United States but sympathizes with the college youth acknowledging that "there is no doubt that even the best of the students are groping in the dark; they have been given nothing in the way of permanent values, and have not the slightest idea what to put in place of the evils—many of them very real, though they exaggerate them—against which they are protesting." Summing up his thoughts he concludes, "Anyway, we are all the more interested in starting as soon as possible a new college which will provide an education solidly based in the Christian faith while at the same time show-

---

January 2013.

34. Warren H. Carroll, "Foreword," *The Best of Triumph* (Front Royal, VA: Christendom Press, 2001), xiii.

35. E. Michael Lawrence, "Introduction," *The Best of Triumph*, xix. The original name chosen by the staff of *Triumph* was *Future*. However, another organization already published a periodical entitled, *The Jaycees' Future*, and threatened to sue if *Triumph* went ahead with its original name.

36. Warren Carroll to Gladys and Herbert Carroll, 17 May 1970.

ing what persons so educated can do even under today's conditions. A truly fresh start is needed in education and we will help try to make it, however small the beginnings." At this point, thanks to some prodding from Sally who was then living in Vermont, they had chosen Vermont as the desired location for their project.[37]

If Sally was an influence on her brother in terms of where to start his school, she was also a help to him in his love of children. First, by supplying him with a niece and nephew on whom he could shower his love in general and his love of reading in particular. Presenting these children with a new "Christmas book" every year and reading to them (and later to Carrie's own children), Warren loved especially the Narnia series authored by his own beloved C. S. Lewis. Buying both of the children the complete set for Christmas, his childlike enthusiasm shines through in a letter home:

> Naturally I was pleased to hear that Carrie did all the dec-
> orating of the Christmas tree, in just the proper fashion!
> Thanks for the pictures, and I do want to keep the picture
> of Carrie with Aslan and of Carrie with Jamie as the little
> drummer boy. . . . It's been a year now since Carrie and
> Jamie got the Narnia books, and here they are still hav-
> ing them read with one more to go, after a rereading of
> another! Hard as it is to compare the books, I am pretty
> well convinced that at least for an adult *The Last Battle* is
> the best and most profound of the series, and will be very
> interested to find if Carrie seems to think so too, from the
> child's point of view. As I think I have said to you, only
> Lewis would have dared to write a children's story about
> the Apocalypse and the Second Coming of Christ. I really
> don't think it's ever been done anywhere else.[38]

---

37. Ibid.
38. Warren Carroll to Gladys and Herbert Carroll, 26 January 1975, Box 7-2B, Folder 6, Archive Collection, Caroline Jones.

As happy as Sally was with the affection and interest her brother bestowed upon her own children, she also encouraged Warren and Anne to take in foster children. Anne's brother Pete recalls that Warren's thoughts on children had changed after being immersed in Anne's warm, large family: "Anne had said that before he came to visit us, he didn't want to have very many children because he had grown up with just one sister. But after he came to visit us he told Anne, 'I want to have a lot of children.'"[39] A large (immediate) family, however, was not what God had in mind for them. Not being able to have any children of their own, they had tried adoption in the summer of 1970, but it hadn't worked out for them. Sally, however, had experience with foster children, having taken in one of her own, and suggested to Warren and Anne that they do the same. Thus, in December of 1971, after having purchased a little house on one and a quarter acres on Bull Run Mountain in the small hamlet of Haymarket, Virginia, Warren and Anne were eagerly awaiting the arrival of Ricky, age seven.

Arriving on the 7th of December, Ricky seemed to fit right in. Warren wrote to his mother that they were having no problems so far and that "Ricky is helping Anne bake cookies."[40] For the next few months, Warren reveled in his dream of fatherhood as he watched seeming progress in Ricky's behavior, disciplining him firmly but with great benevolence and discretion and enjoying a nightly "play time" every evening after returning from work.[41] However, by July of the following year, it had become clear that Ricky suffered from deep emotional problems that were beyond the scope of Warren and Anne to handle, and he eventually returned to his own parents. That this was very difficult for Warren is clear from his own words on the subject to his mother: "We have just been through probably the most difficult period of my life since Columbia, in connection with Ricky, and from that I

---

39. Peter Westhoff, interview by author.
40. Warren Carroll to Gladys and Herbert Carroll, 8 December 1971, Box 7-2B, Folder 4, Archive Collection, Caroline Jones.
41. Warren Carroll to Gladys and Herbert Carroll, 16 January 1972, Box 7-2B, Folder 4, Archive Collection, Caroline Jones.

do know what it means to have to separate from someone you wanted to be part of your family."[42] At some point between July of 1972 and the following January, however, they made another attempt at being foster parents, this time with a boy by the name of Jonny. Though not rebellious like Ricky, Jonny was a child with whom meaningful communication was next to impossible. After two episodes of theft and a few suspensions from riding the school bus for misbehavior, Warren and Anne reluctantly decided to give him up to new foster parents. "On the basis of these two experiences," Warren writes, "we have concluded that we are not Virginia's most promising foster parents."[43]

Even without the boys, however, the small house on Bull Run Mountain was full of life. Following in the vein of many of the *Triumph* people and their agrarian leanings, Warren and Anne began creating their own "homestead." Beginning sometime in 1972, they began to acquire rabbits, chickens, ducks, and geese, and at one point contemplated purchasing a goat—but eventually decided against it as it would tie them down to the daily milking. Instead they obtained their milk from a farmer down the road and made their own butter and cream cheese. For a man mechanically mystified by a blaring car horn in front of the Schmitzes' house, Warren was at least able to put together some rough animal pens. Working out his own design for a chicken house and proposed attached goat shed, he was continually reinforcing it against predators. Particularly troublesome for him were the rabbit hutches:

> Following the death of the pregnant female rabbit on New Year's Eve, caused by an animal breaking through the poorly stapled wire center of the gate to her pen, the last young rabbit we had was killed by an animal pulling up the wire of its pen out of the ground and then, on

42. Warren Carroll to Gladys and Herbert Carroll, 3 July 1972, Box 7-2B, Folder 4, Archive Collection, Caroline Jones.
43. Warren Carroll to Gladys and Herbert Carroll, 11 November 1973, Box 7-2B, Folder 5, Archive Collection, Caroline Jones.

the next night, the remaining female in the same way. We had thought she was safe for the time being because she had dug a deep burrow for herself, but the marauder not only tore up the wire of the pen but dug her out of the burrow. Our male, who survived all disasters, is still alive and Friday I went down to a place out in the middle of nowhere in country Virginia which has rabbits of all kinds— and every other imaginable animal, just about, including horses, calves, goats, a pig, chickens, turkeys, ducks, geese, pheasants, cats and dogs (that's more ambitious even than I am!)—and got another female. Meanwhile we had rebuilt two pens with three thicknesses of wire, wood-slat gates, and huge boulders along the ground, and last night I caught the marauder trying to penetrate (unsuccessfully!) this mighty barricade—a huge German shepherd dog.[44]

Over the next three to four years, Warren defended his rabbits against assorted critters, eventually putting padlocks on all the gates to their pens, built a beehive, planted peach and pecan trees, grew grape vines with the idea of making his own wine, and dug up his backyard dirt in which he planted numerous vegetables. Serving their own homegrown duck for Thanksgiving dinner in 1973, they also ventured into "opossum casserole" using two opossums trapped on their property, and considered the taste just fine: "I suspect possum is like woodchuck. There was certainly nothing the matter with it once it had been thoroughly cooked and tenderized in a pressure cooker, though many people are amazed at the idea of eating it. But then many people even have a prejudice against goose eggs, which are delicious."[45] Even dealing with live bees did not phase this highly intellectual man, who incidentally kept his newly hatched chickens in his study, under a warm lamp, next to his books:

---

44. Warren Carroll to Gladys and Herbert Carroll, 28 January 1973, Box 7-2B, Folder 5, Archive Collection, Caroline Jones.

45. Warren Carroll to Gladys and Herbert Carroll, 25 February 1974, Box 7-2B, Folder 5, Archive Collection, Caroline Jones.

Yes, the bees do arrive in the mail; I agree it sounds odd—
Anne still can't quite believe it. A very interesting moment
comes when you let them out. The books say this is the
beginner's toughest moment, but there's really very little
danger. Somehow that doesn't sound quite as reassuring as
it might. Anyway, you dump them into the hive with sugar
water there to feed them until they get established. Anne
says she will stay in the house with the doors and windows
closed. And I have 'protective equipment' including face
veil, gloves and helmet![46]

Anne's brother Pete recalls the "Warren homestead," and especially—
the bees:

They had all their rabbits and stuff and those miserable
bees. We didn't get much honey. By the time I was out
there they had had them for a while. Warren had all the
gear and everything and all I ever heard him call them
were his "miserable bees." A lot of work and they were
getting no honey. Organic gardening was not a big thing at
the time so people would say, "Why are you doing this—
there are grocery stores?" They thought it was healthier.
If you saw the chicken coop—it looked like something
totally dilapidated even when it was first built. He [War-
ren] would always point to his neighbor who had a coop
perfectly designed and built and he would just laugh at
his. He just thought it was terrific! They ground their own
wheat. They bought wheat from a place that sold wheat as
feed. They would go through it and get all the junk out of
it and then grind it themselves. I helped to sort wheat. He
named his rabbits after queens who had had lots of children, hoping that they would have lots of baby rabbits.[47]

46. Warren Carroll to Gladys and Herbert Carroll, 2 April 1973, Box 7-2B, Folder 5,
Archive Collection, Caroline Jones.
47. Peter Westhoff, interview by author.

Their efforts paid off, however, and pretty soon they were putting up fifty pints of vegetables over a summer and fall, feasting on a rabbit a week, and had one hundred and fourteen blossoms on their peach trees. Yes, that is *one hundred and fourteen*, and we know this number exactly because Warren was so proud of his peach tree blossoms that he went out and counted them—one by one.[48] Besides saving them money on their food bill, working the land gave Warren a sense of fulfillment which he expresses to his mother in a letter dated October 23, 1975: "I feel more attachment to the land, so much of which I have literally remade with my own hands."

During this time of "homesteading" on Bull Run Mountain, Warren and Anne met the Flagg family with whom they became steadfast friends. The Flaggs also raised chickens, and a chicken-slaughtering-and-plucking day became an annual event for these two families. Although the Carrolls spent many wonderful evenings full of delicious dinner and far-into-the-night conversation at the home of George and Carolyn Flagg, the highpoint of their year became the Thanksgivings they spent together. One would imagine memories of Thanksgiving to include turkey, stuffing, and cranberries, but for the Carrolls and Flaggs, the best memories revolve around the game of... Twister. For those who are not familiar with this simple but physically taxing game, it consists of a mat spread out on the floor, on which are printed large, colored circles. A spinner is spun to designate a particular color and all participants must place a hand or foot on a corresponding colored circle on the mat. When one pictures at least four people reaching around, behind, and through the legs or arms of the other players to accomplish these gymnastic feats, the fun of the game can be seen. Picturing Warren Carroll in such a pose, however, is not even imaginable. And indeed, he did not participate in this way. His role in the game is described by Tim, one of the Flagg children:

---

48. Warren Carroll to Gladys and Herbert Carroll, 2 April 1973 and 9 September 1973, Box 7-2B, Folder 5, Archive Collection, Caroline Jones.

Dr. Carroll was a master at spinning the wheel on the twister game to tell us what positions to take. It was extremely entertaining because in addition to spinning the wheel, he was also the referee! If anybody deviated from exactly what was supposed to be done, he would call you out on it and if you argued back he would argue from the rulebook and his interpretation of it and wear you down! There was no doubt the man knew the rules and you dare not cross that line when you shouldn't![49]

Tim's sister, Holly, has similar memories:

It was a really intense game. I was short, only a child, and Pete Westhoff was really tall and there would be these heated debates about whether someone's foot came off the mat/color or not and Warren would get down on his hands and knees and survey the situation very closely. He really took his job seriously. He would say, "No, no, you lifted your foot!" I think Anne just sat there laughing.[50]

George adds, "I think we spent as much time rolling on the floor in laughter as we did playing the game." The evenings would then wind down and culminate in good, solid conversation, lasting late into the night. George elaborates:

Warren was the master of staying up late and would always outlast me. The younger children would be gone first, then Carolyn and Anne, the older children, would drift away. Finally, I would be nodding off at 2:00 or 3:00, but Warren would pick up a book. The discussions woven throughout an evening were priceless and covered church and mankind in every imaginable aspect of past, present,

---

49. Tim Flagg, correspondence with author, November 2016.
50. Holly McShurley, interview by author, 19 August 2015.

and future. Warren was able to bring out of all of us things we didn't know we knew, beliefs, morals, and values that were dormant.[51]

In May of 1972, George Wallace, who was running for president on behalf of the American Party, was campaigning in the state of Maryland. He was shot and paralyzed by a rogue gunman seeking fame, and subsequently forced to drop out of the campaign. The American Independent Party which was begun by Wallace and stood on a strong conservative platform emphasizing states' rights, was now in need of a candidate and they approached Senator John Schmitz, who agreed to run. John secured the nomination at the party's convention in July, and Warren found himself engulfed in a presidential campaign. John's campaign platform had three planks:

> 1) in foreign affairs, we should always treat our friends better than our enemies;
>
> 2) never go to war unless you plan on winning, and;
>
> 3) those who work ought to live better than those who won't.[52]

And Warren had the time of his life:

> John Schmitz's campaign for president in 1972 was an unforgettable experience. I was just forty years old, full of vim and vigor. We hardly ever slept. I wrote every word that came out of Schmitz's office during that campaign [presumably, when he wasn't counting peach blossoms!]. (John was a brilliant ad-lib speaker; he did not need or use speech texts. But every press release was written by me.) Our Eastern campaign secretary, working under Desmond Birch, was my wife's 19-year-old sister, on her first politi-

---

51. George Flagg, correspondence with author, 13 November 2016.
52. Warren Carroll, "Unpublished Autobiography."

cal job. We had a scratch organization put together with less than a week's notice, because the occasion of John's nomination was the shooting and consequent paralysis of American Party leader and founder George Wallace in Laurel, Maryland in July [it was actually May]. Wallace had been expected to be the American Party candidate. We did extraordinarily well, and actually worried Nixon.

As the world now knows, Nixon never could believe the extent of the landslide that was developing for him. He thought we might take away enough votes from him in California to cost him that critical state, with its largest electoral vote in the union. So a couple of days before the election, one of Nixon's legendary bag-carriers offered our Western press secretary, Nelson Ross, a $30,000 bribe to issue a false press release designed to discredit John.

Nelson Ross was not for sale. He turned down the bribe with contempt. He would never even tell us what was in the false press release. So Richard Nixon really *was* a crook, and we can prove it.[53]

Perusing the "Schmitz for President" news releases, written by Warren, one gathers a sense of the topics considered to be of importance to both John and Warren at this time. These issues include, first, a commitment to prosecuting to the fullest degree Jane Fonda for her involvement in destroying the resolve of U.S. servicemen in Vietnam:

> What sort of condition is President Nixon's Justice Department in if it takes them a month and a half to tell the American people that they have "Hanoi Janie" and her violations of law under "active consideration"?[54]

---

53. Ibid.
54. Undated News Release, "Schmitz for President," Box 5-17, Folder 28, Archive Collection, Caroline Jones.

Second, true concern and a willingness to put that concern into action regarding American POWs in Vietnam:

> Now we are supposed to stand up and cheer, or at least feel relief and hope, because North Vietnamese propagandist and self-professed communist Dave Dellinger and his partner, hatchet-woman Cora Weiss, have announced that they will go to North Vietnam to bring back three American prisoners who have cooperated with the enemy by issuing propaganda statements for them. In the meantime, the hundreds of our prisoners who have been tortured, drugged and debased in every manner are rewarded by one presidential candidate who says he would crawl to Hanoi to beg for peace and by another who, through trade with Russia, gives North Vietnam the computer technology to shoot more American boys out of the sky and make them prisoners too. . . . If I were president, within thirty days of my taking office there would be a full Green Beret group and a Marine division knocking on their prison doors to bring those men home—with not one left unaccounted for.[55]

Third, a commitment to life:

> The usual abortion techniques pull the living baby apart, cut him in pieces or pickle him alive in a salt solution. Each of these procedures means a horrible, agonizing death. . . . As a member of Congress, I introduced a Constitutional amendment, H.J.Res.1186, to guarantee the right to life of every American from the moment of conception. . . . No other major party or its candidate has dared take a platform or campaign stand on this issue.[56]

---

55. Ibid.
56. Ibid.

Additionally, Red China as a major supplier of heroin to the youth of the U.S., the danger of coddling criminals, Schmitz as the "author of legislation to allow American citizens to own and trade in monetary gold and make contracts payable in gold," and the sale of wheat to communist Russia, and, maybe somewhat shocking for us in our present political complacency:

> Nothing in the Constitution of the United States establishes the Supreme Court as the sole rightful interpreter of that document. Instead, the Constitution sets up a government of checks and balances in which neither the legislative, nor the executive, nor the judicial branch of the Federal government was intended to be supreme. When one of those branches begins to encroach severely on the Constitutional authority of either of the others, or of the States, even in the name of the Constitution, the integrity of the Constitution requires that this usurpation of power be halted.[57]

And finally, in the newsletter following the fateful *Roe v. Wade* decision:

> On January 22 of this year, the United States Supreme Court handed down the latest and by far the worst in its long series of appalling decisions undercutting the very foundations of the moral order in American life. The decisions in favor of criminals, perverts and pornographers—the decisions striking down so many reasonable and necessary provisions

---

57. Ibid. While in Congress, John Schmitz introduced the first Human Life Amendment to the Constitution. It was House Joint Resolution 1186 introduced on May 3, 1972—before Roe v. Wade. It stated, "An individual, from the moment that he is conceived, shall not be deprived of life, liberty, or property, without due process of law. No state shall deprive any individual, from the moment that he is conceived, of life, liberty, or property, without due process of law; nor deny to any individual, from the moment that he is conceived, within its jurisdiction the equal protection of the laws."

for order, loyalty and discipline in government service and in teaching—the decisions undermining the stability of the family and the parents' right to control the education of their own children—reached their logical and terrible culmination in a decision legalizing mass murder.[58]

Although John did not become America's next president, many Americans loved his message; they just didn't have the backbone to vote for him. This same lack of courage continues to infect our current political process and the rhetoric runs now as it did then: "he has no chance to win and if we don't vote for Nixon, then George McGovern (the Democratic candidate) will win." This line of thought has been the thorn in the side of American conservative politics ever since. It is fear. And Warren was anything but fearful.

So came the time for a parting of the ways between John Schmitz and Warren Carroll. John went back to California while Warren remained in the Washington, D.C. area to work full-time for *Triumph* magazine. But Warren would never forget his friend, godfather, and hero, calling him "the bravest man I have ever known."[59] Delivering John's eulogy in 2001 at Arlington National Cemetery and recalling much of John's sense of humor, Warren spoke of John's quip regarding then-President Nixon's upcoming trip to communist China: "I do not object to the President's trip to China. I only object to the return trip."[60] Then there is John's referral to the party of "but's": "There are right tackles, right corners, right ends, and even right wings in hockey. My position on the team, and yours, Joe [Sobran], is that of 'right but.' The way you play this position of 'right but' is to speak the truth and say it like it is. Then all your friends come up to you and whisper in your ear 'Joe, you're right, but . . . .'"[61] John's sense of humor came

---

58. Schmitz, "Schmitz Newletter," Vol.1, No. 12, Box 5-17, Folder 40, Archive Collection, Caroline Jones.

59. Warren Carroll, "Unpublished Autobiography."

60. Ibid.

61. Ibid.

through the most poignantly though when he jokingly quipped that his tombstone should read:

> I got a million votes for President
> And that was a lot;
> I used to be alive
> But now I'm not.[62]

---

62. Anne Carroll, interview by author.

7

Seeds of Triumph

WARREN'S THOUGHTS AND CONVICTIONS were further developed and fine-tuned over the next few years as he became immersed in the milieu of the folks at *Triumph* magazine:

> In 1973, L. Brent Bozell Jr., . . . brother-in-law of William F. Buckley Jr. and former associate of his in publishing *National Review*, and Dr. Frederick Wilhelmsen teamed up to launch a national Catholic magazine, fittingly named *Triumph*.
>
> Dr. Wilhelmsen was professor of philosophy and politics at the University of Dallas in Texas, after having taught for some years at the University of Navarra in Pamplona, Spain. He was totally bilingual in Spanish and English. He was the finest lecturer I had ever heard. He dressed flamboyantly in a cape, and had more than a little resemblance to the late Bishop Fulton Sheen. He had a rich strong voice. His favorite subject was metaphysics, which ordinarily does not lend itself to oratory. But with him, it did. I will never forget how he regularly made "to be" an active verb, in describing God's action in sustaining everything in being as "izz-ing." He was passionately, lyrically Catholic, as he has made clear in his great collection of essays, aptly entitled *Citizen of Rome*. He was almost as good a writer as he was a speaker. His best articles are

reproduced in the collection, not published until 2001, called *The Best of Triumph*. He convinced me (as my wife had always been convinced) that the strongest argument for the existence and nature of God was that He was the only *necessary being*.[1]

As Warren attests, the heart of the thought of not only Dr. Wilhelmsen, but of all those working for *Triumph* magazine, was captured in the 2001 publication of *The Best of Triumph*. Writing the forward for the book, Warren begins: "*Triumph* magazine was published during the most critical period of American history since the Civil War: from 1966 to 1976. These were the years when America passed through a near-revolution (1968–70) and ceased to be a Christian nation, becoming secular and neo-pagan."[2] In coming to an understanding of the radicalness of the message coming out of *Triumph,* one must understand the radicalness of the folks who worked there. Bill Marshner, an eventual founding faculty member of Christendom College, worked at *Triumph* from 1971 through 1973. This author sat with him in his rather small and dingy office lined with thick, dusty works of theology and strewn with half-empty packages of pipe tobacco. When questioned about his *Triumph* years, he struck a match, put it to his pipe, and settled back in his old, worn armchair. "During all the years I was at Yale," he drawled in between puffs, "I had been cultivating eccentricities. And I had gained the impression [puff, puff] that I was a highly eccentric individual. But when I got to *Triumph!*—I found that I was as ordinary as a cabbage leaf. Because we had real characters, [puff, puff] *unbelievable* characters on staff."[3]

The message issuing forth from this group of rather unusual individuals, cabbage leaves or not, however extreme it sounded, had more solid ground to stand on than any other message of the day because *it* stood on something more solid—the thing most solid in all of human

---

1. Carroll, "Unpublished Autobiography."
2. Warren Carroll, "Foreword," *The Best of Triumph*, xiii.
3. Dr. William Marshner, interview by author, 14 January 2015.

history: the Incarnation. Joining its staff as the magazine's historian, Dr. Warren Carroll posited the question: "Does history have any real meaning or purpose?"[4] For the historian, he said,

> the choice will always remain: either Christ was God, or He was not. Either He rose from the dead—really, physically, with a body that could be touched—or He did not. If He was not God and did not rise from the dead, the beliefs of those who think He was God and did rise have merely academic and psychological interest, and we are back with Tacitus. But if those Christian beliefs are objectively true, then the universe is almost literally turned upside down. A whole new hierarchy of values and of historical significance springs into being.[5]

And the writers and thinkers on the staff of *Triumph* did believe that Christ was God and rose from the dead. And they did not believe this simply as a pious statement to be attested to once a week on Sunday. They believed it with their lives and actions and hence their universe *was* turned upside down—and their magazine reflected this "upsidedownness." Consequently, their politics took on a deeper meaning. It became this message *lived out in the social and political order* and was thus, by its nature, deemed radical by a world which did *not*, at its core, believe in the Incarnation.

Warren denounced this unbelief and its ramifications in the social and political realm and termed the current time period the "age of apostasy,"

> the most widespread, thorough-going apostasy since the church was founded on Pentecost Sunday. This is something much worse than simple heresy; it is the total aban-

---

4. Carroll, "The History of History and the Relevance of Jesus Christ," *The Best of Triumph*, 503.

5. Ibid., 507–508.

donment of Christ and the mockery of God. In C. S. Lewis's striking phrase, we have put God in the dock; we have judged him in the balance of our poor human preconceptions and found him wanting.[6]

Echoing Brent, Warren posited that this apostasy stems from the death of the idea of a Christian commonwealth and that mankind needs to learn that

> Christianity cannot be sustained indefinitely by private devotion alone, but only by public commitment to the building of an explicitly Christian social, economic, and political order.
>
> Christians of the West have tried the other road, the easy road, of putting Christ first only in church, or in the privacy of the home and of their own thoughts. It has not worked. The enemy they would no longer confront in the streets and squares, the market places and the hall of government, is now invading those sanctuaries of home and church, to steal the children of the merely private Christians and make them adepts of the secularist world order.[7]

When looked at through this lens, the American political order was not the answer to the world that it seemed to be, to many if not most Americans. In fact, E. Michael Lawrence, *Triumph's* business manager and later one of the editorial staff, states:

> I would posit that by the time of "Autumn of the country" [written in June of 1968], TRIUMPH had concluded that idolatry—the sin against the First Commandment—was the characteristic blot on America's soul. . . . What was the false god of "the American creed?" . . . [T]he individual

---

6. Carroll, "The West Come to Judgment," ibid., 512.
7. Ibid., 513–514.

American's false god was himself; and American society's false god was itself: America. America as messiah. This was a theme to which TRIUMPH returned again and again.[8]

Lawrence then refers to an article by Bill Marshner on a proposed preface for a "Mass for Independence Day and Civic Observances" in which the American bishops include the statement, "His [Christ's] message took form in the vision of our fathers [the American Founding Fathers]." Marshner clarifies that, rather than saying that the message of Jesus *informed* the vision of our Founding Fathers, the bishops writing the preface had intended to convey something quite different. They had meant that "Christ's message became coherent and took historical form precisely in Americanism."[9] Never one to ignore implications in the subtleties of language, Marshner rightly pronounces this heresy. Summing it up, Lawrence attributes the inability of Americans and American Catholics in particular to stand up against an increasingly corrupt government to the pathology of idolatry.[10]

Based on these beliefs, the main message of *Triumph* becomes twofold. On the one hand, because the American political order includes this sickness of idolatry, one must "transcend the dialectic" between socialism and capitalism, liberalism and conservatism. "Contemporary conservatism and contemporary liberalism are two branches of the same tree," explains Bozell, and it is an illusion to believe that there is an essential dichotomy between conservatism and liberalism in the things that matter.[11] "Catholics should not be overly attached to either of these supposed opposites, but have a social consciousness of their own, bearing fruit in the societies they build."[12] "Modern conservative politics is 'unreal,'" he argues, in the sense that it does not acknowledge that "the proper goal of the orderers of the public life is

---

8. E. Michael Lawrence, "Introduction," *The Best of Triumph*, xxv.

9. Ibid.

10. Ibid.

11. L. Brent Bozell, "Letter to Yourselves I," ibid., 7.

12. Bozell, "Politics of the Poor," ibid., 12.

to help open men to Christ. . . . And they are now suffering the fate which all unrealities must one day suffer."[13]

This conclusion opens the door to the second major message of *Triumph*, and that is the idea that what is needed for the political and social order of a nation to truly express the message of the Incarnation (that is, to be *real*) is what is termed a "confessional state." "A confessional state," expounds Marshner,

> is one in which the church is recognized politically as the true church. What we wanted is for the United States to become a confessional state with the Catholic Church as our established church. . . . The central idea is that the Burkeian tradition of ordered liberty, while good, was not good enough. Key points were missing from America's understanding of the state government and good society, etc. . . . These key points were in the church's teaching and America needed to be reformed and nourished with those points.[14]

Although this line of thinking flies directly in the face of everything entrenched in modern American political thought, *Triumph* (which was originally entitled *Future*) remained positive. In his 1969 article, "Letter to Yourselves," Brent proclaims that

> the future belongs only to those who keep in touch with reality—that is, those who manage to keep open to Christ, who is Reality. You are certainly entitled to observe that the old Christian forms for sanctifying the public life have themselves become obsolete, and thus do not provide a sufficient guide for the future. But that is only to say that the quest for new forms will be difficult, and will require all the energy and imagination

---

13. Bozell, "Letter to Yourselves I," ibid., 10.
14. William Marshner, interview by author.

and grace that are now in us and whatever more time will provide.[15]

Truly transcending the dialectic, another point hammered home by the staff of *Triumph,* was that a political order issuing forth from the message of Christ becomes a "politics of and for the poor." Not to be confused simply with a system of economics aimed at taking care of only the material needs of "the poor," *Triumph's* "poor" meant something quite different. The poor, rightly understood, refers to those who "form the great mass of mankind."[16] Politics, as a Christian vocation, must begin with the premise "that Christ aims to reach all men, and thereupon urges us 'to discover what those conditions are which make a Christian people possible.'"[17] While both capitalism and socialism have tried to provide for the material needs of the poor

> To enter the debate over which system does a better job of distributing material goods—which has always been the main quarrel between capitalist and socialist liberals—is to enter the liberal dialectic, which is a false dialectic. It is false because it tends to reduce politics to economics, to forget that material wealth is only a small part of what the public life is supposed to provide; what it is for. The public life is supposed to help a man be a Christian. It is supposed to help him enter the City of God, and meanwhile it is supposed to help him live tolerably, even happily, in the City of Man.[18]

This thought of *Triumph's* bowl of radical cabbage leaves had a profound effect on Warren, and he came to claim it as his own. In fact, the "watchwords" he chose for the yet ungerminated mustard seed of

---

15. Bozell, "Letter to Yourselves I," *The Best of Triumph,* 10–11.
16. Bozell, "Politics of the Poor," ibid., 12.
17. Ibid., 13.
18. Ibid.

Christendom College are entrenched in *Triumph's* pages. Providing a forward for an article entitled "Liberty and Social Order," penned by Bill Marshner, Warren wrote:

> The idea of liberty as the supreme value is deeply embedded in our social and political order. Most Catholic Americans are not aware that several recent popes have warned in their encyclicals against the idolization of liberty. Liberty is not, and cannot be, an absolute good. Liberty may help some of us to spread truth, but also helps others to spread error. The ultimate question is: How is liberty used? If liberty is understood as rejection of divine, natural, and human law, it is a monstrosity.[19]

In his article, Marshner asks the question, "What is liberty?" If the Christian order is to triumph according to the inferences that can be drawn from the Incarnation, then we must discover the true meaning of freedom, flowing from this same Incarnation, for this is a basic concept for the men of our time and for Americans in particular. The conventional definition of freedom, "liberty is the ability to choose between good and evil," combined with the erroneous idea that the dignity of man consists in this definition of freedom, leads necessarily to a bond between freedom, liberty, and an absence from constraint.[20]

If this false line of thinking is acted upon in the socio-political realm, however, the foundations of society begin to tumble, like falling dominoes set in motion:

> If man's ability to choose between good and evil is the foundation of his dignity, then it follows that human dignity depends upon the absence of constraint. . . . Hence, in order virtuously to choose the good, men must be free of all constraints that would push them toward the good,

---

19. Carroll, introduction to W. H. Marshner's "Liberty and Social Order," ibid., 580.
20. Ibid., 582–583.

whether they be habit, custom, family tradition or blue laws. In fact, logically, all civilization, training, education, moral restriction, all "indoctrination" of the young, become suspect.[21]

This line of thinking culminates in a society in which "liberal man rejects all of what the philosophers call heteronomy, the law that comes from outside, and insists that all law arise in himself.... Finally, if all authority must be rejected ... then the last authority that liberal man is going to get rid of is the authority of truth."[22]

But Warren Carroll had based his whole life on the imperishable nature of this last domino—the domino of truth; "TRUTH EXISTS!" is the first watchword of the college he would found. Far from being simply one domino among many in danger of tumbling to the ground, this pillar of humanity, once knocked from under humanity's intellectual and moral foundations, unleashes terror, misery, and suffering unlike any the world has ever known. In 2010, in a series of lectures given at Christendom, Warren gave a lecture entitled "The Watchwords of Christendom College: Truth Exists. The Incarnation Happened," in which he challenged Christendom students (and anyone else listening) never to heed anyone who tries to say that truth does not exist. "You will know that in a very real sense you are the sons and daughters of truth," he declared poignantly, "who have it and will not give it up nor ever fail to speak for it."

"What happens when you deny all truth and tradition?" he proceeded to ask. As an answer, he described in detail a scene occurring in April of 1975 as the Americans abandoned both Vietnam and Cambodia to the communists. Led by a monster named Pol Pot, the communists in Cambodia formed an organization called Angka Leou. Establishing itself throughout Cambodia, this organization designated all citizens as slaves. No private property of any kind was allowed and children were torn away from their parents at the age of six. Family members were

---

21. Ibid., 583.
22. Ibid., 584.

separated and assigned to work different plots of land. "All religious and social celebrations were prohibited. Marriage required permission from the Angka Leou. There was no escape, because all travel was banned. Any expression of joy was suspect, so no one laughed. . . . People 'withered from loneliness. . . . [A]uthority, loyalty, all sense of identity were monopolized by Angka'."[23] On April 17, the day after the last Cambodian patriot commander left the capital of Phnom Penh with his family by helicopter, the communists marched in:

> "Silent and unsmiling, the communist soldiers filed through jubilant crowds that quickly fell quiet and fearful. Answering cheers and waves with masklike indifference, they stopped traffic, ordered drivers out of their vehicles, and corralled surrendering soldiers into frightened groups, forcing them to disrobe in the streets. . . . The mood in the capital changed as if a switch had been thrown. One of those who felt elation turn to dread over the space of a couple of hours was a French priest, Francois Ponchaud. During ten years in Cambodia, Father Ponchaud had lived among and come to identify with peasants and the urban poor; in the war years, sickened by the corruption, callousness, and social injustice of the Lon Nol government, he sympathized with the revolution. Though he knew from refugees of acts of cruelty in the liberated zone, he still believed that Cambodia could escape its misery with a Khmer Rouge [communist] victory. But now, as he watched the first revolutionary soldiers arrive, doubt became a physical sensation, as if "a slab of lead had fallen on the city. . . .

> Everyone—Cambodians and foreigners alike—thought this had to be Phnom Penh's most miserable

---

23. Warren Carroll, "The Watchwords of Christendom College: Truth Exists. The Incarnation Happened," (lecture, Christendom College, Front Royal, VA, April 29, 2010).

hour after long days of fear and privation," Sydney Schanberg wrote of the republic's fall. "They looked ahead with hopeful relief to the collapse of the city, for they felt that when the communists came and the war finally ended, at least the suffering would largely be over. All of us were wrong."[24]

In one way Pol Pot went beyond anything that any government, communist and Nazi, had ever done or thought of doing in the accursed twentieth century. It was an act of such mindless horror that most people recoil from remembering or even mentioning it, as I do. It was the ultimate product of the denial that truth exists, for it involves the annihilation of all those who believe that it does. Pol Pot and his communists removed every living person except top party officials from his capital city, and he did it that very day.

Not the next week, nor the next month, nor the next day. Not with any notice, not with any time to think or to remember the homes and the loves of the people. That day. That afternoon. Until the sun set, and on through the night. The people of Cambodia were exiled from the world. In a very real sense, they were sent to Hell. Three million people, all gone by the next morning—except for the party men and the soldiers. No other exceptions. None.

Imagination quails before the horrors of that march. Hospitals were emptied, some patients being pushed into the choked streets with needles still in their arms. If they had no beds they crawled, like worms. The roads and streets could not begin to hold them all. They were so thickly clumped together that they could move only a few hundred yards an hour. The soldiers shot any who lagged—and any they felt like shooting. The very small children, the old, the sick, soon began to fall. They died

---

24. Arnold Isaacs, *Without Honor, Defeat in Vietnam and Cambodia* (Baltimore, 1983), 281–283, quoted by Warren Carroll in lecture.

Seeds of Triumph

where they lay, and the driven hordes trampled their corpses.

I used to think that the supreme horror in history was the Aztec human sacrifices. But now I think it was this scene in Cambodia in what Father Ponchaud called the year zero. The devil must have loved every minute of it.

Why would any sane man have done such a thing? Because that is the logical result of denying that truth exists. You come to want to destroy the world which has truth in it. Such is the deadly poison of fundamental skepticism. Do you see now why I tell you not even to listen to the person who tries to tell you that truth does not exist? It is like a lethal plague, a modern black death of the mind. If we believe it, it will take us where the three million people of Phnom Penh in Cambodia went, where the Devil, that "liar from the beginning," wants us all to go, from which Jesus Christ alone can save us. That is why we call Him Savior. Which brings me to the second watchword of our college, "The Incarnation Happened."[25]

This second watchword is encapsulated in an article by the flamboyant Fritz Wilhelmsen entitled "Toward an Incarnational Politics," in which he attempts to unpack the nature of this phrase. To do this, he employs the term "integrism" to designate a manner of thinking which freezes Catholic political order at some moment in the past, usually in the Middle Ages, occasionally the Age of the Fathers or even in the baroque seventeenth century, idealizes it in this time period, and hence despairs of victory in the current political order.

This translates itself into a spiral movement "within," in which the Integrist seeks to incarnate the faith in specifi-

25. Warren Carroll, "The Watchwords of Christendom College: Truth Exists. The Incarnation Happened."

149

cally symbolic ways in his own life, in that of his family, and in that of like-minded fellows. . . . Integrism is elitist by nature. It tends to be excessively moralistic and to read damnation everywhere on the broad screen of the contemporary world: We—the chosen ones—have the key to the truth; we alone know what it means to be Catholic in a truly dense and incarnated fashion.[26]

Although this more-or-less "tribal thinking" is attractive and even possibly necessary as a holding action, concludes Wilhelmsen, it is dangerous in its elitism and also has the potential to damage the command of evangelization and thus turn away from a truly Incarnational politics.[27] In other words, with the Incarnation, politics can no longer remain neutral but must be always currently sacralized in whatever way current Catholics can find. But "because he is so fascinated by his own tradition's historical models, the Integrist cannot react intelligently—imaginatively and creatively—to his own situation in time."[28] Finally, Wilhelmsen throws down the gauntlet:

> The Incarnation of the Son of God in time, united with the dictate to "restore all things in Christ," calls for a sacramentalizing of the real, a hallowing of creation, an extension of the sacramental system by which Christ saves through His church.[29]

In this company of cabbage leaves, Warren was able to build upon his foundation of truth, discovered in his youth and baptized by his entrance into the Catholic Church, constructing the walls and staircases of sound political thought and finding the words which lit the fire under his already-present desire to pass on truth to the genera-

---

26. "Toward an Incarnational Politics," *The Best of Triumph*, 566.
27. Ibid., 567.
28. Ibid., 569.
29. Ibid., 567.

tions to come: "Truth exists! The Incarnation happened!" And the mission "To restore all things in Christ."

Along with the founding of *Triumph* magazine, Brent Bozell established something he called the Society for the Christian Commonwealth, or the SCC, as a sort of umbrella organization for his many existing, semi-existing, and existing as yet only in his mind projects, including the magazine itself and another initiative called the Christian Commonwealth Institute which focused on the field of education. Its goal was to "instaurate the sovereignty of Christ in the social order," which, in Brent's vision, would herald a type of Christian society best exemplified by the historical period of Christendom and experienced contemporarily to a large degree in Spain. To begin working towards this lofty goal, Brent launched an eight-week summer school in Spain beginning in 1970 which drew about fifty students annually, primarily college-age Americans.[30]

Dr. Regis Martin, currently a professor at the Franciscan University of Steubenville, was a student at the first of these summer institutes and has a most vivid memory:

> I was still an undergraduate when, in the summer of 1970, I first laid eyes on Spain, spending seven or so heady weeks in the bright shadow of San Lorenzo de El Escorial, an immense, intimidating pile built by Philip II in the shape of a huge gridiron on which its patron, St. Lawrence, had been slowly barbecued back in the second century. He had designed it that way to honor the martyred deacon whose feast (August 10) fell on the same day his army had defeated the French at St. Quentin, an important victory in Philip's never-ending campaign against the protestant world. That was in the year 1563, the same year that, as providence would have it, the Council of Trent issued its final decrees, thus launching all those wonderful Triden-

---

30. Daniel Kelly, *Living on Fire* (Wilmington, DE: ISI Books, 2014), 157–158. The school was technically run under the Christian Commonwealth Institute, CCI, another of Brent's projects, which was itself under the SCC.

tine warheads aimed at restoring the unity of a divided Christendom.

Those weeks in Catholic Spain were among the happiest of my life, spent in the company of some of the most colorful and contentious people I would ever know. An assortment so captivatingly odd, in fact, that only a God with a sense of humor could account for them. A young Bill Marshner, for instance, who struck everyone as positively, fearfully brilliant (in several languages). When he spoke, in high Yalie hauteur, even the bells of San Lorenzo fell silent. Or Mike Schwartz, a Son of Thunder from the University of Dallas, who was, without doubt, *the* most fiercely self-confident Catholic I'd ever met. Averse to almost everything American (including most English antecedents, because of Britain's barbarous treatment of our Irish cousins), he and I would cross swords not a few times that tumultuous summer. Or Lorenzo Albacete, who was, even then, just about the funniest human being on earth.

There were altogether about fifty of us who managed to make it to Spain that summer, armed with as many opinions as the disparate cities and states we came from. But we were all eager to experience firsthand a culture that offered, in the words of the brochure that first caught my eye, "an organically Catholic life style."[31]

Although Warren was not at this first summer institute (as they became known) in the year 1970, he was asked by Brent to teach a few classes at the summer institute in 1971. At this point, although Warren was still working for John Schmitz, he was keeping an eye open for what the *Triumph* folks and other conservative Catholics were up to on the educational front.[32] He and Anne had also been planning

---

31. Regis Martin, "Remembering Brent," *Crisis Magazine*, March 2015, www. crisismagazine.com/2015/remembering-brent, used with permission.

32. Warren Carroll to Gladys and Herbert Carroll, 19 July 1970, Box 7-2B, Folder 4,

their "great European trip," and so when asked by Brent to give some lectures at the summer institute in 1971, they planned their itinerary accordingly, finishing up at El Escorial in Spain.

At some time just prior to this trip, Warren's skills as a writer, editor, and reviewer were put to the test and involved a book officially authored by Congressman John Schmitz entitled *Stranger in the Arena*. The book was a collection of some of Schmitz's weekly columns, which were being written, of course, by Warren. John then thought it would be nice if Brent would write a forward to the book, which Brent readily agreed to do, contacting Warren and asking him to write the forward and "just put it under my name"—which Warren promptly did. When the book came out, *Triumph* dutifully published a review. But Anne was writing *Triumph's* book reviews at the time, and she passed on the duty to whom else, but Warren, who loaded the review with high accolades and signed it "V. C. Rey" for "Vivo Christo Rey!" Hence, Warren wrote both a forward for, *and* a review of, his own book—without his name appearing anywhere![33]

On March 28, 1970, Warren and Anne embarked upon their much-anticipated "great European trip." Having just read his way through all of Catholic history, Warren knew exactly what he wanted to see and why. Beginning appropriately in Jerusalem (via Basel, Switzerland, to withdraw the necessary cash from their Swiss bank account), they arrived on the eve of Palm Sunday.[34] Inquiring at their hotel the next day as to where to find a Palm Sunday Mass, they were instructed to go into the square and join the Palm Sunday procession which would lead them to the church. The procession was lovely with lots of palm waving and hosanna singing, but also extremely crowded, and as it began to disperse with people going in all directions, Warren and Anne realized that they had not really followed anyone anywhere, at least not to a church where Mass was being said. "Here we

---

Archive Collection, Caroline Jones.

33. Anne Carroll, interview by author, 10 January 2013.

34. Warren was concerned about the economy and thought it may be headed for a crash, hence the Swiss bank account.

are in Jerusalem—on Palm Sunday, nonetheless," they thought to themselves, "and we're going to *miss Mass?*" They went to the Church of the Holy Sepulchre thinking there would surely be a Mass there. They found no Mass but noticed a monk who proceeded to inform them regarding all the particulars of the chapel. Rather than saying Mass afterwards, however, he held out his hand for a donation and then sent them on their way. They eventually ended up in front of the Church of the Flagellation which posted a Mass time of 5:30. Inquiring inside, they found a priest who replied, "Yes, I will say a Mass. But do you want to see my slides first?" Somehow they made it through the slides, with Warren running the slide projector, and finally were able to hear Palm Sunday Mass! The other highlights of Jerusalem included a Holy Thursday holy hour in the Garden of Gethsemane, the Easter Vigil Mass, and a walk to the Holy Sepulcher at dawn on Easter Sunday morning.[35]

From Jerusalem they journeyed to Turkey, finding its most memorable characteristic at this time of year to be the fact that nothing was heated despite the perpetual and miserable rain and cold. "The sights were interesting," Anne remembers, "but we were always so *cold!*" They warmed up on a boat to Ephesus, sleeping so comfortably that they almost missed the disembarking and came close to sleeping their way back to Turkey on the return trip.

Much to Warren's delight, myriads of men, women, wars, and heroic deeds unfolded their stories before him as he visited one historical site or shrine after another. To Rhodes, Corinth, Crete, Germany, Belgium, England, Scotland, Ireland, Norway, Sweden, Denmark, France, and Italy these two pilgrims journeyed rejoicing as history sprung alive for them along the way. In Rome they attended an audience with Pope Paul VI, and in Sweden visited the Shrine of St. Brigid which Warren designated "about the only Catholic thing left in Sweden."[36]

On the Feast of the Sacred Heart, they were at the Shrine of St. Margaret Mary, and in Chartres, held captivated for hours as they

---

35. Anne Carroll, interview by author, 10 January 2013.
36. Ibid.

gazed upon all of salvation history intricately portrayed in every statue, every stained glass window, and the carvings gracing every door and arch. "We've really seen Europe thoroughly on this trip," Warren wrote home to his folks in June, "and doubt we'll be coming back again, at least for a long time."[37]

Equally significant if not more so, although Warren most likely did not know it at the time, was the series of lectures he gave towards the end of his trip to the students attending *Triumph*'s summer institute at El Escorial in Spain. Not only was Warren immersed in a culture whose spires still reflected the last brilliant rays of the setting sun that had been Christendom, but, as the palace of El Escorial is cradled by the mountains north of Madrid, so too was he cradled in the arms of a powerful historical example of the church militant. Embodying this fighting spirit and invigorating all who attended the institute was his friend and mentor Dr. Fritz Wilhelmsen. "He is not only a brilliant man," Warren would declare, "but a real fighter. The martial spirit and top-level intellectuality very rarely go together nowadays, but they do in him."[38]

In his historical research, Warren came upon another man, a Spaniard, who epitomized this same fighting spirit. So much was Warren drawn to this ideal which stands firm and unwavering in the face of overwhelming odds that the story of this man, known to history simply as Pelayo, would become one of his favorites and one that all of his future students would learn to recite almost by heart. It unfolds in volume two of his *History of Christendom*:

> In 683 it had been fifty-one years since the death of Muhammad. Only old men could remember him now; the last of his companions were too old to command armies, or ride with them. . . . Abdul Malik, who succeeded to the Ca-

---

37. Warren Carroll to Gladys and Herbert Carroll, 30 June 1971, Box 7-2B, Folder 4, Archive Collection, Caroline Jones.

38. Warren Carroll to Gladys and Herbert Carroll, 9 September 1973, Box 7-2B, Folder 5, Archive Collection, Caroline Jones.

liphate in 685, was one of the ablest of the commanders of the Muslim faithful. He reigned for twenty years, bringing peace to Islam and terror to its neighbors and targets. In his reign the forces gathered for the climactic Arab assault. The only tangible defenses remaining to Christendom were the waters of the Mediterranean and the walls and the Greek fire of Constantinople. . . . On April 27, [711], Musa's [the new Muslim governor of Africa] chief lieutenant, . . . Tariq, landed at the edge of the Rock of Gibraltar (it is named for him, *jub-al-Tariq*, "mountain of Tariq") with seven thousand men, ferried across the Straits from Ceuta in several journeys by four ships all provided by Count Julian, who accompanied Tariq and took charge of his main base at Algeciras. Tariq quickly defeated the local Spanish forces, and with Musa's approval called up five thousand reinforcements to deal with Roderick [King of Visigothic Spain], now hurrying back from Pamplona in far northern Spain to meet the invaders.

Battle was joined in July at the Guadalete River, beyond Medina Sidonia on the way to Seville—the battle which was apparently to decide the fate of Spain. Relatives of Witiza commanding the wings of the Spanish army betrayed Roderick; they still did not believe that the Muslims, even if victorious, would stay. The Spanish army broke up. Roderick's magnificent white charger was captured in a swamp, where the king's body was probably swallowed up, for it was never found.

. . . Characteristically for a Muslim in that age, Tariq chose the bold course. He decided to conquer Spain—all of it, immediately. Sending his trusted lieutenant Mugaith ar-Rumi with a flying column of only seven hundred men to Cordoba (most of which he took at once, and the citadel three months later), leaving only about a thousand to hold his communications in the south, Tariq marched straight on Toledo, capital of Visigothic Spain, with the bulk of his army. He met almost no opposition.

... Tariq spent the winter in Toledo. In the spring he crossed the high rocky Guadarramas, pushed on over the northern plains of what was to be Castile, past Burgos to Amaya at the foothills of the Cantabrian Mountains in the far north, killing Goths and destroying the principal settlements, while disturbing as little as possible the native Hispanic farming people. . . . The last hope of the Visigoths, the concentration at Merida, was crushed when it fell to Musa June 30, 713, after a year's siege. Every church in the city was looted; its leading defenders who were able to get away, scattered to the four winds. Musa sent Mugaith ar-Rumi and Alo son of Rabah, descendant of a Companion of the Prophet, to report to Caliph Walid that the conquest of Spain was almost complete. . . . In exactly three years, the Muslims had conquered the whole of the Iberian peninsula—a task which had been beyond the powers of Hannibal and was to prove beyond the powers of Napoleon Bonaparte, which had taken Rome at its height the better part of a century to accomplish.

. . . In Rome there was a new pope, consecrated May 19, 715; Gregory, a Roman, the second of the name, resembling his great namesake in the Papacy in more ways than one, intelligent, well-read, articulate—and a saint. He watched the crisis develop, heard the shattering reports from Spain, the grim news of the first penetrations of the Muslims into France, of their preparations against Constantinople, perhaps also of their far victories on the thresholds of India and China. In the whole world he knew or could have known, there was hardly a gleam of temporal hope. This was their hour, the hour of the scourge of God.

We may be sure that he prayed for rescue. Saints always pray.

In Spain there was a man named Pelayo. His name was the proto-Spanish version of the Latin name Pelagius, "man of the sea-shore." He came from the north, from the Asturias, the mountains overlooking the coast at Gijon. He was

distantly related to some of the Visigothic kings. . . . Pelayo
had therefore naturally been strongly attached to Roderick,
and had fought with him at the disastrous Battle of the Guadalete. After the battle he had made his way home, joining
his sister there. Governor Munuza of the Asturias, in Gijon,
sent Pelayo as a hostage with a Muslim party going to Cordoba, the new Muslim seat of government, in 717. As soon as
Pelayo had left, Munuza seized his sister, whose beauty had
evidently caught his eye, and put her into his harem.

South across much of the length of Spain rode Pelayo.
As a hostage, his life was forfeit to his Muslim companions.
Everywhere he saw the signs of their new dominion, their
government, administration, and garrisons. The land where
his Visigothic forebears had dwelt for two hundred and fifty
years must have seemed suddenly, utterly alien. It was Muslim land now; to human eyes the whole world would soon
be theirs.

. . . Eventually Pelayo learned what had happened to
his beautiful sister. He made his decision, his commitment
. . . one man, "lone and far." He escaped. He called for a rising of Spain against the Muslim conquerors.

Hardly anyone in the south paid the slightest attention to him. He made just enough stir to make it worthwhile for the authorities to try to catch him. Search par-
ties went looking for him. In the endless dead-flat plains of
La Mancha, in the broad rolling *meseta* north of the Guadarramas, there were few places to hide. Pelayo rode for
home. At Brece he was almost caught, escaping only by
swimming his horse across the Pilona River and plunging
into the mountains.

It was probably in the winter of 718 that he returned
to the Asturias. Winter among the Cantabrian peaks is
almost as harsh as summer on the way to Cordoba, and
the winter of 717–718 was particularly severe. Pelayo must
have found people who would take him in. He must have
talked of his rebellion, for most certainly he had not given

it up. Finally, early in the spring, when travel was easier, he gathered some 300 fighting men, a mixture of native skin-clad mountaineers and more experienced warriors who had survived the long series of military disasters Spain had suffered in the past seven years. They met in a cave on Mount Auseva, called *Cova dominica* (Covadonga). The assembly elected Pelayo king of Spain. His "realm" was about twenty miles by twenty, the size of a small American county. It was so small that the Muslim authorities did not even hear of it for several years.

. . . The new governor of Spain, as-Samh, led a larger army into France, took Narbonne in 719, but was killed before Toulouse in 721. Undaunted, his successor Anbasa prepared to renew the attack. But first he decided that he should deal with the minor problem in the region of Los Picos de Europa, the Peaks of Europe in the Cantabrian Mountains, which had finally come to his attention. It was time to erase the bad joke of Pelayo's Lilliputian kingdom.

It being almost impossible, and surely not necessary, to get his whole army up the narrow defiles of this region, Governor Anbasa sent his lieutenant Alqama with a detachment, accompanied by the renegade Bishop Oppas. Pelayo retreated to Covadonga, where he stood at bay. He and his men must have had almost no news of the outside world since Pelayo's escape, when the news had been almost as bad as could possibly be imagined. For all they knew, they were the last remaining Christian island in an ocean of Islam. It was May 28, 722. A strong tradition connects the Blessed Virgin Mary in a special way with the cave; it is likely that they prayed particularly to her, last refuge of those who have no other hope. Bishop Oppas came forward to negotiate for Pelayo's surrender. [This is] the dialogue [that] followed [as chronicled by Alfonso III]:

> Pelayo was on Mount Auseva with his people, and the army arrived and pitched their innumerable tents at the entrance of the cave. Upon a mound

facing the holy cave, Bishop Oppas spoke: "Pelayo, Pelayo, where are you?"

Whereupon Pelayo, from an opening in the cliff, responded: "Here I am."

The bishop continued: "I believe that you understand how the entire army of the Goths cannot resist the force of the Muslims; how then can you resist on this mountain? Listen to my advice: abandon your efforts and you will enjoy many benefits alongside the Moors."

Pelayo responded: "Have you not read in Sacred Scripture that the church of the Lord is like a mustard seed, which, small as it is, grows more than any other through the mercy of God?"

The bishop responded: "Truly, so it is written."

And Pelayo said: "Our hope is in Christ; this little mountain will be the salvation of Spain and of the people of the Goths; the mercy of Christ will free us from that multitude."

Pelayo's small force attacked from the sides and tops of the ravines raining boulders down upon the Muslims along with volleys of spears and arrows. Alqama's men broke and fled over the mountains. Some were killed in avalanches, others swept away by rushing rivers. Alqama himself perished, Bishop Oppas was captured, and local governor Munuza was driven out. In the words of the Mozarabic Chronicle of 754, written by a Christian subject of the Muslims in Seville, which nowhere mentions Pelayo or Covadonga, but seems clearly to be referring to the Battle of Covadonga at this point:

"Firmly convinced of the power of God in whose mercy the few Christians who held yonder mountain peaks trusted, after following dangerous and little known paths, having lost many of its soldiers, [the Muslim army] was able to reach the plain by a difficult march and so return to their homeland."

The Muslims wanted to lose no more men in this mountain labyrinth. They had bigger and better tasks before them. Pelayo was allowed to rule his tiny principality in peace for the remaining fifteen years of his life. Its "capital" was the miniature mountain village of Cangas de Onis. A Muslim chronicler scornfully dismissed him and his band of "wild asses": "WHAT ARE THIRTY BARBARIANS PERCHED ON A ROCK? THEY MUST INEVITABLY DIE."

The longest war in the history of the world had begun. It was to last 770 years, interrupted only by truces, never by a lasting peace, and to end in the total reconquest of Spain from the Muslims and the emergence of the Spain of the reconquest as the greatest power in the world for a century and a half: the discovery of America, the champion of the faith, the sword of Christendom, the nursery of half the Roman Catholic Church.[39]

One thousand two hundred and forty-nine years later, Warren Carroll found himself lecturing on the "basic principles of the Christian interpretation of history and the origins of civilization" across the street from El Escorial, the magnificent palace built by Philip II, grandson of Queen Isabel and King Ferdinand of Spain under whose watch the great Reconquista, begun in the cave by Pelayo, was completed. And it was here, at this palace, that Warren's own version of Pelayo's stance against the enemies of the church, began to germinate.[40]

In January of 1973, along with doing fundraising and direct-mail campaigns for *Triumph,* Warren was elected to be the director for the Christian Commonwealth Institute (CCI), which meant he would now be in charge of running the summer institutes. Over the course of the next five summers spent in Spain, his love and enthusiasm for

---

39. Carroll, *A History of Christendom,* vol. 2, 263–274.
40. Anne Carroll, interview by author, 10 January 2013.

Spanish culture blossomed. He was introduced to the Carlists by Fritz, and in the final paragraph of the short snippets of his auto-biography, he recalls:[41]

> Early in the summer [of 1975] Fritz Wilhelmsen and I, with one of his students at the University of Dallas, travelled to Pamplona in the north of Spain, in the heart of the Carlist country, which had turned out with full crusading enthusiasm for the Catholic cause in 1936. . . . We stayed for several days. Fritz had taught at the University of Navarra in Pamplona years before. He was an active Carlist still, despite being an American. (He was at least as much a Spaniard as an American, speaking the language like a native.) We went from bar to bar in the cities (bars in Spain are not in the least like those in America; people don't go there to drink and hide as in America, but to eat, drink, and be merry as befitting Catholic Spaniards). Fritz was greeted with joy all over the city: "Federico! Federico!" We met with Carlist leaders. I was plunged into an utterly Spanish environment—"total immersion," it is called. My spoken Spanish improved markedly, though unfortunately briefly. I used my confirmation name of Paul ("Pablo") since no Spaniard can pronounce Warren. And my enthusiasm for Spanish Catholic culture and history ignited and became a consuming fire.[42]

In Bill Marshner's observation, "He [Warren] became an all-flags flying confessional state triumphalist."[43] Father Mark Pilon, another *Triumph* employee and attendee of the summer institutes, relates that

---

41. The Carlists were the champions of the Spanish Catholic tradition who began their movement following the atheistic spirit pervading Spain in the wake of the French Revolution. The Carlists eventually formed a militia known as the Requetés.

42. Carroll, "Unpublished Autobiography."

43. Dr. William Marshner, interview by author.

Warren returned from this trip with Fritz brandishing a red Requeté cap and sporting a Sacred Heart patch on his jacket—the uniform of the Requetés during the Spanish Civil War. "Strange," he said, "to see this straight-laced Yankee from Maine suddenly emerge as a Requeté!"[44]

In the meantime, *Triumph* was venturing into new educational territory which included both Warren and Anne. As director of the CCI, Warren was responsible not only for the summer institutes, but also for a series of weekend institutes conducted in various cities throughout the United States. Similar in purpose to the summer institutes but condensed into three days, these weekends featured classes in theology, philosophy, and history "followed by synthesis sessions and an attempt to apply the principles learned in the classes to the present situation in the United States,"[45] while also providing good fellowship to like-minded Catholics. Though they started out small, by August of 1974 weekend institutes had taken place in Philadelphia, Milwaukee, Omaha, St. Louis, Denver, San Francisco, Charleston, Boston, New York, New Orleans, Los Angeles, Buffalo, Seattle, Dubuque, Pascagoula, Mississippi; Hillsdale, New York; Hampton, Virginia; and northern New Jersey, with attendance ranging anywhere from eight to fifty students.[46]

Also on *Triumph*'s radar screen was a plan to begin a Catholic grade school and high school to which the folks working at the magazine could send their own children when they had graduated from the local Catholic parish school, which only went through the seventh grade. Hence, in the fall of 1973, after an unsuccessful attempt to enroll Anne in a Montessori training program in Italy, *Triumph* started a pilot school in Warrenton, Virginia, consisting of . . . the eighth grade. Folks who believed in such concepts as "a confessional state" and

---

44. Father Mark Pilon, interview by Dr. Robert Rice.
45. Warren Carroll to Gladys and Herbert Carroll, 28 January 1973, Box 7-2B, Folder 5, Archive Collection, Caroline Jones.
46. When *Triumph* was later forced to fold, the German-Catholic newspaper *The Wanderer* stepped in to sponsor the events and they continued under Warren's direction.

"transcending the dialectic" were not about to send their children just anywhere, and Brent had a daughter entering the eighth grade. They opened their "school" in space provided by the Warrenton Episcopal Church with Anne teaching religion, history, English, and earth science, while other *Triumph* staffers pitched in for math, Spanish, and gym classes. To the eight original students, including Brent's daughter and one other child of a *Triumph* staff member, more were added and by the fall of 1975, it became Seton School in Manassas, Virginia, with sixteen students and two full-time teachers.[47]

The excitement and satisfaction which Warren felt at the prospect of a coming to fruition of at least part of this tremendous vision which had been growing inside him since his youth is expressed beautifully in excerpts from a few letters home during this time period. In October of 1974 he wrote:

> A major expansion of Anne's school is now a strong probability. We expect next fall to move it out of Warrenton, where there are just too few Catholics—and too few people in general—to get a substantial attendance, and move it to Manassas, here in our own parish, where we have the full support of the pastor to set up a school actually including four grades—sixth, seventh, eighth and ninth! We have a good prospect for getting two more full-time teachers of our persuasion—and strong TRIUMPH supporters—which, along with the part-time teachers from the office we have now, would make it possible for Anne to handle four grades and as many as sixty students if we could get that many, though for the first year in Manassas we'd be satisfied with forty. Manassas is also within "striking distance" of several of the closer-in Virginia suburbs of Washington, so we have a chance of drawing children from them too. At this rate, the school could soon become

---

47. The other teacher along with Anne was Miss Mary Baumberger from Colorado. Peter taught part-time. The school is still in existence today boasting 356 students and draws loyal Catholic families from all over the area.

a really significant factor in the education of this area. The most original element in the teaching is the history, told from the Christian and Catholic point of view—an approach with which almost no one is familiar. As I think you know, we wrote the eighth-grade world history text Anne is using from this viewpoint last year, and are now writing an American history text from the same viewpoint, but considering American history in its full sense as including all the Americas, South, Central, and North. Then later we can prepare a text in geography and the culture of different peoples from the same standpoint, and if as we hope we eventually expand all the way through high school, we can introduce a course in politics from the Christian standpoint at the higher high school levels as well. So with the school, as with the institute, we are moving ahead with no end in sight.... The two of us are really back into education in a big way, and truly are breaking new ground. It was the way I always wanted to get back into it—on my own terms, to give what I had found to be so lacking in the conventional educational systems; and it seems that both of us now have the opportunity to do exactly that.[48]

This next excerpt is from a letter dated March 23, 1975, and will be quoted at some length as it illustrates the numerous "goings on" of Warren during this time period, capturing some of that "boyish Maine spirit" which was still very much a part of him, as well as his love and care for his aging parents:

Dear Mother and Dad,

Well, it's really been a long time since I wrote, and maybe we'll have talked by phone before you get this letter; but anyway here goes at last! Actually I haven't been

---

48. Warren Carroll to Gladys and Herbert Carroll, 6 October 1974, Box 7-2B, Folder 5, Archive Collection, Caroline Jones.

home much for the past month—I left Wednesday morning, February 26 to go to Milwaukee in my new capacity as a member of the board of directors of the Society for the Christian Commonwealth, where I got us $15,000 (the donor said only $10,000, but my "pitch" must have worked on him in delayed fashion, since the check we finally got was for $15,000); thence to Dubuque, Iowa, where I had to make plans to market firewood from a woodlot a friend had given us the rights to (I needed grandpa on that one—what I know about marketing firewood is zero!) and also set up a fundraising dinner for the SCC there to be held April 24. I was able to get a half-hour interview with the archbishop of Dubuque about it; thence to northern California where we had quite a successful weekend institute in the San Francisco Bay area; thence to southern California where local troubles had forced me to postpone a scheduled weekend institute, but by the time I left we had *two* scheduled in the area for June; then back here Friday morning March 7. Then I had to leave again Thursday morning the 13 to go to New York to negotiate with the leaders of Catholics United for the Faith, then up to Niagara University where Dr. Wilhelmsen was giving two speeches, to talk with our people there and try to get students for the summer institute in Spain; then down to Gannon College in Erie, PA, where we were having a weekend institute; then down to Pittsburg where our people are desperately trying to keep their new Catholic high school alive; then back here late Monday the 17. This week I have been trying, with only limited success, to catch up on my mail and urgent jobs.

Recruiting for the summer institute is coming well, with 26 definite students (23 tuition-paying, three wives who come tuition free) and five probables out of the 35 or 36 we need. Our plans for an institute in Chile have suffered some setbacks but we still expect to have one there before the year is out, and hopefully in Mexico as well.

The spring institute schedule looks like this: one in northwestern Connecticut the last weekend in April; one in St. Cloud, MN (fifty miles northwest of Minneapolis!) probably the second weekend in May, then the one near Manchester, NH, still definite for the third weekend in May, the 16 to the 18; then one in Harrisburg, PA, the next weekend in May; then one in Long Island the second weekend in June (with maybe one in Charleston, South Carolina, the preceding weekend); then two in southern California the third weekend in June; then departure for Spain June 30—I'm staying the whole time this year, though it's been shortened to six weeks (June 30–August 8) and Anne will be coming over for the last three weeks. I guess I'm going to have to go to every one of these weekend institutes; the last one I didn't go to was a disaster, whereas all the ones I have gone to have worked out well, though some have been very sparsely attended. At the moment I expect to see you Sunday evening May 18, after the Manchester institute, though there's a chance I might have to go down to Brockton, MA, first for an evening meeting of our Christendom course there, and then back up to Maine. I would then stay for Monday and Tuesday the 19 and 20 and come back here Wednesday the 21. Unfortunately Anne can't come with me because her school is still in session up to June 4. And the way it looks now, this will be my only chance to get to Maine for some time. The minute we get back from Spain, we have a special week-long summer institute for families at Front Royal, Virginia, for which we have fifty beds available, and forty-five of them are already booked, this far in advance!

. . . You'd hardly believe the variety of things that we're doing—international (Spain, Chile, Mexico, even Australia), nationwide, local (I'm the president of the Legion of Mary group in our parish, and Anne is secretary), educational at all levels; I'm now planning with a young man who has been in and out of work for us and apparently is definitely going to commit himself to us full time beginning next fall, a major "assault" on the campuses for our apostolate.

. . . It must be a bit difficult for you to explain to inquirers like Dick now what I'm doing! It is without a doubt an unusual kind of work, but I love it and feel far more completely fulfilled in it than in anything else I have ever done—and also have much more responsibility. We are reaching people with a message of real hope, and I know you will agree with me that nothing is needed more profoundly than that in this dark and angry age. Our programs and our courses are occasions of great joy as well as of learning, and of renewed confidence that all will come right in the end. At our San Francisco weekend institute, four of our students were former hippies and Berkeley rebels who still live in a small commune, but after trying every false trail imaginable, had last year become converts to our faith, and in it found what they had been looking for so frantically and often hopelessly all those years. And now they find themselves denounced as conservatives and reactionaries! It is really funny for them considering that they have sampled every liberal, radical and revolutionary cause around. But the point is: there are no politics in Heaven.

Well, tomorrow is forty-three years since I was born out there in Minneapolis. Who could even have possibly predicted the course of my life? But God disposes these things, not us; if He has a job for you and you are willing to do it, it gets done whether anybody expected it or not. Without the foundation you gave me, I could never have made it through to the point where I found out what that job was; for we see all around us those who never have learned the real reason why they were born and why they live. Each period; each generation has its crises and its tasks to be done; and they often differ strikingly from period to period and from generation to generation. Your task was vastly different from that of your parents; mine is in many respects very different from yours. But, as long as we serve the best that we know and the best that is in us, we all serve the same Master. And when we've done our best for as long as we can, we are then entitled to await the reward God will give His faithful servants—including even those who did not know Him, but served Him nevertheless. You have both done great and good work in your time, as I am trying to do in mine; and if it sometimes seems hard for you to understand what's going on now or what I am doing, rest assured—if it's any comfort!—that I'm sure I'll feel exactly the same way come the twenty-first century when people like my brother-in-law Pete Westhoff are taking over. The world goes on and we serve while we can, as best we can, and that is all that is expected of us.

I'm really looking forward to seeing you in May.

With very much love,

Ren

In laying out his plans to his folks, Warren lists two events which became instrumental in the eventual outcome of his "life's work." These were the 1975 summer institute and the special "week-long institute" of that same year in Front Royal, Virginia.

By the beginning of 1975, *Triumph* magazine was in a perilous position due to financial deficits.[49] Drawing its subscribers mostly from the Goldwater supporters of 1964, *Triumph* from its outset garnered only a "sliver of a sliver" (as long-time friend Neal Freeman put it) of the American magazine readership:

> *NR* [*National Review*] had only "a sliver" or the country's magazine readership, and Brent, aiming at *NR's* conservative Catholic readers, was targeting "a sliver of a sliver." *Triumph's* shift from "conservative Catholic" to "radical

---

49. Kelly, *Living on Fire*, 183.

Christian" disappointed (and often angered) such people. Learning of *Triumph*'s founding from *National Review*, and envisaging the new magazine as a second *National Review*, they had subscribed—only to find articles attacking their bishops, their country, and conservatism.[50]

From a height of about 25,000 (and this at its inception), the subscriptions to the magazine did nothing but decline and the staff faced one impending financial disaster after another, finally mailing out its last issue in July of 1975.[51]

Concurrent with the concluding issue of *Triumph* was the final summer institute at El Escorial—and the formal decision to found Christendom College. Having spent five summers traveling the terrain of Spain—Segovia, Salamanca, Toledo, Avila, Madrid, and the Valley of the Fallen—and experiencing at least the cultural remnants of a Catholic confessional state, Warren had become convinced that this six-week immersion must become a four-year program. Fritz's passion for metaphysics, Bill Marshner's pontificating late into the night, professors and students side by side at meals, arguing about and discussing topics that *mattered* to life and to eternal life, with conversation spilling out from the classroom into the bar and from there out into the square in pre-dawn hours—all of this took root deeply in Warren's soul and became an integral part of his vision for a college. And it was at the conclusion of this summer institute, with news of *Triumph*'s folding, that he declared, "This is a sign. I am going to go ahead and start my college."[52] In this way, El Escorial, the palace of Phillip II, grandson of Queen Isabel and King Ferdinand who completed the seven-hundred-year Reconquista begun by the man named Pelayo, was the birthplace of Christendom College and its mission, "To restore all things in Christ."[53]

---

50. Ibid., 153.
51. Ibid., 183, and Mark Pilon, interview by author.
52. Kris Burns, interview by author, 21 November 2014.
53. Anne Carroll, interview by author, 10 January 2013.

In later years, Brent Bozell, who suffered tremendously from bipolar disorder, delved into the topic of God's mercy and wrote a book entitled *Mustard Seeds*. When he died in 1997, Warren wrote an "In Memoriam" for him in which he generously and truthfully acknowledged Christendom College to be a "mustard seed" "gestated in the womb of *Triumph* magazine and the Society for the Christian Commonwealth."[54] And as the courageous Pelayo responded to Bishop Oppas when asked to come down from his cave in the rock and surrender the truth of Jesus Christ to the Moors, "Have you not read in Sacred Scripture that the church of the Lord is like a mustard seed, which, small as it is, grows more than any other through the mercy of God?" so too did the courage and refusal to surrender the truth to an increasingly apostatizing world enable Warren Carroll's mustard seed, firmly rooted on the rock which is the Catholic Church, to bear fruit.

---

54. Thomas L. McFadden, Jr., "Restoring All Things in Christ: A History of the Founding of Christendom College" (Christendom College, 2012), 8.

8

The Watchmen

RETURNING FROM HIS LAST summer as an instructor in Spain, working for *Triumph's* CCI, Warren wrote to his folks:

> Nearly all the faculty at this summer's Institute in Spain agreed to go with me in my parting from [*Triumph*] and even to support a new Catholic educational enterprise to carry on our institute work, under my directions, with an initial contribution of $200.... I am going to work out my plans in detail early in September, but eventually what I intend to do is offer a wide variety of Catholic educational services—speakers, school curriculum, weekend programs, summer programs, study guides and courses for Catholic groups—along with a newsletter and our own college as a long range goal.[1]

Before he could get to work organizing his new idea, however, he was scheduled to run the first week-long mini-institute he was offering in Front Royal, Virginia.[2] This program was geared more to

---

1. Warren Carroll to Gladys and Herbert Carroll, 17 August 1975, Box 7-2B, Folder 6, Archive Collection, Caroline Jones.
2. The property was owned at that time by the AFL-CIO and would, ironically, become the permanent campus for Christendom College.

families who could not attend the longer institute in Spain and offered children's activities, both fun and educational, as well as lectures for the adults. Meals were taken in common and Mass held every day. Among the fifty or so participants, there was great comradery and everyone pitched in to help make sure things ran smoothly, although, even with the best of intentions, not everything always came off as planned. When asked to help out, one young woman of a very intellectual bent who would later become one of the founding faculty, heartily agreed, only to be plopped in the kitchen and told to "start cooking." "But cooking for one hundred people was not what I had in mind," she relates.

> I got there and I didn't know *how* to cook. All I knew how to do was cook a few things. And Anne gave me this look like, "Well, what *good* are you? How can someone not know how to cook?" Because, you know, Anne was the kind of person who could do anything. So I was immediately demoted to the person who washed the lettuce or made the salad and cleaned up the dishes.[3]

This twenty-five-year-old by the name of Kris Popik also recalls that it was either at this gathering, or shortly thereafter, that Warren told her (in response to the definite folding of *Triumph*) "This is a sign. I'm going to go ahead and start my college!" Being single and unattached, she responded, "Fine, sounds good. Let's start a college!"[4]

Having made this definitive decision, Warren Carroll's life now began to resemble that of his character Mark Stornoway in *Banner in the Sky*, who, after surveying the wreckage of his country, made it his job to

---

3. Kris Burns, interview by author, 21 November 2014.
4. Ibid. Warren's initial public announcement of his intention to start Christendom College was in a letter dated November 14, 1975, and printed on letterhead entitled "Catholic Educational Services" from his home address in Haymarket, Virginia. It was addressed "Dear Catholic Lay Apostle." Raymund O'Herron, in correspondence with author, 11 November 2015.

find the redemptive remnant who even yet could cause it to live and grow and build anew, for a juster and a truer future. He was not surprised that he had not found them quickly. They were so few and the others so many. But now, perhaps, he had a better knowledge of where and how to look. From Cairncannon he had come to Pemaquid, and from Pemaquid to Portland, and from Portland to Boston, and from Boston to New York, and from New York to Washington, and from Washington to Pittsburgh and Duluth, and from Duluth to St. Louis and New Orleans, and from New Orleans to Texas and Colorado and the Far Ocean shore of Washington State.[5]

The weekend institutes, begun by the now-defunct *Triumph* magazine, were picked up by the staunchly Catholic newspaper *The Wanderer* and became known as "Wanderer Weekend Forums." In letters home to his parents during the fall of 1975, Warren assures them that he and Anne will be alright financially and keeps them updated on his progress:

> In just two weeks after leaving the TRIUMPH offices, I have already arranged to speak (for a fee) at two independent weekend programs during November and have received a commission for an article in a Catholic quarterly, even before the invitation to New Hampshire [to speak at Magdalen College] and to Minnesota [to meet with the editor of *The Wanderer*] came in yesterday. So it looks as though, as on previous occasions, my period of unemployment is going to be very brief.[6]

---

5. Carroll, *Banner in the Sky*, 104.
6. Warren Carroll to Gladys and Herbert Carroll, 16 September 1975, Box 7-2B, Folder 6, Archive Collection, Caroline Jones.

So Warren began crisscrossing the country in the manner of Mark Stornoway from Philadelphia to Syracuse and from Syracuse to Milwaukee and from Milwaukee to Phoenix ... And like Mark Stornoway, he was garnering support for his long-desired project, making contacts, fundraising, and laying out his vision. In addition to conducting the *Wanderer* weekend forums, he spoke at other venues including meetings of Catholics United for the Faith and local parishes in the Northern Virginia area.

On the writing front, along with writing articles for local Catholic newspapers and submitting his first article to a publication known as *Faith & Reason* (which would come to play a significant role in the college project), Warren finally had the time to begin serious work on the first of a projected five volumes of his Catholic history, and, by Christmas of 1975, was able to bring the initial chapters to Maine to submit to the scrutiny of his mother. Anne, too, had been writing—a history textbook for the high school level which would be published in March of the following year. Together, Warren and Anne offered "Catholic Educational Services," (with letterhead printed up) offering seminars, lectures, research, newspaper columns, private school organization, curriculum materials, and college guidance.[7] Quoting Pope Pius XI, they declared, "There can be no ideally perfect education that is not Christian education."[8] In this brochure, Warren offers weekend programs, speaking engagements, summer programs, help in starting an apostolic school, and ultimately (his word), Christendom College (also his words).

Amidst all of this bustle (and the chickens, rabbits, ducks, miserable bees, and fruit trees), arrived what must have been for Warren a dose of much-awaited encouragement: he was given his first donation for the college. Received on October 22, the $150, he says, "will

---

7. Warren Carroll to Gladys and Herbert Carroll, 19 February 1976, Box 7-2B, Folder 6, Archive Collection, Caroline Jones.

8. Raymund O'Herron, personal papers, "The Apostolic School."

be used to cover preliminary costs—postage, stationary, prospectus."[9] And by January 7 of 1976, he had collected $2,000.[10]

That January, while he was collecting money, Warren was also collecting future faculty. As may be predicted by this point, all of the first founding faculty, as they came to be known, had been in some way influenced by *Triumph* magazine. The most unusual of these stories involves one of the first three paid employees of the college, Ray O'Herron. "I first met Warren," he explains, "at a weekend institute in Harriman, New York, in February of 1975."

> My connection to him arose oddly enough—through *Triumph* magazine. But instead of working for it—I was burning it. I was visiting my brother and he was burning old magazines, clearing out a room. I was out at the incinerator throwing stuff on the fire and among the stuff was a set of old *Triumph* magazines. I saw a cover title that mentioned "conscience," and I thought to myself, "I've been thinking a lot about this. I'm gonna take this out of the pile and read it." So I rescued three magazines. I read them, and I was astounded to see that there were people out there who actually thought about the church and the faith and their relation to the world the same way I did. I had never encountered this in print anywhere and I was fascinated by it.[11]

Through the magazine, Ray became aware of the weekend institutes put on by the Christian Commonwealth Institute and subsequently found himself captivated by Warren and others as they expounded upon these Catholic truths, rarely seen in print.

With a background in electrical engineering and a master's degree in philosophy from Catholic University, Ray was teaching math

---

9. Warren Carroll to Gladys and Herbert Carroll, 23 October 1975, Box 7-2B, Folder 6, Archive Collection, Caroline Jones.

10. Warren Carroll to Gladys and Herbert Carroll, 19 February 1976, Box 7-2B, Folder 6, Archive Collection, Caroline Jones.

11. Raymund O'Herron, interview by author, 14 January 2015.

and physics at that time at a diocesan high school in Endicott, New York. "I was over-awed," he says, "by these people and what they were talking about because I didn't know anything about these subjects." On the last day of the institute, both Warren and Ray, being of that group who stick it out to the bitter end, found themselves alone in the parking lot. Warren's car, however, would not start and he looked around, most likely with that same look on his face which had caused the little Terri Schmitz to burst into peals of laughter and which said, "I have absolutely no idea what to do." Luckily, the practical-minded Ray was somewhat handy with cars. So he offered to give Warren a hand, cleaned off the battery cables which were terribly corroded, and jumped the dead battery. "Even though this help failed to get the car started, the event was significant," says Ray, "because it made Warren remember who I was."[12] Nine months later, those corroded battery cables worked their magic at another of the weekend institutes, this time in Buffalo, New York, where Warren came face-to-face with Ray again, stared at him for about two seconds, and then said, "Oh, Ray O'Herron, nice to see you again!" Because of those battery cables, and this second meeting, Ray's name and face were now ensconced in Warren's permanent memory.

Early in 1976, the diocese in which Ray was teaching announced that it would be closing his high school. So, knowing that Warren was involved in the educational aspect of the Society for the Christian Commonwealth, Ray wrote to him explaining his situation and asking him if he knew of any place where he could teach philosophy from a Catholic perspective. Five days later, Ray heard back from Warren who said in effect, "Well *I'm* planning on starting a college. Are you interested?"[13] "I can't tell you it's a sure thing," Warren wrote, "but I do think it is a good prospect."[14] Ray's letter of response was a combination of amazement and joy:

---

12. Ibid.
13. Ibid.
14. Warren Carroll to Raymund O'Herron, 29 January 1976, personal papers of Raymund O'Herron.

> I was so stunned by the prospect that I had to set the letter
> down at that point and walk around a bit before resuming.
> The hope of teaching Christian philosophy in a deeply
> Catholic atmosphere had seemed impossible of being ful-
> filled till then. . . . Again, we are really joyous at this turn
> of events and feel that our prayers and our friends' prayers
> for us have been answered beyond our expectations and
> that divine providence has been merciful to us. Thanks
> ever so much for your kindness and your confidence and
> we look forward to joining the task.[15]

"All this," reminisces Ray, "from glancing at the headlines of *Triumph*
magazine—which I was throwing in the fire!"[16]

Kristin (Kris) Popik had been a philosophy student studying under Dr. Frederick Wilhelmsen (of El Escorial fame) at the University
of Dallas, and she attended the second of the Spain programs put on
by *Triumph* in the summer of 1971 as Wilhelmsen's assistant. It was
here that she met Warren for the first time. When Warren became
the director of the Christian Commonwealth Institute, he put her
in charge of activities for the students attending these summer programs as a sort of social director. "I was in charge of planning [the
side] trips," she says. "Getting everyone on the bus, telling them
what to see, how to use the local currency, what places to visit in
the towns, and not to drink too much at the discos."[17] She was also
recruited by Warren to participate in his weekend institutes and got
to know him better through these programs. By January of 1976,
she was teaching philosophy at Niagara University in Niagara Falls,
New York. "I don't remember how early I signed on to the college
project," she says,

---

15. Raymund O'Herron to Warren Carroll, 4 February 1976, personal papers of
Raymund O'Herron.

16. Raymund O'Herron, interview by author.

17. Kris Burns, interview by author.

but it was probably during the fall of '75 or very early winter of '76. At first he [Warren] was just talking about the idea of a college and it was not certain that anything would come of it, so even expressing interest in joining the endeavor was not really a commitment. But definitely by spring of '76 I was intending to be part of the college—*if* it actually got started! I thought it would be an exciting adventure and I knew that I would be disappointed if it succeeded and I had not been a part of it.[18]

Bill Marshner had the closest connections to *Triumph*, being already a member of its staff by the time Warren began to work for the magazine in 1973. "My personal story," he begins, "goes back to the year 1966, when I attended one of the very first meetings of the Philadelphia Society."

Brent Bozell was there and so was Dr. Frederick Wilhelmsen. I got talking to them, and I learned that they were hatching this magazine called *Triumph*. At the time, I was a graduate student at Yale in Near Eastern languages with an interest in Biblical studies, theology, and so on. And I was sort of wending my way into the Catholic Church. I was Lutheran. I started reading *Triumph* before I was a Catholic, and I got a good polemical understanding of the mess emerging at the end of Vatican II. So I subscribed to the magazine, and a few years later I decided to come down from Yale and work for the magazine. That would have been 1971. I had converted by then; I came into the church in '67.[19]

So Warren and Bill Marshner got to know one another initially within the offices of *Triumph* which moved, soon after Marshner be-

---

18. Kris Burns, correspondence with author, 30 October 2015.
19. William Marshner, interview by author.

gan working for them, from the cosmopolitan atmosphere of Washington, D.C., to a rural property in Warrenton, Virginia, where, according to Marshner, "we were obviously rusticating." In one of these two locations, Warren learned more of the personality of this man he would eventually hire to teach theology when he happened to overhear one of Marshner's phone conversations, which was easy to do given the resonance of his voice. Engaged in a loud and boisterous theological argument with whoever was on the other end of the phone line, Marshner boomed, "NO! NO, you can't *say* that! That's HERESY!" This went on and on and poor Warren, who was used to Maine manners and reserve, listened with a growing amount of trepidation. It must have been with some surprise and no small amount of wonder when he finally overheard the conclusion to this tirade: "Yes, yes, mother, I love you too," said Bill and hung up the phone.[20]

Not being the type who enjoyed "rusticating," and feeling the call of great Beethoven symphonies bellowing from the bowels of the Kennedy Center, Marshner moved back to Washington after about a year, finally leaving *Triumph* altogether because of the length of the commute. He went to work for *The Wanderer*, and when this newspaper took over the weekend institutes, Marshner went along and was therefore once more working with Warren to instruct students in the glorious Catholicism which had united them at El Escorial.

At some point during the first half of 1976, while Marshner was finishing up his doctoral work at the University of Dallas, he found himself once again on the phone, this time with Warren on the other end of the line rather than in the next cubicle, and was offered a job. To Warren's question he replied, "Sure, I'll teach at your college." Did he expect that the college would actually get off the ground? "Absolutely not!" is his response.

Jeff Mirus, who began writing articles for *The Wanderer* during his freshman year in college, also became a *Triumph* subscriber around that same time, writing an article for the magazine sometime in 1969

---

20. Kris Burns, interview by author.

Mrs. Gladys Hasty Carroll with her young son, Warren.

Warren with his sister, Sally, in the living room of the "house on the hill" built across from the original Hasty homestead.

Graduation from Berwick Academy in 1949.

Bottom row, far right, Miss Marie Donahue.

College debate team 1952–1953. Bottom row, far left is Warren Carroll and bottom row, third from left is Jerry Handspicker.

California State Senator and
U.S. Congressman John G.
Schmitz, godfather of Warren.

Marriage to Anne
Westhoff, Wiggins,
Colorado, July 6, 1967.

The Palace of El Escorial in Spain.

Warren Carroll with Bishop Thomas J. Welsh,
a key supporter of Christendom College
who was instrumental in obtaining the
permanent campus.

Wearing the famous plaid
suit in his original office at
Christendom College.

With his hard-working
typewriter.

Dr. William Marshner,
founding faculty member.

Raymund P. O'Herron,
founding faculty member.

Dr. Kristin Popik Burns,
founding faculty member.

Jeffrey A. Mirus,
founding faculty member.

Board member
Dr. Sean O'Reilly who
was instrumental in
obtaining the permanent
campus.

From left to right: Onalee McGraw, Warren Carroll, William Marshner,
Ray O'Herron, and Anne Carroll.

William Carrigan and Anne Carroll.

Mr. George Meany, president
AFL-CIO.

Miss Regina Graham,
one of the first major donors to
Christendom College.

Dr. Warren Carroll lectures in Classroom 1 of the original Regina Coeli building.

Cathy O'Donnell, Fr. John A. Hardon, and Tim O'Donnell attending a
book signing for Dr. O'Donnell's book *Heart of the Redeemer*,
first published in 1989.

Dr. Damian Fedoryka introducing the college to Saint John Paul II.

Dan Arnold, Warren Carroll, Mark Gallagher, and Tim O'Donnell
sing favorite Irish fighting songs at the annual St. Patrick's Day party.

Singing *O'Donnell Abu* and *Roddy McCourley*, "true to the last, true to the last!" are Dan Arnold, Paul O'Donnell, and Warren Carroll.

Pope Saint John Paul II to Warren Carroll,
"You have done a great work for the Church."

Warren with his best friend and third president of the college, Tim O'Donnell.

Warren Carroll with Cardinal Arinze.

Warren and Anne attend the Christmas
dinner at Christendom College in 1999.

Reading the Easter Proclamation for the last time
at the 2010 St. Patrick's Day celebrations.

Delivering one of his last lectures at Christendom College.

Warren is laid to rest on the beautiful grounds
of his beloved Christendom College.

Tim O'Donnell
sings "Bonne Charlie."

Mr. Kieran DuFrain plays a tribute to
the late Dr. Warren H. Carroll.

Christendom College campus, 2017.

or 1970. When Jeff graduated from Rutgers University in 1970, Brent Bozell offered him an editorial job on the magazine staff—which Jeff turned down in favor of graduate school and an eventual job as a professor. In 1975, while teaching at Pembroke State University in North Carolina, he started his own publication, a Catholic interdisciplinary quarterly which he called *Faith & Reason*. In October of that year, Warren submitted an article for publication which Jeff accepted.[21] However, as Jeff recalls,

> He [Warren] explained his situation, what he was trying to do, and the fact that he had no regular income. So he wondered if *Faith & Reason* could pay for the article. Typically academic journals don't pay, but I wanted to help, so I sent him what little I had ($100, I think) and asked him not to tell other writers that we paid! Warren clearly appreciated this, and so he sent me the prospectus he had developed for Christendom and asked me to comment on it. Apparently he liked the comments and thought we were on the same wavelength, because shortly thereafter, he asked me to become one of the founding directors of the project, and invited me to join the faculty.[22]

Since Warren mentions in a letter to his folks dated February 19, 1976, that he is trying to get the editor of *Faith & Reason* "for my college faculty, and think I may succeed," Jeff's official incorporation into the founding faculty must have been sometime between that date and March 28 of that year when Jeff's journal merged with the college to become "Faith and Reason, The Christendom College Journal."[23]

Although quite a young professor, Jeff had already realized that he was, in his own words, "a fish out of water" at Pembroke because of his

---

21. Warren Carroll to Gladys and Herbert Carroll, 23 October 1975, Box 7-2B, Folder 6, Archive Collection, Caroline Jones.
22. Jeffery Mirus, correspondence with author, 19 October 2015.
23. Warren Carroll to Gladys and Herbert Carroll, 28 March 1976, Box 7-2B, Folder 6, Archive Collection, Caroline Jones.

strong Catholicism. "The idea of a new Catholic college was a natural fit with my own interest in Catholic teaching and publishing," he says, and "I was a 'starter' by nature; it has never bothered me to strike out on my own. The time was ripe, and I thought that as a team we might be able to do this. I was certainly excited by the prospect!"[24]

And what did Warren say to these folks whom he was gathering into his vision? Well it must have been something along the lines of what Mark Stornoway said when he met anyone who would listen:

> I think of America today ... as a large party of emigrants on a long, long trek through wilderness, with no turning back but no end yet seen or even imagined. And here rising before us is an immense wall of mountains, seeming to grow higher and higher the longer we look upon it, each peak one more apparently insoluble problem—problems of a divided and increasingly hostile world, of an uncertain and often aimless people, of despair and crime and sordidness and fear, above all of a sense that we have lost our historic destiny, our place in the sun, and cannot find it again. So we camp below the escarpments, looking up, looking—for a pass. How do we find it, and cross it? ... We will say there are five hundred in our wagon train—men, women, and children, the old and the lame, the young and the reckless, the fearful and the wise, every variety of human being. All recognize the necessity of finding a pass, even though some in their hearts still do not really wish to risk the search for it. We have, fundamentally, three courses of action.
>
> We may take from among our number One Man, set him up on an axletree and shower him with our praise and our hopes, commission him on our behalf to go and find the pass, with a lonely death as the price of failure and everlasting fame as the reward for success. The chances are that he will not return; as every mountain climber knows,

---

24 Jeffery Mirus, correspondence with author, 19 October 2015.

at least two men with a stout rope between them are far safer than one alone upon a mountainside, however well-equipped and however skillful that one may be. If our One does return, it is virtually certain that the pass he says he has found will prove to be no pass at all, only a byway of his own imagination, created in the conscious or unconscious hope that with it he may win from us the devotion and support that is essential to his quest. For one alone may defy mountains, but cannot conquer them. . . .

Or we may agree that since the problem of the mountains concerns all of us, all of us ought to share equally in its solution. We may select committees, with strictly proportional representation from each sex and age, each health and strength and ability grouping, each level of experience, which will sit on the ground looking up at the mountains and try to decide which two look as though they might have a pass between them, and then take a vote on the proposed routes. Having voted, we may then pack our belongings, hook up our wagons, and trundle off in a body along the plurality path, with periodic stops to reconsider. When the way becomes steep we may hook all the wagons to the trail of the stoutest that is pulled by the strongest team and driven by the surest hand, and let that team and that hand pull until all strength and sureness is gone from them, and then replace them by the next strongest and surest, and so on and on until there is no strength or sureness left in all our company and what we thought might be a pass is shown to be no pass, and we cannot go on and we cannot stay where we are, and the weakest lie down on the cold ground to cry, and the others stay to share their misery—and in the end, like those who starved not so far below Donner Pass one winter in California a century and a quarter ago, we begin to eat each other in fire-hollowed caves under snowdrifts forty feet deep.

But there is a third course. We may search among us for our best, not our one best but our few best—perhaps five out of that five hundred, choose them for what they are and not what we think perhaps they ought to be, give them the bare essentials of what they must have to climb, and promise them only this: that if they find their way through this mountain range, we will give them the same opportunity, when we arrive at the next one, to do it again. And then we can let them go . . . to find and mark the trail, and stake out the pass, knowing that in the very act of doing so they will have their fulfillment.

This is allegory, but it is also history. It is only thus that mountains have ever been scaled and passes found and trails marked, in the real as well as the figurative sense—not by lone men, not by large groups, but by small, resolute bands who take on the challenge of the summits with uplifted hearts, rejoicing in their freedom to meet it on its terms and theirs and no one elses's, and sustained in all their efforts by the comradeship of the trail—and there is nothing closer than such comradeship.[25]

And so Warren had chosen his five: Ray O'Herron, Kris Popik (later Burns), Bill Marshner, Jeff Mirus, and himself. And this resolute band began their climb to find the pass through the muck that was higher education, to raise Catholic higher education to its true majesty, to mark the trail so that others may follow them, and to sustain their mountainous efforts in the joy of shared comradeship. And, as all mountain climbers are, they would be tested, and would be forced to remember that they five out of the five hundred were chosen for who they are, and not for who they might in the future think one another ought to be. There are always obstacles when one blazes a trail.

In a letter to Ray dated January 29, 1976, Warren lays out the status of his plans thus far: "It will probably be called Christendom College. A lawyer is working on the incorporation right now, I have some initial financial contributions in hand, and as soon as we are in-

---

25. Warren Carroll, *Banner in the Sky*, 94–97.

corporated will begin a widespread fund-raising effort with the target date for opening September 1977."[26] Next, knowing that faculty were not the only watchmen he needed to gather, he began putting together his board of directors, along with both an academic and a financial advisory board.[27]

By March 28, the letters home were no longer typed out on the old "Catholic Educational Services" letterhead, but on new, official "Christendom College" letterhead which listed down the left hand side a board of directors consisting of himself, Anne, Jeff Mirus, and two new watchmen: Dr. Sean O'Reilly and Dr. Onalee McGraw. Of Sean O'Reilly, Warren writes that he is a very highly regarded neurologist at Georgetown Hospital "with whom I have been working for a year and a half in a discussion group and other activities in this area."[28] Onalee, a subscriber to both *Triumph* and *The Wanderer,* recalls that her own introduction to Warren had occurred around 1972 or 1973 when she was doing some lobbying for Citizens United for Responsible Education for which her husband, Bill, was the chairman. Calling the offices of U.S. Congressman John Schmitz, she was answered by one Warren Carroll who "gave me some advice about lobbying," she says.[29] Little did she know that a few years later, she would be attending lectures by this same man at St. John's Catholic Church in McLean, Virginia, along with a small group of families which included the family of Sean O'Reilly.

---

26. Personal papers of Raymund O'Herron.
27. These boards consisted of the following people: Board of directors: Dr. Warren H. Carroll, Anne W. Carroll, Dr. Onalee McGraw, Dr. Jeffery A. Mirus, Dr. Sean O'Reilly; Academic advisory board: Dr. Frederick D. Wilhelmsen, Dr. Donald J. D'Elia, Dr. Rupert J. Ederer, Dr. Robert Herrera, Rev. Dr. William Most, Rev. Cornelius O'Brien, Dr. Peter Sampo; Financial advisory board: John J. Carlin, L.L.B., Dr. Leo E. Becher, Dr. Robert P. Blume, Mrs. Regina Graham, Mr. Thomas May, Mr. Joseph P. Wall.
28. Warren Carroll to Gladys and Herbert Carroll, 19 February 1976, Box 7-2B, Folder 6, Archive Collection, Caroline Jones. He is mistaken: Sean was working at George Washington University Clinic.
29. Onalee McGraw, interview by author, 14 January 2015.

> Warren Carroll gave his lectures at St. John's every
> month—over a period of about a year and a half—on
> the history of Christendom. And that was before he had
> written his book. He was doing his research. We had the
> benefits of the lectures that presented the intellectual
> historical foundations and why this was so important to
> found the college—because there's a body of knowledge
> in the history, the philosophy, the theology of the church
> that needs to be transmitted to this generation of today;
> because there's been this disconnect with Vatican II, the
> aftermath, the failure to implement a true proper fullness
> of doctrine. And now we need this college. He was a his-
> torian, and he went back after his conversion and studied
> the whole history. He was brilliant. That was what made
> us so grounded in his vision. It wasn't just that he had told
> us this vision. We had heard him speak. So he inspired us,
> and he inspired Sean O'Reilly.[30]

Onalee, who was chairman of the board for the first two years,
vividly remembers that at the very first board meeting "somebody
said, 'Who's going to take the minutes?' And nobody said anything. So
finally Warren said, 'Oh, what the . . . *I'll* take the minutes.'"[31]

With first donations in pocket and his core of watchmen on his
side, Warren was ready to announce his vision to the public at large.
It came in the form of a "prospectus," sent out at the beginning of
April to every name Warren could possibly come up with as having
any interest in his project. Because Warren and Anne were living on
a shoestring and putting every penny into their educational projects,
the initial draft of the prospectus was not Xeroxed (too expensive),
but copied on an old mimeograph machine, of which they had been
given use free of charge.[32] Anne's brother Pete, who was living with
the Carrolls at the time and acting as Warren's "secretary," dutifully

---

30. Ibid.
31. Ibid.
32. Peter Westhoff, interview by author.

took the original to the shop and watched as the first few copies came out just fine. "I called Warren," says Pete, "and said, 'they look great!'" So the mimeograph machine rolled out the copies—the rest of which came out horribly. Undeterred, Warren sent them out anyway, only to hear back from his first major donor, Regina Graham, who called with the not so enthusiastic comment of, "You know, these are not very presentable."[33] Presentability, however, was not the first concern of Warren Carroll. The man with a mission loved truth and did not much care *what* it looked like on paper—as long as it was presented in all its entirety. Already, the watchmen, on their arduous climb, were beginning to trip over the rocks of one another's personality traits. They may not have been causing falls as of yet—but they were beginning to bruise toes.

The prospectus laid out quite clearly the extent of the ruins of Catholic higher education with "misguided educational philosophies" too deeply entrenched to be reformed. It rightly characterized these institutions as "secularized, groping, undisciplined, without a clear sense of purpose and without doctrinal or moral foundations."[34] Although on great terms with Bishop Thomas Welsh, in whose diocese the college would be located, Warren was quite strong in his insistence in the college's autonomy, "not subject to ecclesiastical control."[35] "It will, however, be submissive to the guidance of the local ordinary regarding the orthodoxy of the Catholic doctrine taught at the college."[36] Warren had had dealings with modern "academic freedom" and its resulting chaos, and wanted none of it. "Rejection of the magisterium of the Roman Catholic Church and of the pope on any question of faith or morals, or defiance of the authority of the pope as head of the church," would be grounds for automatic termination.[37] Far from cre-

---

33. Ibid.
34. Warren H. Carroll, "Christendom College, A Prospectus," Haymarket, Virginia, 1976, personal papers of Raymund O'Herron.
35. Ibid., 10.
36. Ibid.
37. Ibid.

ating a rigid, somber institution of higher learning, Warren, himself a naturally joyful person and with experience of the added joy the faith brings, envisioned that this joy, which will never be understood by the worldly but which he had imbibed during his summers in Spain, would permeate the life of the college:

> Throughout the history of the Catholic Church, those actively engaged in apostolic work have known the deep satisfaction and strengthening and joy of fellowship with their brothers and sisters in Christ joined in building up His Mystical Body. That apostolic fellowship and Christian joy will mark the whole life of the Christendom College community, bringing together faculty and students in common service to Our Lord and Savior as they seek to understand His truths more fully. Informal conversation and social interaction between faculty and students will be a vital part of this life of the community and a source of much additional learning, mutual inspiration, and moral guidance. Students and faculty will work together in building up the campus and operating its facilities.[38]

And finally, the prospectus unfolded Warren's great dream of rebuilding and restoring:

> Time and again in history, the church and the faith have been rebuilt from the ashes of secular or heretical destruction. Time and again the church and the faith have been proclaimed dead and buried, only to rise again. For the church is Christ's and the faith is Christ's, and Christ does not die. Most of the damage to Catholic higher education which could have been done, has been done. The ruins lie all around us. But the destroyers do not know what to do with their victory, for all the roads away from the truth of

---

38. Ibid., 6.

Christ end only in darkness. It is time for the rebuilding to begin.[39]

But, like all great visionaries whose minds are vast places of creating and building, Warren often had to be brought back to the reality of the things that are; to the world of men who did not see what he saw. And as he crisscrossed the country with his endless energy and optimism, his spirit was sometimes squashed by these men. He would set up his table at events—and no one would show up. Or if a brave soul did venture over to the sign advertising "CHRISTENDOM COLLEGE," he might screw up his brow and say, "Oh, Christian Dome," or "Kristen Dum—ahhh," and nod his head while shrugging his shoulders and walking off in another direction. "People can't even *pronounce* the word," Warren complained in exasperation to his wife.[40] "Our college takes its name," he would later explain, "from the word which embodies the Christian social and political ideal: a society, a culture, a government in which Christ the King reigns. To help extend His reign, insofar as His grace strengthens us to do so, is the heart of our mission."[41]

There were more doses of reality to come. At some point, Warren found out that you had to be approved by the state to open a college and to grant degrees legally. So he traveled down to Richmond to meet with the folks at the Department of Education. Coming home discouraged, he said to Anne, "There is so much they want us to do. We can do most of them, but they want us to have this library with such a large number of books."[42] So he added "book collecting" to his already gargantuan list of things that needed to be done. He donated all of his own books and then began scavenging in other places. "Very happy to hear you have rescued more books from the trash,"

---

39. Ibid., 3.
40. Anne Carroll, interview by author, 31 January 2013.
41. Warren H. Carroll, "Christendom College Report," vol. II, no. 2, February 1977, personal papers of Raymund O'Herron.
42. Anne Carroll, interview by author, 31 January 2013.

Anne wrote at one point to Ray.[43] They sent out the word, "We need books," and people began mailing them to Warren's house in Haymarket where they piled up in corners. All the members of the founding faculty donated substantial parts of their personal libraries.[44] By the opening of the college in the fall of 1977, Warren had managed to collect at least seven thousand volumes, some of them "out-of-print volumes of great value for Christendom College studies."[45] Far from allowing obstacles to turn him away from his God-given path, Warren turned them into opportunities. Hence, his goal now became the "building of one of the finest collections of orthodox Catholic materials in the United States."[46]

In August of 1976, almost exactly one year before the proposed opening of the college, the final week-long institute held in Front Royal, Virginia, became a magnet, drawing together those who had been reached by Warren through *Triumph*, *The Wanderer*, and the pro-life movement, or had heard him speak elsewhere. Onalee remembers the final day of this week vividly:

> Warren had a certain limited number of people; not people with money but really dedicated. So Warren said, "I think I've got $30,000 and if some of you guys can help me I have this dream. I want to share with you that we need to have a college." So he laid it all out. He waited until the last day so we had all had our courses and our meals with Kris Burns struggling with these large pots. I still remember—I don't know how she even turned one of them over to clean, it was so big! I don't know how they stuck her with that. She wasn't even married, what would she know about cooking? But that would be typical because this was

---

43. Anne Carroll to Raymund O'Herron, 4 January 1976, personal papers of Raymund O'Herron.

44. "Christendom College Report," vol. II, no. 7, July 1977, personal papers of Raymund O'Herron.

45. Ibid.

46. Ibid.

a band of people, not intimate, but who had a dedication to a belief. There wasn't anything about personality, "I don't know this person over here," but we knew our cause and we knew we all believed in it. So we said, "I don't know what we're going to do in this world but here is a man with a visionary plan, so let's go with this." This man had done a lot of thinking and that was obvious. He had the ability to say, "Let's make something new that will exist as a positive force." That was his vision, that was what he was unveiling there. I think maybe he had $30,000 or something like that but he said, "if we can just get this $50,000, then we can start."[47]

By the beginning of August, there were two pressing tasks on Warren's agenda in addition to fundraising and recruiting students: the selection of a site for the school and its incorporation. Articles of incorporation for the Christendom Educational Corporation which would oversee the development and operation of Christendom College were submitted to the authorities on August 30, and Christendom was officially incorporated as a non-profit according to Virginia law on September 3.[48] After an intense search for a site for the campus, undertaken mainly by Ray, Warren, and William Smythe, a vacant diocesan school building was settled upon in Triangle, Virginia, about an hour's drive south from Washington, D.C. The former school, run by the parish of St. Francis of Assisi, had been forced to close because of lack of funds for needed renovations, and so St. Francis's pastor, Fr. Angelus DeMarco, agreed to lease the building to the college for a period of two years. Charging $1,000 per month year-round would enable them to make the needed repairs and re-open their school.[49]

---

47. Onalee McGraw, interview by author. Warren had collected about $25,000 at that time.

48. Warren H. Carroll to Directors, Advisors and Potential Faculty of Christendom College, 26 August 1976, personal papers of Raymund O'Herron. See also "Christendom College Report," vol. I, no. 1, September 1976, ibid.

49. Raymund O'Herron, interview with author.

The use of six classrooms and a chapel, however, left the students with nowhere to actually *live*, and so Warren and Ray began additional negotiations to lease an apartment building three miles away in Quantico, Virginia, a tiny, somewhat dumpy town completely surrounded by the Quantico Marine Base.

With all major aspects of "starting a college" at least begun, the watchmen entered their final year of preparation. At the end of September, Kris Popik left for Rome and the Angelicum where she would be the first woman to gain her Ph.D. in philosophy from the prestigious institution. Bill Marshner spent the year at the University of Dallas working towards a doctorate in theology. Jeff Mirus finished the 1976–1977 academic year at Pembroke State University in North Carolina. And Ray O'Herron, who had moved his family to Manassas, Virginia, in August of 1976, spent the year teaching algebra and religion for Anne's Seton School during its second year. So the brunt of work for this last phase fell most heavily on the shoulders of Warren and Ray. The site for the college was announced formally in "a nationally distributed press release on November 15, following a preliminary local announcement" by Fr. DeMarco.[50]

And then, in the little house in Haymarket, with all of its rabbits and peach trees and its miserable bees, they waited. They waited for money and they waited for students. And as the months passed, each number climbed in what must have been felt as a painfully slow process. Anne's younger brother Pete had moved out to Virginia in 1975 presumably to work for *Triumph*, but it folded right around the time he arrived, so he coached and taught math and typing at Seton School and worked part-time for Warren as his "secretary." Ironically, he was both "the admissions department," which consisted of Warren, Anne, and himself, *and* the first student officially enrolled in the college. It must have been a strange experience to admit oneself into one's college of choice! This "admissions department" would sit around their kitchen table scrutinizing the applications which trickled in, won-

---

50. "Christendom College Report," vol. I, no. 3, November 1976, personal papers of Raymund O'Herron.

dering "how many of these students are going to be normal?"[51] Of course, "normal" is a relative word—when you are Warren Carroll. How many "normal" people start colleges? And an application came in for one Peter Scheetz. There had been an ongoing debate regarding the dress code with Ray proposing shirts and ties for the men and Kris insisting that "you can look nice without a tie." So following the application of Mr. Scheetz came a letter from his mother—which included cut out pictures of mostly polo shirts from the Sears catalogue pasted on a sheet of paper, asking, "Is this O.K.?" Warren, Anne, and Pete looked at one another. "His letter of recommendation is from his *square dance teacher,*" moaned Warren. "But he is from Colorado—he must be all right," returned both Anne and Pete. And so it went. Pretty much anybody who applied was accepted.[52]

With his indefatigable optimism, Warren had set his sights on an enrollment of fifty students for the first year. He proposed this number to Ray early in 1976 but dropped the number on Ray's advice:

> On Kris's recommendation I have decided to raise the tuition fee to $2,000 while lowering the room and board charge to $1,500, to be more in line with existing institutions. This enabled me to reduce, in the initial budget, the number of students expected for the opening classes from fifty to forty, in line with your suggestion that fifty was too large a number. I personally do not believe it to be too large—I think we might even get more—but if it impresses even you who are so sympathetic with and interested in the project as too large, then doubtless it would impress many others in the same way. Having recruited forty students last summer for our program in Spain— quite expensive, and with no academic credit at all—and knowing the opportunities I have and will have to speak to people all over the country who are desperate to find a sound college education for their children, I am sure

---

51. Anne Carroll, interview by author, 31 January 2013.
52. Ibid.

that fifty is a realistic figure, particularly when you keep in mind that we are accepting beginning students in two classes rather than just one. Magdalen College now has over one hundred applications! But forty is the figure that will now go into the prospectus. Better to aim too low than too high—then you can claim more credit if you exceed expectations. In any case, I believe we could actually start with as few as thirty.[53]

But "realistic" was not Warren's strong point. And even the number forty began to look unreachable. In February of 1977, he reports that the "number of students who have either made a definite commitment to enroll . . . or are strongly leaning towards such a commitment, has risen from six to fourteen."[54] In March this number was nineteen, and by May, Warren reports a "definite number of thirty."[55] In reality, Christendom College opened with twenty-six students. Somewhere in those last number of months, Warren must have lowered his expectations, for Anne reports that he finally said he would start with twenty-five students. No less. And he got twenty-six. But if he started with a goal of $50,000 and fifty students, and his number for students had to be lowered, his budget was on track. By June of 1977, just two months before the projected opening date, Warren reported at the second board of trustees meeting (the first had occurred in January) a fund of $52,000 to date. And in his optimism "President Carroll reported the revenues of over $115,000 are expected during the first academic year. A fund-raising target of $100,000 for that year was proposed. This would more than meet the projected operating deficit, permitting the accumulation of funds for the permanent campus to begin."[56] Maybe—in Warren's Dunnybrook world.

53. Warren H. Carroll to Raymund P. O'Herron, 4 March 1976, personal papers of Raymund O'Herron.

54. "Christendom College Report," vol. II, no. 2, February 1977, ibid.

55. "Christendom College Report," vol. II, no. 5, May 1977, ibid.

56. "Christendom College Report," vol. II, no. 6, June 1977, ibid.

In the meantime—what were Warren and Anne *living* on? Surely they did not eat the bees! Writing to Ray back in January of 1976, Warren admitted that "the problem, of course, is money," and, after attempting to manipulate figures in the best of lights, asked Ray for his "absolute rock-bottom figure" for living expenses as he offered him a job as a college professor.[57] Neither Anne nor Warren was taking a salary at this time, although Warren did take a small percentage of the funds he raised, besides earning a bit for his *Wanderer* forums and also doing some side work for Congressman Larry McDonald from Georgia.[58] By the fall, things were looking up somewhat so that in November, Warren could add to Ray's salary for teaching at Seton School, the first official salary of a Christendom College employee, making Ray the first paid employee of the college.[59] Even so, Pete remembers overhearing Anne one day say quietly to her husband concerning their finances, "the wolf is not at the door—*yet*." "So they were not destitute—yet," Pete says.[60] But these were people who believed in something and were willing to make the necessary sacrifices ... and God provided, as He has promised to do.

The summer of 1977 pulled the watchmen together. A torch of truth was ignited, and Christendom College became a reality. July saw the arrival of Kris and Jeff to Virginia and the first official meeting of the founders to discuss the curriculum (minus Marshner who was busy being brilliant and did not appear until a few days before the college opened). *This is to say, no meeting of all the founding faculty together had occurred until one month prior to the opening day!*[61] This is unbelievable; a college is expecting students in one month's time and the five founding faculty have not all met together to discuss, not only the curricu-

---

57. Warren H. Carroll to Raymund P. O'Herron, 29 January 1976, ibid.

58. Anne Carroll, interview by author, 31 January 2013.

59. Warren H. Carroll to Raymund P. O'Herron, 30 November 1976, personal papers of Raymund O'Herron.

60. Peter Westhoff, interview by author.

61. Obviously, the founders had corresonded, especially during the spring of 1976, to discuss items such as curriculum. There had also been meetings of two or three of the five, but never one including Bill Marshner.

lum, but the administration in general. This is unheard of in the world of academia. But it happened. What happened? Some well-planned, well-thought-out meeting of the minds? Absolutely not, says Kris:

> About a month or so before we started, I remember this meeting we had about the curriculum. We still didn't know what it was! There was a little bit of an argument—everybody had their ideas. Ray had made up these square pieces of paper for the different courses we should have and then he had this chart with the number of courses a student would take each semester, etc. . . . So he wanted to work with these squares and this chart to figure things out. It was a really good idea, but everybody was sort of impatient with that. We knew in general what we wanted to do, but it is amazing to me that we were having this discussion a month before we were going to start! We were all really pretty unprepared to do this college. Nobody really knew what they were doing![62]

Jeff attributes this remarkable ability to pull together at the last minute to the self-reliance of these five: "The project would never have gotten off the ground if each person hadn't been remarkably reliable."[63]

And curriculum was not the only thing tackled during that last hectic month. The school had eight classrooms, six of which the college was allowed to use. Two would be used for classes, one for the library, one for a study room, one for the dining area, and one *for the kitchen*. But there *was* no kitchen! Since the lease for the building gave the college official occupancy as of August 1, all of these renovations had to be done at the last minute. With the help of board member William Smythe, along with assorted St. Francis parishioners skilled in plumbing and electrical work, the kitchen was indeed completed, but

---

62 Kris Burns, interview by author.

63 Jeffrey Mirus, correspondence with author, 22 October 2015.

in the rush, a vent hood for the stove was not sealed correctly—and so the first time it rained, the kitchen flooded.[64]

The nucleus of folks who had formed around Warren possessed that same spirit of sacrifice and reliability without which there would have been no college. While Bill Smythe was installing a kitchen and Ray O'Herron was putting together bookshelves, Onalee McGraw was searching her own home for furniture to bring to the campus. "I had a little white dresser," she recalls, "and I said, 'This would look nice next to such and such.' So I brought that in. Whatever we had, we gave to Christendom. Sometimes we would skip a vacation and give the money to Warren."[65] Students pitched in as well, students who hadn't even attended the college yet because there was as yet no college to attend! They arrived early to help clean the building, catalogue the books, move furniture, and assist with building maintenance. Sister John Eudes O.P. was hired as a librarian and Mrs. Shirley Carosi of Triangle as the college's cook.[66]

Finally—the students arrived. Twenty young men and six young women. It was September 11 of 1977. As Anne puts it, "Five faculty and twenty-six students were willing to take a chance. Most of the people there the first years were pioneers, and they knew it. It took some courage."[67] Warren himself expanded on the thought of his wife in a column of the "Christendom College Report" entitled "From the President to the Students at CC," in which he wrote:

> We of the staff of Christendom College can and will do
> all in our power to carry out our teaching responsibilities
> well, in the broadest Catholic sense of teaching. But our
> efforts would inevitably be futile without students who

---

64. "Christendom College Report," vol. II, no. 6, June 1977, and vol. II, no. 7, July 1977, personal papers of Raymund O'Herron, and Anne Carroll, interview by author.

65. Dr. Onalee McGraw, interview by author.

66. "Christendom College Report," vol. II, no. 9, August 1977, personal papers of Raymund O'Herron.

67. Anne Carroll, interview by author, 31 January 2013.

will respond to the faith, to the broadened and brightened and come-alive view of it which it is the task and privilege of the Christendom College staff to present. There is nothing automatic about that student response. There is no magic of argumentation or charisma that can bring any student into the fullness of joy of a Catholic community and the fullness of participation in Catholic study without an openness to what is being offered, a willingness to put aside previous conditioning, to take a risk, even "a leap in the dark"—hoping and trusting that it will turn out to be light at the end.

That is what the first students at Christendom College have done. They came to an institution that did not yet exist, no more than a dream on paper. They came to share in a vision, to make a journey, that few, before they came, understood in more than the vaguest way. Yet they were willing to try. They were willing to open themselves. Now that they are here, nearly all of them are finding Christendom College an experience like none they have ever known before—an experience with unlimited promise.

Undoubtedly our future holds many problems—many crises. But I hope that no one associated with Christendom College in these first days will ever forget the spirit that is among us now and the way we have all responded to it, for I firmly believe that spirit is of God, and that whatever the future brings, He will never forsake us.

Let us build on the foundations we are now laying together, in His Holy Name.[68]

Warren's faith in these young people was not disappointed! Under the direction of Kris, who eventually earned the title "director of student life," these twenty-six students poured their energy and talents into

---

68. Ibid.

laying the foundations for an astounding number of events and activities, many of which continue at the college to this day. These included a drama club, (which currently produces two professional plays each year), a nascent "athletic department" consisting of soccer and basketball games played against Seton School and a ping-pong tournament, a talent show dubbed "The Coffee House," a literary journal called *SPARK*, and a Mardi Gras celebration which culminated in square dancing directed by Pete Scheetz from Colorado, probably wearing his polo shirt from the Sears catalogue. On the spiritual front, the students and faculty participated in the Shield of Roses to pray for an end to abortion and the annual March for Life in Washington, D.C., where to date, the students from Christendom College have led the March four times. In one sweet moment from that first year, the students and faculty came together for a Christmas party at which gifts were exchanged and the students were presented with a popcorn maker. The evening wrapped up with teachers, students, and guests all singing Irish and Spanish folk songs.[69]

Nor was Warren disappointed in the students' ability to meet challenges. They cooked for themselves on the weekends, had competitions to see which room could keep their utility bill the lowest, shoveled the snow when needed, pitched in with the maintenance, and walked, rode a bike, or caught the "school bus" back and forth between the dorm and school building. And for the most part, this was all done without complaining. Well, there were a few complaints. "They eat rabbits!" was an exclamation from Ed Sullivan of California. And one young man, when marked down on an examination, later complained in an exasperated manner to his friend Pete (Anne's brother), "Your brother-in-law thinks there is a Christian significance to Alexander the Great! There is *no* Christian significance to Alexander the Great!"[70] As a point of interest, the "school bus" was a bus used by Aquinas School, in the town of Woodbridge,

---

69. "Christendom College Report," vol. III, no.1, January 1978, personal papers of Raymund O'Herron.

70. Peter Westhoff, interview by author.

to transport their grade school kids. But the pioneers ate humble pie and rode with these kids back and forth to their classes. There was one run to drop students off in the morning and one run home after classes. One more run was made in the evening for those who had stayed later. Sister John Eudes, the librarian, began working in the library before the bus runs began. She rode her bicycle back and forth.[71] A nun in full habit pedaling her bicycle across the Marine base—Warren must have been pleased.

For their part, the faculty were hit with their own frustrations. To begin with, *there was no administration!* "Warren *was* the administration," chuckles Ray in amazement. "We had competence as teachers, but no competence as administrators, and we all suffered because of this. We just did things as they came up!"[72] There wasn't even a secretary. The second year, a student came who had worked in an office, and hence, secretarial work was promptly plopped in her lap. "Now think about this," says Kris:

> Warren had taught for a year as a graduate student in Indiana. Jeff had started some teaching. I had done about three or four years of teaching in college. Ray had taught in a high school. Marshner was still a graduate student. We mostly had experiences in colleges because we had *gone to college as students.* So when we were trying to figure out how to do things we would say, "well at *my* college we would do it this way." I was bringing up the University of Dallas, Warren was bringing up Bates; everyone was talking about their own college experience. Nobody had a clue! All we knew is what we had seen as students or when we taught, what we saw.[73]

---

71. "Christendom College Report," vol. II, no. 7, July 1977, personal papers of Raymund O'Herron.

72. Raymund O'Herron, interview by author.

73. Kris Burns, interview by author.

Adding another perspective to their lack of experience in starting a college, Jeff comments, "By worldly standards, that was certainly true. Not having the requisite experience, we would be regarded as foolish upstarts. Still, it would be my tendency to emphasize the opposite side of the same coin. At a deeper level, and I'm sure Kris would agree, the reality was this: we knew *exactly* what we were doing; and Whom to trust in doing it."[74]

Based on their individual talents and temperaments, they fell more or less naturally into certain positions. Warren took care of fundraising and bookkeeping, Kris and Ray were jointly responsible for discipline, with Kris also taking care of student activities and Ray shouldering the entire areas of maintenance and mechanical anything. Jeff concentrated on the academics. And Bill Marshner? He was more or less just brilliant. For illustrative purposes, this author relates the following exchange with Kris:

> Kris: "Around the second year, the winter, we got this idea that we had better make up an administrative structure. Normally there would be a VP of this and a VP of that, but we only had five people! We had the idea to eventually hire more people and we thought we should at least have some sort of administrative positions in place. Even if we all had four jobs, at least we would know what the jobs were. So I did up this chart. Ray was really practical and could fix things. Everybody else was more or less a spacey, academic type. So Ray was operations and Jeff was academics and I was director of student life, and Warren was treasurer, fundraising."
>
> Me: "And Marshner?"
>
> Kris: "Marshner did . . . a . . . Marshner was . . . a . . . er . . . Marshner! Are you *kidding*! (we both break into peals of laughter) We're not *that* crazy!"

---

74. Jeffrey Mirus, correspondence with author, 27 June 2016.

"Marshner was just this brilliant guy," adds Jeff, "and we didn't want to burden him with administrative details so he could just think." Kris continues,

> We had meetings every Friday afternoon to say, "O.K., how did things go this past week? What do we have to do next week?" We were flying by the seat of our pants! I remember one meeting towards the end of the first semester saying, "Hey guys, it's coming up to the end of the semester. We're going to have to do something about report cards." And Warren says, "Oh, not *another* thing to think about! Oh, what am I going to do about that!" But Jeff said, "Well, I've thought about this and I'll take care of it." There was a lot of conflict because everybody had strong ideas about how things should be done. So at these meetings we would say, "No, you can't do this" or "You can't do that." Then we would have to work it out. This was very hard on Warren because he is the kind of person who doesn't pay too much attention to the details. You know, he was on this crusade and he would say, "O.K., we're going to do this!" and we would say, "Yeah, but how are we going to EAT on the way?" And then he would get a little ticked because you brought that up. But we were only fighting about the details, not the common goal. We were fighting about the best way to do "the thing" that we had all agreed should be done. This was kind of remarkable. Warren used to talk about the fact that it was the grace of God that held us together and that God wanted us to succeed.[75]

And God's providence was evident. For instance, very early on in that first year Warren, opened up a bill from the heating oil company. They wanted the whole years' worth paid in advance. The amount was $5,000—which they didn't have. "What is this?" questioned Warren, "And where is it going to come from?" So he prayed. And in the

---

75. Kris Burns, interview by author.

next postal delivery a donation came in—for the exact amount.[76] But I believe that Warren expected this type of care from Almighty God. Not in a presumptive way, but in that manner of the "poor in spirit" who are vibrantly open to God's gifts because they themselves exist on a level of radical giving. Because he had known for so long that this was the area to which God was calling him to exercise his talents and gifts, he had a firm and unwavering trust that God would help him out. This attitude was not felt from the beginning, at least not to the degree that it was by Warren, by the rest of those involved. By way of highlighting the uniqueness of Warren's role and the seeming impossibility of what he accomplished, I offer the following thoughts from those who lived through this time with him:

> Your ordinary practical person would never think of starting a college. It just would never happen. He was a romantic in the sense of wanting adventure, looking for joy, setting high goals and never thinking you can't achieve them.
>
> —Anne, wife of Warren

> Warren, I don't know anyone else anywhere who could have done what you have done.
>
> —Ray O'Herron, founding faculty member

> The main thing about Warren is that no one else would do this. Other colleges might start, but with huge funding and large committees or sponsored by an order. Warren had friends but he himself started the college. He is the sole founder.
>
> —Kris Burns, founding faculty member

---

76. Anne Carroll, interview by author, 31 January 2013.

> Warren had the idea of founding a college which, contrary
> to all prudent opinion, got off the ground.
>
> —Bill Marshner, founding faculty member

> There was a *Wanderer* forum in Harrisburg, Pennsylvania.
> It was promoting the college and was not well attended.
> And on the way home Warren said to me, "Do you feel
> that we are on to something really big here?" And my
> thought was, "absolutely not." His thinking was that it was
> something big—it was going to succeed. The poor atten-
> dance just made him work harder.
>
> —Pete Westhoff, brother-in-law of Warren

No matter their doubt that the vision of this rather odd and unre-
alistic man from Maine would ever become a reality, when it did, the
pioneer watchmen who joined him in his hunt for the pass over the
mountain of Catholic higher education proclaimed him vindicated.
In "A Tribute to the Founder," printed in the "Christendom College
Report" of August 1977, they wrote:

> While it is true that the ultimate success of Christendom
> College will depend upon the co-operation and hard work
> of the entire founding team, there can be no question that
> the credit for its successful initiation belongs to Dr. War-
> ren Carroll, founder and president.
>
> The idea of the college grew large in Dr. Carroll's own
> mind before anyone else had even thought of it. The organi-
> zation of personnel, assignment of duties and, most impor-
> tantly, the inspiration throughout the preliminary months
> came solely from this remarkable and dedicated man. Fur-
> ther, the fundraising and nearly all of the student recruiting
> were planned and carried out personally by the president.
>
> Something of the true picture may be seen in the fact
> that no one on the staff began to devote full time to the

college project until this summer, whereas Dr. Carroll has worked overtime on it for well over a year—with virtually no pay.

Dr. Warren Carroll and his wife, Anne . . . have stood as beacons in the field of Catholic apostolic education. If he (or she) knew in advance about this article, it would never have been printed. It has thus been the sole secret of the staff in an atmosphere of unqualified loyalty and trust. In our judgment, however, even this secret should be told.

As Kris Burns sums it up:

It was Warren's courage to go ahead and do this thing. He was definitely the type of person that didn't feel like he needed to go to school to know how to do this. He trusted in God and he had us to help with the details, to say "we have to do it *this* way." But I just find it amazing that, looking back on it now, these five people who really did not know what they were doing, would attempt this thing. And secondly, that they would succeed.

9

The Conquest of Darkness

When later I became founding president of Christendom
College . . . [I] faced no less than ten years of wearing,
crushing struggle to keep it alive and forging ahead despite the worst the world and the Devil could do.[1]

–Warren H. Carroll

EVEN WHILE SHOULDERING THE weight of founding a college,
Warren's love for travel did not wane, and in the spring of 1976, he,
Anne, and Pete embarked on an extended road trip. Stopping in Flor-
ida (to visit Disney World), Mississippi (to meet with Dr. Edgar Hull,
one of Christendom's first major donors), New Orleans, and Houston
(where they visited relatives), they drove through the desert areas in
the north of Mexico and then to Mexico City. As Anne relates:

We visited the Tenochtitlan pyramids, but the main goal
of the trip was the Shrine of Our Lady of Guadalupe. This
was the original basilica, not the modern shrine. We attended Mass and prayed and were awestruck by the devotion of the people—going across the courtyard on their
knees, for example. Warren took a photo of the tilma and

---

1. Warren Carroll, "Unpublished Autobiography."

we marveled at the brightness of the turquoise color in the photo, even though the church was dark. While we were at Mass, a thief picked the lock on our car and stole my suitcase, Pete's suitcase, and a smaller bag we had. He left Warren's suitcase—didn't have enough hands, probably. So Pete and I had limited wardrobes until we reached my family's home in Colorado, where Pete had clothes and I could fit into my sister's. In my suitcase were notes for a speech I was going to give on the way back to Virginia on how to start a Catholic school. We joked that if a new Catholic school was suddenly opened in Mexico City, it was probably started by the thief![2]

On this trip, Warren was also gathering information for his next book, *Our Lady of Guadalupe and the Conquest of Darkness* (which would be published in 1983). Before learning of the rape of Cambodia by the monster Pol Pot (described by Warren in chapter seven of this book), he had believed the supreme horror of history to be the human sacrifices carried out by the Aztecs which the Spanish conquistador Hernán Cortés had shockingly discovered in Mexico in June of 1519.[3] In his gripping, spell-binding manner, Warren narrates the aftermath of Cortés's discovery:

> Once there was a world within the world, self-contained, complete within itself. On its every side were impassable barriers made by the gods: to the north, an utter desert which that world called Mictlan, dead man's land, where one can traverse sun-blasted miles without seeing a single living thing; to the east and west, the endless sea; to the south, sodden, almost impenetrable jungle, the domain of Tlaloc the rain god. Like a cup held in these iron hands were the good lands, where the tall corn waved green and

---

2. Anne Carroll, correspondence with author, 27 June 2016.
3. Warren H. Carroll, "The Watchwords of Christendom College—Truth Exists. The Incarnation Happened."

gold, bright flowers bloomed, and lakes shimmered in the sun. Some twenty million people lived there. Almost fifteen million of them were ruled by the empire of the Mexica (who came, much later, to be known to historical writers as Aztecs) with their capital at an island city with a population of three hundred thousand or more: Tenochtitlan, Cactus Rock, where salt Lake Texcoco and fresh Lake Chalco joined.

They had reached the first stage of civilization, which is cities and writing, though their writing was still in the process of development out of pictures. They were in touch, although distantly, with the somewhat older civilization of the Mayas at the edge of the southern jungles. Oddly enough, they had never invented the wheel; but they used human porters very efficiently, and their city built on water was an engineering marvel. There was no apparent, external reason why they should not have been growing as other civilizations like them grew, from ancient Mesopotamia and China to classical Greece and Rome: seeking truth and justice, honoring virtue even when not practicing it, questing for the divine.

But this self-contained, isolated world had taken a very different course.

The Aztecs, like the Mayas, counted by twenties. Each of their months had twenty days, making eighteen of them in a year, with five days left over. Each twenty-day month had its festival dedicated to one of their gods. Most of these festivals were marked by sacrifices, ranging from one to thousands. The sacrifices were of people—usually adult men, but fairly often children as well.

Every Aztec city and large town had a central square, from which a high pyramidal temple rose, and four gates opening upon four roads approaching the town in straight lines extending at least five miles, each ending at one side of the temple pyramid. On each side of the temple pyramid was a steep stairway to its top. The whole structure was skillfully tapered inward, suggesting even greater height than the 90 to 100 feet that was common. Month after month, year after year, in temple after temple, the sacrificial victims came down the roads to the steps, climbed up the steps to the platform at the top, and there were bent backwards over large convex slabs of polished stone by a hook around the neck wielded by a priest with head and arms stained black, never-cut black hair all caked and matted with dried blood, and once-white garments soaked and stained with innumerable gouts of crimson. An immense knife with a blade of midnight black volcanic glass rose and fell, cutting the victim open. His heart was torn out while still beating and held up for all to see, while his ravaged body was kicked over the edge of the temple platform where it bounced and slithered in obscene contortions down the steps to the bottom a hundred feet below. Later, the limbs of the body were eaten.[4]

Into this hellish world, marched Cortés who, with his band of three hundred valiant men, drove straight into the heart of this people. At odds of ten thousand to one, they battled their way into the keep of the two chief Aztec gods, "Huitzilopochtli, the Hummingbird Wizard, called Lover of Hearts and Drinker of Blood, and Tezcatlipoca, the Lord of the Dark, the Smoking Mirror, god of phantoms and monsters, demiurge of creation, 'He Who Is at the Shoulder' as the tempter. . . . Nowhere else in history has Satan so formalized and institutionalized his worship with so many of his own actual titles and symbols."[5]

---

4. Warren H. Carroll, *Our Lady of Guadalupe and the Conquest of Darkness* (Front Royal, VA: Christendom Press, 1983), 7–8.

5. Warren H. Carroll, *A History of Christendom*, vol. 4, *The Cleaving of Christendom* (Front Royal, VA: Christendom Press, 2000), 23–25.

The fantastic three months that followed the first entry of
Cortés into Mexico City provide one of the great climaxes
of history, rivalling the taking of Jerusalem by the First
Crusade, the reconquest of Seville by King St. Ferdinand,
the massacres of September and the Thermidorian reaction in the French Revolution, the Battle of Waterloo, and
the Red October of 1917 in Russia. Yet this one is unique,
different from all the others, in the incredible speed with
which it had developed. The other climaxes marked cul-
minations of chains of events going back for years or centuries. But Cortés and his army had been in Mexico less
than seven months. On November 8, 1519, Cortés entered
its capital as the honored guest of the absolute ruler of fifteen million people, as one who might be a god, or at least
the emissary of a god; by November 15, Montezuma [the
Aztec Emperor] was Cortés' prisoner, and Cortés was—
however precariously—ruling Mexico through him. Yet
Cortés, too, was a prisoner of the Hummingbird Wizard,
because he was unable to free the beautiful city from its
hideous grip without provoking an uprising that would
cost him his conquest.[6]

After two months of stepping cautiously around Montezuma in an
attempt to explain that the God of all men did not want human sacrifice, Cortés finally sprang into action and confronted the emperor:

> I have often asked you not to sacrifice any more souls to
> your gods, who are deceiving you, but you have not been
> willing to do so. We have come to beg you to give us leave
> to remove them and put up Our Lady, Santa Maria, and a
> cross. If you do not give permission, they [indicating his
> men] will do so anyway, and I would not like them to kill
> any priests.

---

6. Carroll, *Our Lady of Guadalupe and the Conquest of Darkness*, 44.

There is every reason to believe that Cortés was telling Montezuma no more than the simple truth about what his men, who had been watching and hearing the human sacrifices in the temple next to their quarters for two full months, were threatening to do.

Montezuma said he would see about it, while warning that any removal of the gods would lead to all-out war. He secured permission for the erection of an altar, a cross, and an image of the Blessed Virgin Mary in a room within the temple itself. It was cleaned and washed with lime; Father Olmedo said Mass there every day; an "old soldier" was stationed to guard the room (Can it have been only one? What a duty!) and the Aztec priests were ordered to keep the room clean and candles burning before the Cross and the image of Our Lady and to decorate it with branches and flowers, but without touching the altar.

Who but Hernán Cortés ever arranged it so that the acolytes of Satan would have to burn candles to the Blessed Virgin Mary, on the orders of their earthly sovereign? The Devil hates above all to be laughed at, and there has rarely been a better laugh at his expense. Perhaps we may even dare to imagine a smile on the lips of Mary herself.

It was more than the Hummingbird Wizard could stand. The priests came to Montezuma and told him that Huitzilopochtli had spoken, and the daily Mass must go from his temple at once, or there would be war.

Cortés replied that the Christian knights of Spain would gladly fight for the Lord God and for the Mother of God. He called his men to arms, and they marched straight on the temple with drawn swords. Up the tall steps of death they climbed to the platform at the top. With a slash of keen blades they ripped through the veil that hid the monsters from profane view.

"Oh God!" cried Cortés, "Why dost thou permit the

devil to be so grossly honored in this land?" He bowed his head, and added, as though in prayer: "Accept, O Lord, that we may serve Thee in this land."

The chief priests came running and panting to the scene. Cortés told them he had come to cleanse and purge their shrine to evil, and place there the image of the Mother of God. The priests told him that the people were already taking arms against the Spaniards for what they were doing. Cortés sent a messenger to warn the rest of his men, and ordered up forty reinforcements. Then he turned and faced the Hummingbird Wizard. Its obscene bulk rose up before him as though to fill the earth and all the sky.

Somewhere near the door was a metal bar. Cortés seized it. He swung it over his head. "I pledge my faith as a gentlemen, and swear to God that it is true," wrote Andres de Tapia, a valiant young officer of pale complexion and grave countenance, who has left us the best record of this supreme moment, "that I can see now how the Marquess [Cortés] leapt up in a supernatural way and swung forward holding the bar midway till he struck the idol high up on its eyes, and broke off its gold mask, saying: 'We must risk something for God.'"

A few days later the priests removed the idols from the great temple in deathly silence. True to this word, Cortés ordered their shrines cleaned. . . . The Spaniards erected two altars and brought up images of the Blessed Virgin Mary and of St. Christopher. Heavily escorted by armed men, a cross, followed by the two images, was carried up the great staircase, scene of the unprecedented horror of Tlacaellel's sacrifice of the eighty thousand in 1487. The Spaniards sang *Te Deum laudamus*. Father Olmedo stepped forward.

I will go up to the altar of God,

The God who gives joy to my youth.

> The soldiers of Christ took off their helmets. Holy
> Mass was said; Jesus Christ came, body, blood, soul, and
> divinity, to His altar now standing, like a meteor fallen
> from Heaven, in the very heart and center of what had
> been the keep of the Hummingbird Wizard.[7]

While compiling this story of the darkness unleashed by Satan on the Aztec people, Warren was fighting his own battles. From his time spent at Columbia University, to his knowledge of the inner workings of communism, through his fight in the pro-life movement, he was fully aware of the nature of evil. Moreover, as a Catholic convert and historian, he had voraciously devoured stories of saints and their diverse battles against evil. Firmly believing that his fledgling college commanded its own place in this cosmic battle of good and evil, and being a devoted "watchman," he remained acutely aware of the possibility of attacks. This strength in keeping watch, however, was combined, in a unique and sometimes baffling way with a certain optimistic naiveté regarding the ordinary and practical ways of the world. And it surfaced rather quickly.

In the February 1978 edition of the "Christendom College Report," Warren reports that, due to the college's first major foundation grant in the amount of $10,000, the college "will enter its second semester without a deficit or a debt."[8] However, just one month later, at the board meeting held on March 4, the conclusion is that "Christendom College now has only sufficient funds on hand or due in soon to get through the month of March," and that "it would appear that a loan of at least $10,000 will be required before May 31 unless at least that much money can be raised by then, over and above the responses to the March fund appeal."[9] By March 14, the projected deficit for the end of the 1978–79 school year was, depending

---

7. Ibid., 53–55.

8. "Christendom College Report," vol. III, no. 2, February 1978.

9. "Financial Report for Christendom College Board of Trustees," March 4, 1978, personal papers of Raymund O'Herron.

on whose scratched out numbers on a piece of notebook paper you chose to use, somewhere between $47,200 and $100,000. In Ray's calculations, the college could remedy this situation by, among other measures, raising tuition, raising room and board, releasing Sister Eudes, and releasing himself! Truly a watchman, Ray actually put forth his *own dismissal* from his dream come true—to save the college. The reply from Warren is telling. To the first two suggestions, he replies, "Never." He agrees to saving an annual $8,000 by releasing Sister Eudes, but next to the "release Ray" suggestion, he boldly scrawls, "NO." By the faculty meeting of April 4, Warren had come up with a solution to the college's financial woes which he termed non-negotiable. He "will forfeit his house rather than endanger the college."[10] This man was willing to sell his own home—to provide truth to others. That is the nature of truth—it is a light which burns inside the soul and will not be hidden under a bushel basket—even at great cost to the one who is enlightened by it from within. Luckily for Anne and Warren, this step was not necessary. By the official May faculty meeting, the watchmen had applied for a "loan of at least $10,000 from the diocese or the bank" (secured by a partial lien on Warren's house).

Besides scrounging for money, they were also scrounging for students for the upcoming school year, listing prospects under all possible headings including: "Now enrolled, definite or highly probable for second year," "Now enrolled, uncertain but possible for second year," "Applied and accepted for 1978–79," "Definitely promised for 1978–79," "Special indications of intent to apply," and "Telephone call or visit within past two months."[11] Ray recalls:

> After the first year, I thought the college was not going to last. In fact, I thought we would probably not be able to open the second year. We were $40,000 in debt. By Warren's own projections of enrollment and expenses, we would not pos-

---

10. Agenda for April 4 faculty meeting, 1978, personal papers of Raymund O'Herron.
11. Agenda for May 2 faculty meeting, 1978, personal papers of Raymund O'Herron.

sibly be able to do this. Kris and I had a very ugly and memorable knock-em-down argument with Warren about what had to be done if we were going to open the second year. He had engaged a fellow to teach a one-credit course, and we said we just can't afford to pay this guy. Warren was always anxious to discern where the threats to the stability of the college would come from. He remembered from reading saint's life after saint's life and saw how much trouble people in the church give to the founders of these things. So he was always wary that danger would come from within. Maybe this made him not willing to objectively look at the arguments that Kris and I were making. So we went to talk to him and it went on for several hours. Finally, Kris left and it went on for several more hours. Finally, I guess Warren realized something had to be done and he cut that guy out and did some more things.[12]

Besides the ever-looming ominous cloud of financial ruin, there was another question, shoved to the back recesses of the everyday running of the college, but persistent in its nagging nonetheless. This was the question of a permanent site for the college. From the outset, the parish board of St. Francis had made it clear that the college could lease the buildings for two years—no more. The parish was going to use the rent money from Christendom to upgrade their school and then restart it. Warren, however, possessed a disconcerting characteristic—he often did not look at the face of the person with whom he was speaking, focusing instead on the ground in front of him. Ray believes that this habit kept Warren from properly reading the body language and expressions of those he dealt with, resulting in Warren's occasionally missing the complete meaning of a conversation. In the case of his meetings with the board of St. Francis, this characteristic led him to miss the definitiveness of the terms with which the offer of rental was made, and he held onto a hope that the college would be able to remain in Triangle for a third year. Well into the first academic

12. Raymund O'Herron, interview by author.

year, when the subject was broached at the weekly faculty meetings, Warren would suggest that the parish might extend the lease. When told flat out, "Warren, they're not gonna extend the lease," he would grumble, "Oh, yes they will."[13] It became clear, however, that the parish meant what they had said when Onalee McGraw received a phone call from Bishop Welsh (in whose diocese the parish was located), who said, "I'm calling because you guys are going to have to find a new place. Triangle wants their school back."[14]

Providentially, says Onalee, the search for a new campus fell on Ray's shoulders. Because Ray had arranged for the rental of the busses to carry the students back and forth from the dormitories to the campus, he had been dubbed "director of operations." And it was either Warren or the "director of operations" who would have to take responsibility for this job. "Warren was busy," says Ray, "so I stepped up—this is how we got 'assigned' to things at the time."[15] The one requirement from Warren's point of view was that the campus remain in the Diocese of Arlington. Bishop Welsh had been very supportive, and this ecclesial support was a necessity for such a new operation. So Ray wrote to many realtors, two from each county in the diocese. Replies came in. "We looked at a chicken farm on the other side of Winchester," he says, "and a place outside of Leesburg where people go to 'slim down.' Also, a small estate of Brent Bozell's that he was selling at the time out in Huntly."[16] Finally, he was shown a property that he recognized. It was the same property, owned by the AFL-CIO, at which Warren had organized his two week-long institutes in the summers of 1976 and 1977. Hence all of the founding faculty were already familiar with the property and buildings and thought it perfect!

Then came the negotiating process. The AFL-CIO consisted of two mega-labor unions, the American Federation of Labor and the

---

13. Raymund O'Herron and Kris Burns, interview by author.
14. Onalee McGraw, interview by author.
15. Raymund O'Herron, interview by author.
16. Ibid.

Congress of Industrial Organization, which had merged in 1955 and were now under the leadership of their president George Meany. They had been using this particular piece of property as a school to train young Latin American labor leaders to resist communist infiltration of their unions—something the communists had already done in Europe. Like Warren, George Meany was a staunch anti-communist—but he was also an extremely tough negotiator.[17] The original asking price for the property was $450,000, which was absolutely impossible for a school hanging on by its financial fingernails. So a meeting was called, which Onalee terms "unforgettable," at which a small group—including Bill and Onalee McGraw and Sean O'Reilly—discussed how they could possibly move forward on this property. In the end, Warren went to see Bishop Welsh who was a friend of Cardinal O'Boyle of Washington, D.C. Cardinal O'Boyle, in turn, just happened to be a personal friend of George Meany. O'Boyle then went to Meany and pleaded for the college, assuring Meany that these were "good people" and asking him to lower the price. Meany lowered it—to $275,000. "Weeeellll," says Ray, "we didn't *have* $275,000 or any possible way of borrowing it."[18]

Then board member Sean O'Reilly took his turn at bat. "For whatever reason," says Sean's wife, Anne, "they decided that Sean would be the best person to get the down payment. He had a sabbatical [that year] which he gave up. He thought it was the right thing to do."[19] The first thing he did was to go and see *his* good friend Cardinal O'Boyle and ask O'Boyle to negotiate with Meany to hold the property for the school while they tried to come up with the down payment. Meany gave him a certain date until which he would hold the property for the college. So with a sense of urgency, Sean went from bank to bank— "Sorry," they said. He went from individual to individual—"Sorry," they said. "Eventually," says wife Anne, "there was no one left." But providence again provided, and William Carrigan, a former donor to *Triumph* magazine, entered into the picture. As Anne tells it:

---

17. Ibid.

18. Ibid.

19. Anne O'Reilly, interview by author, 21 October 2015.

There was nobody left but Mr. Carrigan. Sean didn't know Carrigan. Everyone said to Sean, "You're wasting your time, he won't do it." But Sean said, "There's nobody else, I have to work with him to persuade him." Sean knew Carrigan had the money, but also that he had worked hard and didn't want to give his money to an organization that wasn't worthwhile. Sean spent hours and hours talking to him on the telephone. Carrigan was in his eighties at the time. Sean would talk about Catholic education and how wonderful it was and how they needed to do what they could and Carrigan, who was very slow in his speech, would nod his head, "Yes, yes . . ." Finally, time was getting close. So Sean said, "I'm gonna have to push him. I can't beat around the bush any longer." So he went back and said, "Either you believe in Catholic education and you're going to help us, or you don't mean what you say" (or words to this effect), and Carrigan said, O.K., he would lend them the money.[20]

But Carrigan's financial assistance came with a caveat: Warren had to be able to raise the $75,000 down payment. If he could do this, Carrigan would carry the $200,000 mortgage. "Warren managed to get $75,000 and probably not a penny more" and the purchase contract was signed on March 9, 1979.[21]

Christendom moved into its new, expanded, and permanent campus in the summer of 1979. George Meany died in January of 1980 and is buried in the "Gate of Heaven" Catholic cemetery in Silver Spring, Maryland. Because William Carrigan charged such a high interest rate on his loan, nothing was paid on the principal for years, and the loan amount did not really decrease. Finally, when Carrigan was well into his nineies, the current college president, Dr. Tim O'Donnell, went to him and said, "You know, Mr. Carrigan, you're not going to be

---

20. Ibid.
21. Raymund O'Herron, interview by author.

able to take it with you."[22] This must have resonated with the elderly man because he proceeded first to cut the interest rate on his loan, and then designated that whatever amount the college still owed at the time of his death would be forgiven. Carrigan died in 2000 at the age of ninety-eight, and the entire amount of the loan still owed was considered paid.[23] In front of the new St. John the Evangelist Library on Christendom's campus stands a monument to William Carrigan which reads: "Without him . . . Christendom College would not exist today."

Sean O'Reilly died of a heart attack in 1982. "He wasn't with the college very long, but he saw it over that hump," says Anne. "He would say to me, 'Every day this college survives is a miracle.' It is ingrained in my mind. 'Where do we get the money for this?' 'How are we going to do that?' It was really, really hard. But it was in God's providence, and it was meant to be. And thanks be to God for Mr. Carrigan and his trust in them."[24]

Wrapping up the college's second academic year was the board of directors meeting held on May 13, at which the college adopted its first official administrative structure. Appropriately, there were five positions, with Warren holding that of president, the others being the director of finances and development, the director of academic affairs, the director of student affairs, and the director of operations.[25] So, heading into their third year of operation, this group of dedicated Catholics "camping out and playing at having a college," as Kris describes it somewhat jokingly, was looking more and more permanent and college-like. They now owned their own campus, the incoming class brought with it a number of solid leaders, and a new spirit began to pervade. These folks were building something wonderful together—and they knew it.[26]

---

22. Robert Rice, interview by author, 19 August 2015.

23. Ibid.

24. Anne O'Reilly, interview by author.

25. The administrative structure of Christendom College, May 1979, personal papers of Raymund O'Herron.

26. Kris Burns, interview by author.

Proving to the world that they were indeed a new force to be reckoned with, Christendom held its first commencement on May 4, 1980, awarding two students, Mary Stuart and Leo White, their bachelor of arts degrees. In the May edition of the "Christendom College Report," Mary wrote the following tribute—which certainly must have gladdened the heart and spirit of Warren and added a gleam of pride to his already dancing eyes:

> When you find something new and beautiful, you want to run and show your friend—"look what I found!"—to share your joy. When that "something" sets you free, you want to shout it from the roof tops with delight.
>
> That is how I felt when I "found" Christendom. Suddenly I began to learn the answers to my own and so many friends' questions about life and about faith. I yearned to share with them what they needed to go to God, to see the truth, to be happy.
>
> The "Christendom experience" that I have found across three years has been a rare, exciting interweaving of truth and beauty on the loom of grace and charity. Since it is in the context of daily Mass, Rosary, and the example of others to do God's will, perhaps the multicolored, multi-patterned tapestry has been woven by the loving hands of the Mediatrix of Grace.
>
> The threads are such courses as logic, metaphysics, philosophy of man, and ethics to show the mind the order of the world, then literature and culture to add the color of human experience. The surprises are an all-the-mysteries-you-ever-would-want-to-know-about-but-did-not-pay-any-attention-to-before doctrine class, a history sequence that proves you never knew history until you truly considered BC and AD, and a once very lazy high school girl suddenly "turned on" to learning, "turned on" to the challenge of truth.
>
> But I am by no means primarily an intellectual crea-

ture. "My heart was restless," as St. Augustine says, and that restlessness was calmed by the love of God, found here in so many ways. It shines through the dedication of the teachers, the goodness of the students, the love and joy we find together as a community.

And what now? I take my tapestry with me. It illustrates the sources of grace and truth, so that I may go forth with St. Peter and all the apostles "always ready with a reason for the hope" that is in me.

If God is calling me forward to "greater" things than Christendom, as I believe He does all our life, then they must be tremendous! The great sorrow of parting with each beloved member of this community is only consoled by the faith that, as Dr. Carroll says, this unfailing well of strength and love will not diminish through distance and time. This well-spring of grace has given the bright rosy hue to my whole tapestry.

If the watchmen began to relax, thinking their path now cleared of stumbling stones—they were mistaken. In the spring of 1980, a team from the Virginia State Council on Higher Education came to review the college. This was necessary, according to Virginia law, to grant Christendom the power to confer degrees. Because of some points brought up by this site visit committee, along with the ever-present financial fingernail biting, a plan was developed by the executive committee of the board of trustees to transform Christendom College into a cooperative.[27] Membership in the existing board was "self-perpetuating," meaning that vacancies were filled or new members added by a vote of the existing members. Given that great care had been taken by Warren to assure that the original members of this board shared deeply in his purpose and vision, this arrangement almost guaranteed the protection and perpetuation of both purpose and vision. In the

---

27. Warren H. Carroll to all members of the board of trustees, 3 April 1980, personal papers of Raymund O'Herron.

cooperative proposal, however, future vacancies on the board would be filled from among the current members by a vote of all members of the new cooperative. The unique fundraising possibility here was that membership in the cooperative was granted to those willing to invest or donate at least $1,000, or render services which equaled that amount, for which they received a promissory certificate. This certificate could be redeemed at a future time if the holder so desired to cease his or her membership, and the money would then be returned.

The great concern for Warren, however, was that an expanded member group with the power to elect individuals to the governing board (the board of trustees) might endanger all he had fought and worked to achieve. And he voiced his concerns, quite forcefully, in a nine-page memo to the board on April 3:

> The original purpose, for Christendom College, is profoundly *apostolic*. Our education is designed above all to form Catholic lay apostles. Needless to say to all of you, this means that the education given must be of high academic quality. But the *apostolic* character of that education is vital, and that requires the rigorous application of the educational principle of *integrating the Catholic understanding of truth throughout the curriculum*. This principle, in my view, must be preserved at all costs. But this principle is very little understood and appreciated today, even by many personally good Catholics. The danger of the weakening and eventual loss of Christendom College's original purpose and mission through the cooperative proposal does not come from any real likelihood of takeover by outright heretics, but rather from the gradual dilution or even the sudden elimination of board members marked by a commitment to, and a clear understanding of, the lay apostolate and the above-stated educational principle which serves it, and their replacement by new members who have much less of this commitment and understanding, but regard themselves as more "practical" and business-oriented.... I do not mean to say or imply that such a shift

away from apostolic commitment is certain or even probable, if the cooperative proposal is adopted. I do regard it as distinctly possible, and therefore a serious risk which should be run only if the survival or reasonable growth of the college clearly requires it.[28]

Warren went on to propose alternative means for raising funds and for acquiring additional dormitory space for the growing number of students, the other pressing issue on the table at the time. He concludes, however:

Whatever the final decision of the board may be, I will loyally abide by it. At the same time, I owe it to Christendom College and to you to state my concerns fully and to tell you frankly, now and in the future, to what extent those concerns have been resolved by further developments, and to what extent they continue to exist. Let us all pray God's help in arriving at the decision that is best for those we serve—those wonderful young people here who make Christendom College so joyous and uplifting a cause for which to strive.[29]

Given his experiences in higher education, and an intellect which could pierce through to the fundamentals of things, Warren's concerns are certainly understandable. But there were also the practical realities of day-to-day life, and the college needed funds immediately— which normal fundraising practices just weren't producing. In a memo of their own in response to Warren, some of the founding faculty stated their own reasons in favor of the proposal, saying that Warren's

---

28. Ibid. According to Ray, the supporters of the new proposal shared this concern and it was addressed by limiting those who could serve as directors to members of the corporation who had been approved by the board of directors prior to being accepted as members.
29. Ibid.

concern about continuity of curriculum orientation was "misplaced:"

> It is the function and work of the *teaching* faculty to retain
> the Catholic emphasis and liberal arts orientation of the
> college. This is not the work of the board, under either
> the present or the proposed cooperative corporate and
> governing structural arrangements. The hiring of faculty
> remains properly under the direct and sole control of the
> college administration.[30]

Furthermore, while Warren remained ever optimistic regarding the future financial status of the college, these faculty members disagreed:

> The financial position of the college as projected in your
> memorandum to the board members should the co-op
> proposal *not* be adopted is too precarious to be a basis for
> planning:
>
> 1. It depends on there being almost no expansion in the
>   academic area.
>
> 2. It depends on minimal or no expansion of the admin-
>   istration, contrary to the course forcefully urged on
>   us by the state site team.
>
> 3. It ignores the $200,000 debt owed on the present
>   campus, due and payable in four years from now.
>
> 4. It creates a heavy debt structure, encumbering all
>   campus equity and encumbering future tuition in-
>   come needed for operational expenses. We were re-
>   peatedly warned of the dangers of this approach by
>   the state visiting team.
>
> 5. It supposes (p. 8) that the thirty students to be added

---

30. Kristin Burns, William Marshner, and Raymund O'Herron to Warren Carroll, 10 April 1980, personal papers of Raymund O'Herron.

next year will all pay full tuition, which is certainly
not the case. . . .

And the list went on . . . "In short," they concluded:

> We think the cooperative proposal is a good one for the
> college, and that it is necessary for the survival and growth
> of the college, since we do not have backers and trustees
> who are as well-connected as those of other colleges. We
> hope that you understand our position and also our re-
> quirement in conscience to make our opinion known. We
> also pray that you might, and respectfully ask you to, con-
> sider what we have said and consider whether you can in
> conscience agree with us and support a vote by the trust-
> ees in favor of the co-op proposal at this meeting.[31]

It may have seemed to Warren that his small, resolute band of
mountaineers—who took on the challenge of blazing a trail to the
summit sustained by the joyful spirit of shared comradeship—was beginning to disintegrate. Those who were close to him concur that he
took these disagreements personally.

> The pressure of the disagreements was very difficult, es-
> pecially on Warren because he was the "dad." He was in
> charge. So there was enormous pressure on him. He would
> have some idea that was kind of ridiculous, and he would
> have knock-down arguments with us. And he took this kind
> of personally, like we weren't quite on board with him. And
> all we were saying was that, "We think maybe it's best to
> do it this way or that way." Then afterwards he would see it
> and say, "O.K.," and he never held a grudge. . . . Sometimes
> we'd compromise. But it did wear him down, I think.[32]

---

31. Ibid.
32. Kris Burns, interview by author.

What is truly the grace of God and speaks to the characters of all those involved is that, in all of the troubles and all of the arguments, they all state repeatedly that there was *never any personal animosity.* All of these people shared Warren's vision and cared deeply about the school, and, although it takes strong personalities to do something like this and those personalities will sometimes get in the way of one another, they were all humble enough to make sacrifices, relinquishing personal view points when necessary to accomplish a great good. One good example is that of Dr. Sean O'Reilly, who, shortly before his death, wrote a letter to the board apologizing for anytime he might have become too angry.[33] Warren shows forth this same humility and self-sacrifice when, at the board meeting of April 12, the matter of the cooperative was finally settled. It is officially recorded in the minutes that:

> Dr. Carroll then presented his comments in the context of his memorandum to Dr. Pepin dated April 3, 1980. He stated that he was persuaded by the executive committee that the need for financial growth is so great he now withdraws his previous objections to adoption of the Cooperative Plan Proposal, although he does retain some misgivings. . . . He withdraws his objection only because of the overriding need for raising funds . . . [and] urges all to maintain vigilance against any weakening of the apostolic basis for the college's existence.[34]

So the Christendom Educational Corporation was re-structured and the cooperative membership drive was successful, bringing in somewhere around half a million dollars and providing a much-needed respite from the dark financial storm clouds.[35] The site visit

---

33. Anne O'Reilly, interview by author.

34. Governing Board of Christendom College, Minutes of the Meeting of 12 April 1980, personal papers of Raymund O'Herron.

35. A large percentage of this money was later lost through an imprudent invest-

had also been a success, with the committee recommending that the "Council of Higher Education grant provisional approval to Christendom College to confer the bachelor of arts degree." This provisional approval would last for two years, at which time the college had to obtain accreditation from the Southern Association of Colleges and Schools.[36] A few comments from the committee stand out:

> The staff organization is very good (comparable in organization to other larger institutions), but the functions have too few people fulfilling them. I was rather impressed when I first saw your administrative organization chart, but then I turned the page and found that two people were doing all the jobs![37]

> There appears to be a degree of camaraderie among students and between students and staff that is not prevalent on many college campuses. . . . The commitment of the entire college community to the fundamental mission of the institution is evident.[38]

---

ment, at which point each investor had to be called and the situation explained. Jeff Mirus took on this most difficult task, urging them to "stay the course with us, promising we would raise the money needed for them to exit without harming the college if they chose to do so later. Some took their money immediately, and we were able to let those people redeem their promissory notes. But the key was to keep that to a minimum so that this did not bankrupt the college. We were able to keep it at a minimum, and between the summer of 1983 and my departure in May of 1985, we had essentially recovered the losses, and the college was no longer in imminent danger of collapse." Jeff Mirus, correspondence with author, June 2016.

36. Commonwealth of Virginia Council of Higher Education to Dr. Warren Carroll, 12 May 1980, personal papers of Raymund O'Herron.

37. Raymund O'Herron, "Transcription of Notes with Site Inspection Team of the State Council on Higher Education," 28 March 1980, personal papers of Raymund O'Herron.

38. Commonwealth of Virginia Council of Higher Education to Dr. Warren Carroll, 12 May 1980, personal papers of Raymund O'Herron.

> You have a good start. You are at the point now of
> being in what the computer people call a "survival mode."
> But you may not be in an "operational mode." You've got-
> ten by your Dunkirk, but you're not ready by any means
> to invade Africa, let alone retake France. Your logistical
> problems are paramount. You have a lot of steps to take.
> You have to get your War Plans Department working.[39]

One logistical task necessary for the "invading of Africa" and plopped in the lap of the "war department" was where to put the incoming students. Heading into the 1980–81 academic year (the college's fourth year of operation), the existing dormitory space was not adequate to house the new students, and this had been one of the issues bandied about during the board restructuring discussions. While the new cooperative had raised substantial funds, not every-one agreed on how they should best be used. Not only was new space needed for dormitories, but the "retaking of France" would require additional space for recreation, a larger dining area, expanded li-brary and kitchen facilities, and modification of the chapel.[40] Propos-als put forth ranged from simply purchasing a few already existing residential homes across the street from the campus to purchasing an old plantation mansion known as Scaleby to moving the school into an existing campus in Washington, D.C. which was on the mar-ket for $1.2 million.

In the end, the war department chose to invade France in small steps. The two neighboring homes were purchased as dormitories,[41] and when more space was needed, temporary trailers were added.[42]

---

39. Exit interviews with Raymund O'Herron and Kris Burns, 28 March 1980, per-sonal papers of Raymund O'Herron.
40. Kristin Burns, William Marshner, and Raymund O'Herron to Warren Carroll, 10 April 1980, personal papers of Raymund O'Herron.
41. "Christendom College Report," vol. 5, no. 1, October 1980, personal papers of Raymund O'Herron.
42. The trailers were added in the fall of 1981 and remained as girls' dormitories until January of 1983.

Students made do with the existing administrative/classroom space, waiting in a line at the beginning of each semester to purchase their books from what can only be described as a large closet, the line spanning a short second-story hallway and winding down the rickety staircase into the "common room" which functioned as a combined dining hall, study area, meeting place, and, when necessary, dance hall. Daily Mass, although not required, was well attended. However, arriving in the nick of time usually meant that the student or faculty member squished himself into the small area in the back of the chapel and stood for the duration or attended Mass on the sidewalk leading out of the small building. They didn't care. They went anyway.

Mark McShurley, who worked with Warren early on in the Admissions Office (which had not come all that far as of yet from Anne and Warren's kitchen table experience), relates that some students, upon arriving at the campus for the first time on opening day, simply turned around and went home. "They had never actually been here," he says. "They had only seen pictures. They turned right around and went home that same day! I had a few instances where the parents wanted to take their child home, but the child wanted to stick it out."[43] It was tough. "Here I was trying to sell an unaccredited school that barely looked like a summer camp! But it dawned on me as I got into this—all that time that Warren had spent on those weekend institutes was paying off because many of the early students had attended or their parents had attended." Mark's wife, Holly, one of the now-grown Flagg children who had snuck a look at Twister-judge Warren to see whether he had noticed her foot slide for a moment off of the red circle, experienced exactly what she expected upon arriving at Christendom for her first year. Having attended Anne's Seton School, she knew how things in this small, dedicated Catholic world worked:

> The first day I was there, it just confirmed to me that, yeah, this is about right. This is just like Seton. Because there was no water or electricity in the trailers! So the

---

43. Mark McShurley, interview by author, 19 August 2015.

girls all moved over to this house, and we were sitting around—sort of in the semi-darkness. And they were all surprised—except me. I just thought, "This seems about right. This is a thing that would happen at Seton." It was just a glitch, and it was restored by the next day. But this was opening day![44]

Eventually, a new girls' dormitory was constructed, and in the winter of 1983, the girls moved all of their belongings out of eight very ugly trailers and into a *real* college dorm. Petrine Construction, a construction company started and run by Dr. O'Reilly's son, Frank, not only built these new accommodations, but went on to triple the campus over the next twenty-five years, adding more dormitories, a student center, large kitchen and dining hall, gymnasium, the beautiful Chapel of Christ the King, and the St. John the Evangelist Library, which boasts approximately 112,000 volumes, fulfilling Warren's dream of a top-notch library.[45]

New buildings were not the only thing being added. Additional faculty began trickling in, giving added support and reinforcement to the weary but steadfast trailblazers. A number of these dedicated men and women spent only a short time as part of Warren's vision-become-reality, but two of them committed themselves to their core and remain to this day. Dr. Robert C. Rice, a convert to Catholicism and charter subscriber to *Triumph* magazine, remembers reading the first notice that a college, teaching in the vein of *Triumph*, was going to begin. He recalls shouting to his wife, "Mary Alice, *this* is where I want to teach!" Having been led to the Catholic faith via the Real Presence of Jesus in the Eucharist, reading the Apostolic Fathers, Aquinas, Augustine, Cardinal Newman, G. K. Chesterton, and Ronald Knox, and finding support for his faith in *Triumph*, Rice was a perfect fit. And Warren agreed. "Oh, a *Triumph* man!" he exclaimed when they met for the first time. "How interesting!" It was then just a ques-

---

44. Holly McShurley, interview by author, 19 August 2015.

45. This was the number as of 2017.

tion of convincing Robert that there actually *was* a college at which to teach. "The college, physically, didn't seem much of a college," Robert smiles:

> There was just an old wire fence around the grounds, and only four insignificant buildings visible. My impression was, "Where's the college?" But then I saw the students. There were maybe seventy-five students all together, but, amazed by their piety, I saw some of them kneeling outside of the chapel because of the overflow. I sat in on classes and I thought, "This is truly remarkable!" . . . Dr. Carroll offered me a teaching position, but I asked for one week to pray about it, since I had a family to support. So I went home [to Ann Arbor, Michigan] to talk to Mary Alice and we prayed about it. And a very remarkable thing happened. I was back at work on the Middle English dictionary and I was reaching for a book on a high shelf. As I was reaching, I heard an authoritative voice in my head and it said, "Don't worry, it's all right." I understood that this was the will of God. So I called Mary Alice and said, "Don't worry—it's all right! We're going to do this." And I called Dr. Carroll and accepted the teaching position. This was April of 1981. We arrived in August.[46]

Eventually becoming vice president for academic affairs and chairman of the English department, Robert was also a trailblazer—literally. The campus grounds spanned seventy-five acres and sat on the outside curve of a horseshoe-shaped section of the peaceful, meandering Shenandoah River. Viewing all this natural beauty, Robert envisioned walking trails, overlooks, and picnic areas. When he approached Warren about it, his reply was, "Great! Go ahead—do it!" "There was no question of setting up a budget or anything," he relates. "There was no budget for these kinds of things!" So he and the new

---

46. Robert C. Rice, interview by author.

director of finance and development, Richard Seelbach, studied topographical maps and planned out some trails. Robert then bought some appropriate tools and announced to his classes his plan for "blazing the Christendom Trails." He asked for and got over a dozen student volunteers the first and subsequent weekends. And so Visio Pacis was created as the first vista overlooking the beautiful Shenandoah River, and Angels Rest as the first cleared picnic area. Later, unsure of how to get additional help, Robert approached Ray O'Herron (now also wearing the hat of disciplinarian), who wholeheartedly agreed to assign delinquent students to "Dr. Rice's Saturday work crew" as creative punishment.

Arriving in January of 1985, Dr. Timothy O'Donnell became a bright ray of light for Warren, who had quickly taken Tim into his heart as a son. As did most of the early members of Warren's mountain-scaling team, Tim had made his way into the Christendom family via the branches and shoots of that same seed—*Triumph* magazine. Tim's brother-in-law, whose parents were subscribers, had attended the first summer institute in Spain. Tim's future wife, Cathy, was fourteen at the time and, for a birthday gift, was given a trip (accompanied by her mother) to visit this brother of hers in Spain. "I turned fifteen in Morocco!" she exclaims gleefully. Two years later, Cathy and her sister attended the 1973 institute. Having already met and begun dating Tim, she had a strange experience. Tim, having been raised in a family culturally immersed in its Irish heritage, had loaned his new girlfriend a book entitled *Fighting Prince of Donegal*, a story of Red Hugh O'Donnell who played a major role in the politics of late sixteenth-century Ireland. Stepping into one of Warren's lectures there in Spain, Cathy began to hear of the story of this same Red Hugh O'Donnell. "Wow," she remembers thinking, "I had never heard of this person and now here is his name again!" Approaching Warren after his lecture, she conveyed this information to him and "He was *thrilled*. . . I think that's what put Tim on his radar," she states.[47] She wrote home to Tim, "I met this guy, Dr. Carroll, who talks just like you do! He makes you

---

47. Timothy and Cathy O'Donnell, interview by author, 21 May 2015.

look normal. But he thinks he's going to establish a college. I can't imagine anyone who seems less likely to found a college!"[48]

For his part, Tim flew over to Spain that summer—not to attend the institute—but to visit his girlfriend. Their combined memories include Warren in his plaid, gingham suit jacket with the bursting buttons, bustling around while practicing his eccentric habit of looking intently at the ground, the 8 a.m. morning beer and brandy drinking (which Tim termed "eccentric"), and the swords.[49] "I loved the swords!" exclaims Tim. "Everyone got swords!" Even though his intention had been to visit his girlfriend and not to gain the "Spanish experience," he found himself drawn into it all:

> I remember a lecture with Wilhelmsen, early in the morning, and he was smoking a cigarette and getting all caught up in "BEING" and talking about being, and not noticing that the cigarette was getting shorter and burning his fingers. And all of a sudden he shouted, "Damn it! I *burned* myself!" And I said to myself, "This is *so* strange!" But at the same time it was so joyfully Catholic that it did have a big impact on me. I've always had a real love for Ireland and so the connection between Spain and Ireland—especially where their history as two Catholic nations linked—that really got me into the whole Spanish thing.[50]

Cathy encountered this man, Warren Carroll, who had seemed so odd to her in Spain, a few years later while attending a Christian Commonwealth Weekend Institute at Loyola Marymount University with Tim, now her husband. Because Cathy's parents were very politically active in southern California politics, and Warren had worked for the political dynamo California Senator John Schmitz, they ended up knowing many of the same people, and Cathy remembers Warren

---

48. Ibid.
49. Cathy did not drink—she was under age—but looked for milkshakes instead.
50. Timothy and Cathy O'Donnell, interview by author.

staying at her house at times. Most likely prompted by their combined love of Irish history, Tim later sent Warren a copy of his master's thesis on the Nine Years War. Warren wrote back eagerly, exclaiming, "You have the exact same vision of Catholic history that I have!" whereupon he expounded upon his plans for the college and urged Tim to join him in his endeavor. Tim wrote back explaining that he intended to pursue a doctorate in theology, not in history. "I don't care what field you are going into," Warren shot back. "I want you to teach at my college!"[51]

So Tim and Cathy moved to Rome where Tim earned his doctorate in theology from the Angelicum. And Warren continued to write to them occasionally, at one point sending words of encouragement stating, "Don't worry, you'll always have a place here."[52] Although Tim remembers this encouragement as very sweet, both he and Cathy came from large, Catholic families in southern California and had no intention of relocating to the small hamlet on the Shenandoah River. Tim eventually got a job teaching at the same Loyola Marymount University where he had first met Warren. Soon, however, reality began to set in. Loyola Marymount was quite a liberal university and, although Tim felt like he was doing a lot of good there while managing to slide under the liberal radar, he could see that he would not be able to teach from a truly Catholic perspective—as his heart was calling him to do. And Warren continued to write, asking, "Are you going to come?" Tim was given a final shove when, at a Loyola Christmas party, he and Cathy couldn't even make it past the cocktail hour as they had nothing in common with the many ex-nuns and priests also in attendance. They left and found another place to have dinner. They also decided that it was time to find out what Christendom College was all about.[53]

Hence, in November of 1982, they boarded a plane bound for Virginia. Their experience was similar to that of the Rices, who actually put them up for the night of their arrival. Awakening that first

---

51. Ibid.
52. Ibid.
53. Ibid.

morning, Tim looked out across the fields and inquired, "Where is the campus?" "This is it," replied Robert Rice (most likely chuckling to himself remembering his own similar thoughts). And, like Robert, Tim and Cathy spent the next few days sitting in on classes, marveling at the young kids reading St. Thomas Aquinas, and were moved by the students kneeling on the hard concrete outside of the chapel because of the overflow from the daily Mass. "This is like Ireland or Poland," thought Tim:

> And it struck me that all these kids crammed in there stayed and prayed after Mass. Their devotion was impressive. And then going to the common room for lunch afterwards—the laughter, the noise, the conversation—it was normal Catholic conversation. And I thought, wow, if there is hope for the future it is not going to come from my big University. It will come from a little place like this where the faith is actually being lived.[54]

Later that night, reviewing all the events of the day between them up in the Rice's attic, Tim and Cathy came to a conclusion. "Playing devil's advocate, I was giving all the reasons why we shouldn't come," says Tim, "and then Cathy said, 'You're resisting the Holy Spirit.' And I said, 'You're right—we'll come.'"[55]

The bright ray of Irish O'Donnell sunlight arrived just in time for Warren. As the core of this very good-hearted but strong-willed group of people expanded—so did the possibility of disagreement (vehement at times), factionalism, and confrontation. In his own chronology of his life, put together sometime in the 1990s, Warren refers to two "counter-coups" and a "year of struggle." This period of darkness for him begins in 1983, the same year as the death of his father, at age eighty-five, and also, quite fittingly, the same year as the publication of his novel, *Our Lady of Guadalupe and the Conquest of Darkness*. Following

---

54. Ibid.
55. Ibid.

the dethroning of the Hummingbird Wizard by Cortés and his men, Part II of this book relates the appearance of the Blessed Mother to an Aztec native Saint Juan Diego. Under her title of "Holy Mary of Guadalupe," she inspired the baptism of approximately nine million Aztecs in less than twenty years in this land which had formerly been kept in the oppressive darkness of the Hummingbird Wizard.[56] Warren knew the power of the Blessed Mother. Relying on her help and protection, he had founded his college under her patronage as Our Lady of Fatima:

> On May 5, 1917, Pope Benedict XV had urgently requested all Christians to beg the Virgin Mary to obtain peace in the world and to solemnly entrust the task to her alone. Then, just eight days later, on May 13, 1917, Our Lady appeared to the children in Fatima. She asked everyone for prayer and reparation. Our Lady warned of the evils to come, but she also assured us: "In the end, my Immaculate Heart will triumph. Russia will be converted, and there will be peace." From this, Dr. Carroll understood her to mean that ultimately Christendom would be rebuilt. It was because the college hoped to play some small part in that Divinely-appointed task of rebuilding that Our Lady of Fatima was chosen as the college's patron.[57]

It may well have been, therefore, by her power enfolded in God's providence that the college was able to defeat its own darkness, which Warren considered to be at times of a diabolic nature. But he suffered greatly during this time. As he used to point out regularly while teaching his classes, one man can indeed make a difference. But one man can also shoulder only so much, and he had reached his limit. By the spring of 1985, with great weariness but also remarkable humility, Warren recognized not only that the burden had become too great for

---

56. Warren H. Carroll, *Our Lady of Guadalupe and the Conquest of Darkness*, 108.
57. Tom McFadden, correspondence with author, 13 May 2014.

him, but also that his shortcomings hindered him in exercising his duties as president of the college. Jeff Mirus remarks,

> He cared deeply about the vision of Catholic education, but he didn't care if it was realized without him being in charge. This is an extraordinarily rare quality. He believed that someone with better administrative abilities needed to take over and especially someone who had gifts that he did not have as far as the social aspects of promoting the college, raising funds, and so on. He knew that there had been many battles that we had gone through inevitably in the early years, and that any lingering tensions were partly tied to him. Stepping down could be a way for people to put these behind them. Also, he had a real desire to simply be the chairman of the history department and write his books.[58]

Having made the decision to step down as president, Warren now prepared to take some time away. He had expected Tim O'Donnell to arrive in time for the fall semester to shoulder a large amount of his teaching load, but because Tim's leadership was needed at a critical time on a Catholic news program, his coming was delayed until the spring. "That was really hard on Warren," recalls Cathy, "because he was really anticipating this and waiting. When we asked to delay it one semester he said, 'Well, O.K., but you're going to have to teach five classes.'"[59] As it turned out, the O'Donnells were in for a few surprises:

> When we came in '85, we found out that Warren was planning to step down and there would be a new president next year, which was really a shock to us because we were really there for Warren. Then Jeff Mirus and Tom Mangeiri left. It felt like everyone that we had connected with left.

---

58. Ibid.
59. Timothy and Cathy O'Donnell, interview by author.

Then Warren announced that he was taking a sabbatical the first semester of the next year because a new president was coming in. Christendom was in a time of upheaval, and it was hard for us because Warren was not around.[60]

The man chosen to take Warren's place as president was Dr. Damian Fedoryka, a philosopher well versed in the thought of Pope Saint John Paul II. Although his being a phenomenologist in his philosophical approach rather than a Thomist caused some division amongst the faculty (who were Thomists across the board), Dr. Fedoryka added greatly to the college during his seven years as president. Of significant importance was the publicity he gained for the college "in the highest circles in the Vatican through several trips to Rome and personal audiences with [Saint] John Paul II, and [guiding] . . . it to full accreditation by SACS on December 10, 1987."[61]

Dr. Fedoryka was also at the helm during what many term "the college's darkest hour." An aspect of factionalism had grown to such an extent that it became severely divisive amongst everyone—faculty, board members, and students alike. Many of those who were there at the time thought they were witnessing a deep crisis—one which could have destroyed the college. Understandably, Warren suffered greatly from this division, praying for God's grace to protect his little family. In the end, Dr. Fedoryka, now shouldering the weight of his own burdens as the president, was able to steer the college through these imperiled waters, pilot it forward, and the contention subsided.[62]

---

60. Ibid.

61. Thomas L. McFadden Jr., *Restoring All Things in Christ*, 20. Though Dr. Fedoryka did not publicize the intimacy of his relationship with St. John Paul II, he and the pope were on very close terms, having extended, private meetings together on a number of occasions.

62. This paragraph is intended solely to portray the sufferings Warren experienced while trying to carry out God's will in his life. It is not the author's intention in any way to assign blame to anyone involved. As has been said, these were good people with sometimes very different viewpoints.

Every cloud, as the saying goes, has a silver lining, and Warren's sky, once darkened with impending financial failure and fierce disagreements, began to clear, giving way to the warm rays of a newly dawning day. And in many ways, Tim O'Donnell, and the love and knowledge of the Irish culture he brought with him, embodied the light of Warren's brightening horizon. It is probably safe to say that nestled in the memory of every Christendom alumnus is at least one St. Patrick's Day—celebrated in the college's unique fashion. And I believe it is also safe to say that this celebration was the highlight, liturgically speaking (the college was not open for Christmas or Holy Week and Easter), of Warren's academic year. And he played a prominent role! Standing in front of the old stone fireplace, now graced by portraits of G. K. Chesterton and Hilaire Belloc (which commanded a central position in the original "common room"), he belted out his favorite Irish fighting songs. Unable to sing even one note in the proper key and completely tone deaf (especially noticeable in the small chapel during Mass), he didn't care and sang to his heart's content—at the top of his lungs. The Irish embodied the fighting spirit of the church he loved, especially during their long periods of persecution under British rule, and he was inspired and energized by this spirit. Tim settled naturally into this milieu, donning his Irish cap, grabbing his guitar, and joining wholeheartedly in the revelry. Many a student can describe the scene: Warren in his suit, button about to burst, glasses askance, holding high his Irish songbook and belting out the words to "Bonnie Charlie" or "The Foggy Dew" with a smile on his face reaching from ear to ear, eyes sparkling with spirit, and periodically raising a fist in solidarity with the fallen Irishmen he certainly considered to be his own comrades in arms. The faculty loved it! And the students loved it! Ray O'Herron and Tim O'Donnell joined right in as did any number of students bringing with them their guitars, bagpipes, tin whistles, and joyous spirit.

At the beginning of the festivities, Warren read out the Easter Proclamation of 1916, the document issued by a group of Irish patriots led by Pádraic Pearse, proclaiming Ireland's independence from Great Britain during the Easter Rebellion of that same year. Since

1171, when Henry II of England first landed on Irish soil, contention between the two countries has been almost continual. "There was then," says Warren, "no heresy, no doctrinal difference like that which developed when England under Henry VIII became protestant while Ireland remained Catholic. It was that difference which ultimately raised the struggle between England and Ireland to a far higher plane, on which by and large it has ever since remained."[63] Two of Warren's favorite stories recounting battles pitting Catholics against British protestant rule involved Hugh Roe O'Donnell, known as "Red Hugh" (the same Red Hugh of whom Cathy had heard—both from her boyfriend, Tim, *and* from this strange fellow Dr. Carroll in Spain), and Prince Charles Edward Stuart—better known as "Bonnie Prince Charlie."

As Warren retells the story, Red Hugh came to prominence as the son of Hugh Duv, head of the principal family and clan of County Donegal, in northwest Ulster and northern Connaught. Kidnapped in 1587 by the English Lord Deputy John Perrot, he managed to escape on Christmas Eve of 1591 using a file smuggled to him in Dublin Castle.[64] Soon formally installed as "The O'Donnell," or head of the clan, he set to work uniting his countrymen in an uprising against "English rule in the name of the Catholic faith."[65] For the next ten years, Red Hugh and Hugh O'Neill, "The O'Neill" of the principal family and clan of Ulster, fought courageously, at one point appealing to the great Catholic monarch Philip II of Spain: "Our only hope of re-establishing the Catholic religion rests on your assistance. Now or never our church must be succored."[66] Five months later, the reply from Philip arrived: "I have been informed that you are defending the Catholic cause against the English. That this is acceptable to God is proved by the signal victories which you have obtained. I hope you

---

63. Warren H. Carroll, *A History of Christendom*, vol. 3, *The Glory of Christendom* (Front Royal, VA: Christendom Press, 1993), 110.

64. Carroll, *A History of Christendom*, vol. 4, *The Cleaving of Christendom*, 461–462.

65. Ibid., 463.

66. Ibid., 464–465.

will continue to prosper, and you need not doubt that I will render you any assistance you may require."[67]

Buoyed by this promised support, Red Hugh and Hugh O'Neill dealt to Queen Elizabeth the worst English military defeat of her long reign at the Battle of the Yellow Ford.[68] Handed further defeat by her own Earl of Essex with whom she had sent "the largest army ever to cross the Irish Sea," Elizabeth was furious and replaced him with Lord Mountjoy. The long-awaited Spanish army finally set sail, eventually landing and securing the port town of Kinsale, and these three forces prepared for what Warren calls "the most decisive battle in the history of Ireland:"

> It was the day before Christmas by the old Julian calendar still used in the British Isles; Red Hugh O'Donnell intended to give the destruction of Mountjoy's army before Kinsale to the Irish people as a Christmas present. There were violent thunderstorms all night. In the misty dawn some of the attackers lost their way, and others unexpectedly met a strong English position at a ford. O'Neill withdrew temporarily to try to reassemble his men. So the Irish did not reach the position which del Águila [the Spanish commander] was watching, at which their arrival was to serve as a signal for a Spanish sally. There was no sally. Mountjoy, observing the confusion of O'Neill's Irish, launched a cavalry charge. Just then O'Donnell came up, but Mountjoy attacked him at once from another direction. Red Hugh's troops, in the confusion of the moment, broke and fled. The Spaniards, whose iron discipline was world-famous, never came out of Kinsale at all. In three hours the Irish host was gone, fleeing where no man pursued.
>
> Mountjoy proved himself one of the greatest generals in English history by his triumph against the odds at Kin-

---

67. Ibid., 465.
68. Ibid., 466.

sale. The Irish and the Spaniards certainly should have won. Neither Juan del Águila nor Red Hugh O'Donnell nor "the great O'Neill" could ever really explain why they had lost.

But lost they had. On January 12, 1602, del Águila surrendered Kinsale in return for permission to take his men and their arms and go home. (A courier carrying a letter from King Philip III to del Águila ordering him to stand fast was intercepted.) On January 16, Red Hugh O'Donnell took a ship for Spain to try to persuade Philip to send another Spanish expedition—now Ireland's only hope. But this was highly unlikely after such a debacle, and never came close to materializing. George Carew, president of Munster, made sure that it would not materialize by sending an agent named Blake to poison Red Hugh in Valladolid. He died a holy death in Simancas in September 1602. He was only twenty-eight years old. He lives in the memory of the Irish, forever young, bold and high-hearted. His song "O'Donnell *Abu!*" almost became the Irish national anthem.[69]

Fleeing England during the Glorious Revolution of 1688, King James II, the rightful king of both England and Scotland, but a recent convert to the Catholic faith, was betrayed by his daughter and his best general, and was given refuge by King Louis XIV of France. His grandson, Bonnie Prince Charlie, was raised in Rome, but never gave up the quest to regain his rightful place as Scotland's Catholic king. Returning to Scotland in 1743, his fortune followed closely that of Red Hugh. Becoming the leader of an uprising against English rule, Charles memorably declared to the Highlanders: "I am come home, sir, and I will entertain no notion at all of returning to that place from whence I come; I am persuaded my faithful Highlanders will stand by me."[70] The Scots rallied and

69. Ibid., 479–480.

70. Warren Carroll, "Bonnie Prince Charlie" (lecture, Christendom College, Front

On September 16, 1745, Prince Charles called on the city of Edinburgh, the capital of Scotland, to submit to him, as it did submit on the following day. On October 30, the prince announced, at an acrimonious council of war, that he was committed to the invasion and conquest of England as well as of Scotland. He was in England early in November and on November 16, proclaimed James III at market cross in Carlisle in the north of England. Carlisle surrendered to him on November 18 as he rode into the city on a white horse.

The next day, Prince Charles made triumphant entry into Manchester, where a whole regiment was enlisted. On December 6, Charles reached Derby in England, only about a hundred miles from London. That day was called "Black Friday" because of a financial panic in London caused by the approach of Charlie's army, but it was the blackest of days for the prince and his adherents, because it was then that the decision was made to abandon the invasion of England and retreat to Scotland. Charles deferred, even when all his instincts told him to press on . . . Frank McLynn says of this critical decision:

> The debate about Derby can never be satisfactorily resolved. The fact remains, as one historian of the issue has shrewdly pointed out, that the Scottish leaders would never have agreed to continue to London, whatever the cogency of the prince's arguments. States of mind were to be all-important after Darby . . . The prince, who had trekked at the head of his army on the way south, now rode depressed and sullen on horseback in the rear. . . . He never truly recovered from the trauma of Derby.[71]

Royal, VA, February 26, 2008). An audio recording of the lecture may be accessed at https://media.christendom.edu/2008/02/bonnie-prince-charlie/
71. Ibid.

Eventually, sensing the loss of spirit which had pervaded the fighting Scots, the English pursued them and dealt the Bonnie Prince his final disaster at the Battle of Culloden, the last battle ever fought on British soil.[72]

Warren, having committed all of this history to memory, must have felt united in brotherhood with his defeated comrades as he belted out in his signature off-key, raspy voice one of his favorite songs, "Sound the Pibroch," at those St. Patrick's Day celebrations:

> By dark Culloden's field of gore,
> Hear how they cry "Claymore! Claymore!"
> Bravely they fight, can they do no more
> Than die for Royal Charlie?
> No more we'll see such deeds again,
> Deserted now each highland glen,
> And lonely kilns are o'er the men
> Who fought and died for Charlie!

"I have been to Culloden," says Warren. "Of all the many battle-fields I have seen, it is the saddest. . . . If you ever go to Scotland, try to visit Glenfinnan where the Scots rallied to their true king, the last Catholic king of the English-speaking peoples, and try to visit the battlefield of Culloden in the north, where the Scots so bravely gave their lives for him. . . . There you too can commemorate Bonnie Prince Charlie, your last king."[73]

In summing up much of the war of Irish Catholics against their tyrannical English rulers, Warren states:

> The people of Ireland had from the beginning almost uni-
> versally rejected the change of religion in England. Only
> a tiny minority, prompted in almost every case by love
> of gain or desire for office, had adhered to the protestant

---

72. Ibid.

73. Ibid.

church in Ireland, whose bishops were mere place-men who rarely if ever ventured out among the overwhelmingly Catholic people. In Irish-speaking areas there were no protestants at all, for hardly any protestants could be found who spoke their language. But the Irish were, as ever, cursed by political disunity. Their chieftains could not seem to comprehend bringing the Irish people together as Catholics to fight to preserve the religion they professed.[74]

As divine providence and humble watchmen would have it, this curse did not take hold in the unfolding of Warren's vision. Christendom College was granted unity, and danger was overcome. As Ray states:

> This is why it survived. Because everybody, donors, parents, founders, faculty, administration, students, what they call interested parties—all were on the same page as far as what the college was for, what it was supposed to do, and how it should be structured. And that gave us an enormous inner strength against all the natural difficulties that naturally beset us in administrative differences. And I think that is still true today.

---

74. Carroll, *A History of Christendom*, vol. 4, *The Cleaving of Christendom*, 382–383.

10

"You Have Done a Great Work for the Church!"

WHILE THE TRAPPINGS OF founding and running a college formed the exterior structure of much of Warren's adult life, the hearth fire of this structure was kept burning with the kindling of his loves. First and foremost—he loved his God. Enthroned only slightly under God and faith came (fittingly—if one understands the nature of the Catholic faith) his ever freshly romantic love for his wife, Anne. However, it was also apparent to most who knew him that he also dearly and deeply loved his students.

He had discussed the topic of how to reach young people, who were becoming hardened and turned in on themselves more and more by a culture gone bizarre, with his mother as far back as the early 1970s when he was still working for Senator Schmitz. Groups of emotionally charged college students lobbying to end the draft would show up in Schmitz's offices, ready for a fight. Far from taking a dogmatic approach, Warren tended to sympathize with some of these young people and thought the best way to reach them was with "new approaches to the old values."[1] "So, oddly enough," he wrote to his mother, "just at

---

1. Warren Carroll to Gladys and Herbert Carroll, 17 May 1970, Box 7-2B, Folder 6, Archive Collection, Caroline Jones.

the point when you for the first time seem to have completely given up on our college youth, I am slightly more optimistic about them than I have been in the past."[2] Warren's approach was not to argue and castigate, but simply to present the truth—in all of its glory—and let the students' hearts be inflamed with the love of this truth. And it worked.

One of the things Cathy O'Donnell noticed when she and her husband first visited the college was the love and respect the students had for Warren. "They would be walking and they would say, 'Hello, Dr. Carroll.' I never thought he would be the kind of person who could relate well to the students. But to see the love and affection that they had and the way everyone made sure to greet him, even with his head down, was remarkable."[3]

Having been a student of Warren, this author would like to add her own observations in a first person account.

> As Kris Burns has said repeatedly—he was the dad. I think all of the students felt this. I know I did. But he was the kind of dad who commanded respect and love *because he was who he was*—not because he asked for any of these things. Often you wondered if he even knew your name because of his quirky characteristic of keeping his eyes glued to the ground. We students had a running joke that he knew us by the color of our shoelaces and sometimes contemplated switching these laces between us to see what would happen. Would we completely confuse him? Well, it was funny to think about, but at the same time, we would have done *anything* for him. He inspired us. He made us want to be better people. And he filled our minds with stories—of heroes, of martyrs, of those whose lives seemed wasted, but who became saints of Heaven because they said yes to God or they just refused to give up. He opened up the past for us as events came alive and people moved, were faced with choices, and made decisions which decided destinies.

---

2. Ibid.

3. Timothy and Cathy O'Donnell, interview by author.

And we could *see* the hand of God working constantly to bring goodness out of the evil that is the effect of original sin. But even more than this, we were shown that even when evil *does* seem to triumph—it is the character and the soul of the individual person that matters. This is how good triumphs over evil—in the individual human person. "One man can make a difference," he would tell us. And then he would show us how.

His lectures were electric. More than one eye dropped tears onto notebook paper as shivers were sent up and down the spines of students trying desperately to keep their pens moving as quickly as Warren's steamrolling narrative. Sometimes you just had to put the pen down and listen, hoping that a fellow student would lend his notes later for you to fill in your gaps. The names cascade through our memories: Philip II, Whittaker Chambers, Charles V, Clovis, Queen Isabel and King Ferdinand, Cortés, Charlemagne, St. Thomas More, John Sobieski, Bonnie Prince Charlie, Charles Martel, Ignatius, Danton, Alexander Solzhenitsyn, Joe McCarthy, and of course— Pelayo. But even as these names stood tall, and we were required to learn the details and significance of them all, Warren taught us something even more important—and he taught it by example. Every day, he was front and center in the chapel for Mass, belting out hymns in his characteristic off-key voice. Every day, he bustled into the chapel just in time for Rosary, tapping students on the shoulder as he made his way up to the front row, whispering in his raspy voice, "Tom, you take the first [mystery]. Jenny, you take the second." And because of his rock-solid faith, we knew. We knew that if he were alive in communist Russia in the twentieth century, he would have gone to a concentration camp rather than deny his faith. We knew that he would have been on the ships at Lepanto, fighting and dying for his faith if God requested it of him. And we knew that, were he alive in Spain in 718, he would have stood fast with Pelayo's band of thirty men perched on a rock.

We knew that he loved heroes—yes—but more than that,
we knew that he would become one if it were asked of him.
And in his own way, it was.

Warren ate meals with the students, he prayed with the students, and he stayed after class to answer any and all questions of the students. In fact, one sat up a bit taller in one's chair if Warren's response to his or her question was a resounding, "Good question!" He played ping-pong with the students, and he came to the dances. No, he did not dance—he was content simply to stand against the wall watching his "children" have a good time, all the while his eyes sparkling with pride. "You loved him in a different way," says Mark McShurley.

He wouldn't be called personable. But you saw that he was determined, and that he really did care for the students even though he wasn't warm and fuzzy about it. He just loved the fact that his students married each other. Every time he heard about an engagement, he just loved it. He was very fatherly in that way. The students loved and respected him even though they laughed at his foibles. He was goofy! And the students made fun of his goofiness, but with great respect. Even sometimes we who worked for him weren't exactly sure he knew who we were![4]

In fact, Mark was working for the college when he decided to ask permission to date his future wife, Holly, a student at the time. In true "dad" fashion, Warren counseled him, "I expect you to be a gentleman, and if you're not—you're out of here!" "He said this dead seriously," recalls Mark. "It was like getting Holly's father's permission!"[5]

Even if he might seem oblivious, Warren was often a very perceptive person, keeping much of what he observed and overheard to himself. During the time he was president of the college, his office was right

---

4. Mark McShurley, interview by author.
5. Ibid.

next to the common room—basically the only room large enough for any group of students to congregate in the college's early days . . . talking, studying in groups, playing backgammon, strumming guitars, or plunking out tunes on the piano. Since there were only two real classrooms, and these were on the second floor of the main building (which came to be called the Regina Coeli Building), most students passed through the common room nearly every day throughout the day. Meals were served here, Mass was held on Sundays, and other assorted organized activities took place within its walls. What all of these students coming and going most likely did not know is that Warren could hear right through the wall separating his office from this room always filled with activity. "You don't realize it," he said to Holly one time, "but I can hear everything that goes on in the common room when I'm in my office." "And that is how he knew a lot of the life of the college," she states. "He always looked down and so people thought he wasn't listening, but he was—and was very in tune to what was going on."[6]

One consequence of Warren's loving and responsible fatherly heart, combined with a vision of what this love and responsibility were called by God to produce, was that all his energy was focused on a single goal. Even with a deep faith, a person who possesses these characteristics can sometimes lose patience with those who fill his life on a regular basis. With staff and students alike—Warren was not always what one would call personable. In fact, his interaction with people has been described at times as "gruff," "crotchety," "abrasive," and "curmudgeonly." "Warren was a choleric man," says Thomas Storck, who taught at the college for a short time. "I think he tried to be fair, but he could be abrasive. But he was deeply Catholic and would modify or temper the cynical attitudes and judgements from his previous life in the light of faith."[7] And the same walls which allowed Warren to listen in on the students' conversations in the common room worked in the other direction as well. Warren was accustomed to spending many a night on an upper floor of the Regina Coeli Building, typing

---

6. Holly McShurley, interview by author.
7. Thomas Storck, correspondence with author, 13 October 2016.

away furiously at his latest book. "One night," relates Sharon Hickson, "a bunch of the kids were downstairs, and they could hear him typing. He was a fanatic typist, and he would sound like a machine gun. But he kept cursing, because he missed a word or something. He didn't know anybody else was in the building."[8]

There is a story which this author remembers personally, and which embodies the tunnel vision of this tender-hearted man to a tee. It is re-told here with the permission of Mary Catherine Pegis who, along with Warren and a classroom full of history students, was the key player. It happened during an evening class. Warren was at the front of the classroom, with his back to the wall containing the only door into the room. The door was slightly to his right. Although he could not see the door while lecturing, for the room full of students facing him, it was, of course, in full view. His lecturing resembled his typing ("five hundred years in five minutes" as one student jokingly put it), and on this particular evening he was going at full speed, with students, heads down, writing as furiously as they were able. Then the door opened just a crack, and a frog came flying through the air—thrown into the room by Mary and Tom Ehart—and it landed with a plop on the floor. Warren must have seen some activity out of the corner of his eye, but he continued lecturing without a pause. One by one, the students noticed this large green blob looking a bit dazed and giving an occasional hop. But Warren continued to lecture. Finally, when it became obvious to all that there was indeed a frog hopping around the classroom, Warren stopped. Watching his face to see how he would react, the students did nothing for a moment—until he began to laugh, and then the entire room erupted in laughter. But Warren did not know what to do next. I think he realized that giggling at a hopping frog in the midst of a lecture was not exactly a professional thing to do, so he quickly tried to contain his laughter and continue the lecture. But he simply couldn't do it! Wavering between uncontrollable bursts of laughter and a comic attempt to straighten his face, appear stern, and go on with the lecture just made the whole situation

---

8. Sharon Hickson, interview by author, 19 August 2015.

even more hilarious to the students who, while suffering from cramps in the side from so much laughing, also felt for him and so were making their own valiant attempts at straight faces. Finally, he was able to gain control over his urge to laugh, and he continued with the class. Anyone else would have stopped the lecture, picked up the frog, and either thrown it out of the window or taken it downstairs and thrown it out of the door. But Warren was so engrossed in his topic that I don't believe his mind could make the transition to this untimely but harmless practical joke. At the same time—something in him appreciated the comical situation and wanted to react normally with laughter. But he truly did not know which one to do! I believe, however, that situations like these, added to all of his singular qualities, just made the students love him more. This is attested to by their own memories.

> I also remember Dr. Carroll coming to have lunch with us. At that time, we were only about one hundred students. He would tell us stories, we would ask all kinds of questions, and by the end of the meal, we had solved all the problems of the world. He would join us for the Rosary, which he led, and evening prayer. He attended parties with his wife and was just a presence of calm and strength. It seemed to me that we all really felt he gave us the power and the courage to fight the good fight. He was able to empower us to carry the faith wherever God was calling us. He is truly one of the humblest people I have ever met.
>
> —Sister Eileen Tickner, class of '81

> My favorite memory of Dr. Carroll [is] the day I made him laugh while teaching modern American history. ... The class was filled with seniors swamped with theses, eager to graduate, and too tired to stay awake for a class that began right after lunch. In this particular class, Dr. Carroll was berating the class because ninety percent of us had flunked a quiz. Since his quizzes were only worth

one point of our final grade, not too many of us took them seriously at the time. During this tirade, Dr. Carroll said that the answer that had disgusted him the most was that the soldiers charging the beaches drowned in underwater barbed-wire [this particular battle had nothing to do with water or barbed wire]. Knowing the answer was mine and seeing the look of disgust on his face, I couldn't contain myself and burst out laughing. Dr. Carroll then proceeded to sit down and laugh until he cried.

—Caroline E. Pollock, class of '03

The first time I heard Dr. Carroll teach a class was during my high school visit to Christendom. . . . The students were very helpful to me and made their recommendation of which class I should attend in no uncertain terms. Dr. Carroll's "History 201." All I can really remember from that day was being very intimidated when I left Dr. Carroll's classroom. "I'm not sure I can handle college here," I remember thinking. "That guy I just listened to for an hour and fifteen minutes seemed brilliant, and he didn't pause for one moment during the whole lecture. I doubt I will be able to write notes fast enough to capture what he was saying, let alone understand it." He didn't take any excuses from the students either. . . . Later on during my visit, I attended a student activities event at which Dr. Carroll was present. "There is that intimidating teacher again," I thought. But I was amazed at the reception he received from the students. At one point, they were chanting with vigorous respect and affection: "DC! DC! DC!" I looked up and saw Dr. Carroll, a.k.a., DC, smiling from ear to ear. This was the first time that I learned another lesson that would continue to be re-learned throughout my time at Christendom: "Don't be fooled by Dr. Carroll." This brilliant man, who at times might seem like he was missing something because you were not even sure if his eyes were open, was not missing anything! . . . As a student and later as a staff member, I was repeatedly impressed that Dr. Carroll's insight was not limited to people and events in history. He also understood and valued the people and events around him in the Christendom community. Immediately following Christmas break during my junior year, he addressed the student body and told us, "I don't mean to sound egotistical, but since I thought of starting Christendom College in my living room, it was my idea, and therefore I know better than anyone else what Christendom College should look like." He went on to reprimand us for not acting in accordance with his idea of Christendom. Dr. Carroll pointed out, quite correctly, that in our attempts to make things better by "complaining," we had been too negative and divisive during the previous semester. It was exactly what we needed to hear, and the complaints virtually stopped from that day until my graduation. Dr. Carroll was the greatest teacher of my life.

–Tom McGraw, class of '93

My most vivid memory of Dr. Carroll is of the many times we saw him kneeling in the front pew of the chapel.

–Jennie McGuire, class of '02

Part of what most likely drew the students to their brilliant, but sometimes bumbling, father figure was his own attitude towards them. He had such a deep trust in divine providence, not only for himself and for the establishment of the college, but also towards the students whom he considered to be hand picked by God for immersion in the milieu that was Christendom College. As he stated in one "Christendom College Report:"

I firmly believe that God had a special and unique reason for sending each person to Christendom College who has come here—students, faculty, and staff. The students going out at graduation are sent upon the mission which, whether they knew what it was to be or not (usually not), they came to Christendom College to prepare for. A long march and many battles lie ahead for each graduate in his or her personal apostolate. He or she will need and pray for much of God's help in sustaining the fortitude and the courage required for the march and the battles; along the road, no matter what the strife, whatever sustenance the enduring Christendom College community can offer to its graduates will always be ready for them.[9]

The summer of 1992 was a momentous one for Warren. Tim O'Donnell had lived and studied in Rome and knew it well, so he decided to organize a pilgrimage to Rome for the students, as well as some adults. Warren, who was not about to miss a trip like this, went along, and together he and Tim led the group, taught classes, and toured Italy. "We kept saying we were trying to do the Spain thing," says Tim, "and he absolutely loved it!" There was a very poignant moment which Tim recalls:

> I remember one night, we were in Assisi, and we were standing in front of the Basilica of St. Francis. It was evening twilight, sundown. Warren was smoking his very first cigarette! And the sky, the stars, everything was painfully beautiful. We were gazing at the illuminated façade of the basilica, and Warren was quietly reflecting on God giving him the grace to found this college. And it was so sweet. But then he also spoke about God's providence in sending me to the college.[10]

After Assisi, the group traveled back to Rome to attend the canonization of St. Claude de la Colombière, which occurred on May

---

9. "Christendom College Report," vol. 4, June 1981, personal papers of Raymund O'Herron.

10. Timothy O'Donnell, interview with author.

31. The following day, the group was touring the Vatican radio studios when Tim got a call from Bishop Dziwisz, private secretary to John Paul II, the pope at the time. The members of the group did not know what this meant. They had put in different requests to see if they could attend an audience with the pope, but had heard nothing. "The pope wants to meet with you," explained Bishop Dziwisz. "Can you come tomorrow?" "No, we're *leaving* tomorrow!" exclaimed Tim. "It *has* to be today!" "Be at the bronze door at 11:00 a.m.," was the response from Dziwisz. So they showed up at the appointed time, wondering if maybe they would get to attend a papal Mass or something. They were admitted to a waiting room where they prayed the Rosary and sang hymns. Tim continues the narrative:

> We had been singing and praying the Rosary, and I think we were on the third mystery, the descent of the Holy Spirit, and the door opened and the pope walked in! It was a private audience! And everyone fanned out—there were about forty of us. And he said, "You all are from Christendom." And he went around, and I introduced him to everyone, and he greeted everyone. Finally he came to Warren and I said, "This is the beloved founder of our college." And of course, Warren was down on his knees. And he kissed the fisherman's ring and then got up. And I said, "Holy Father we want to thank you for all you have done for the Church and what you have done for the Church in our country." And he said, "No, I thank *you. You have done a great work for the Church.*" So Warren was there to hear that from the Vicar of Christ. . . . Then he gave us his blessing. We were all on our knees, and then he left, and we were all crying like babies. It was an amazing experience; a great, great moment.[11]

Anne, who had not gone on the trip in order to be at Seton's graduation, describes her husband when she met him at the airport the next

---

11. Ibid.

day: "He looked like he had gone to Heaven," she says. "The meeting was totally emblazoned in his mind. He felt very close to John Paul II. When he wrote the final volume of his history, John Paul II was one of the heroes of that volume."[12] In this same volume, Warren wrote, at the age of seventy-seven, an appendix entitled "Mission," in which he says:

> The college became my mission. I was its founding president and brought it into being. Every time now, in retirement, that I visit its campus, somebody thanks me for founding it. Pope John Paul the Great knew what I had done; when I was introduced to him in 1992 as its [Christendom's] founder, he said to me, "You have done a great work for the Church"—words which will go on my tombstone when my mission is completed. It was so that I could found Christendom College that my guardian angel held me on that railroad trestle without a railing in Lewiston, Maine, when I was at Bates College.[13]

Returning from his thrilling audience with the pope, Warren was immediately engrossed in a second momentous event. Dr. Damian Fedoryka had decided to step down as president of the college—and Tim O'Donnell was approached by the board to take his place as the third president. "I had been involved in every facet of the college except fundraising," says Tim, "so I said I would accept on the condition that I could continue to teach. And they agreed."[14] Tim's yes was extremely important to Warren. The relationship between the two cannot be over-emphasized and was one of only a handful of relationships Warren considered intimate. Anne has memories of this time period:

> It was just before the feast of Saints Peter and Paul, and we had them [the O'Donnells] at our house for dinner. We

---

12. Anne Carroll, interview by author, 14 March 2013.
13. Warren H. Carroll, *A History of Christendom*, vol. 6, *The Crisis of Christendom*, 810.
14. Timothy O'Donnell, interview by author.

were sitting outside, and Warren told Tim that the board was going to offer him this position. Tim said, "I need some time to pray about this decision and prepare for it." But by the end of the conversation, he was prepared! He was born to have that job. . . . Warren always said, "He is the best possible successor." He loved Tim and Cathy—he really loved them. The times he would spend at their home were for him like being next door to paradise. And Tim was exactly the right person [to carry on Warren's vision], and he is what makes Christendom College what it is today. Warren started it, but Tim built it. It is what it is because of Tim—his character, his personality, his love for the faith and everything else. And Warren would want that tribute to him to be in this kind of book. That was important to him—that Tim be honored for everything he has done for the college.[15]

For his part, Tim also felt the incredible bond shared between him and Warren. "He was a fatherly figure to me," he ponders. "But he was also a friend. He used to say to me, 'Tim, you're my best friend.'"[16] Their bond grew out of the solid foundation of a shared love of the faith, was nourished by devotion, loyalty, and compatibility, and bore fruit in the embodiment of this faith that is Christendom College. "He would come over almost once a month for dinner," relates Cathy.

We'd stay up and talk 'till 3:00 in the morning. And that's how I learned history, because I didn't have a good history background. He'd say, "Have you ever heard about Cova Donga?" or some other topic, and I'd say, "No!" and you could see the rolodex in his eyes, and he'd start into the story. I felt like a little kid enrapt in these stories. He continued to do this throughout our relationship. He would spend the night in the study on a little sleeper sofa so he

---

15. Anne Carroll, interview by author.
16. Timothy O'Donnell, interview by author.

didn't have to drive all the way back to Manassas, and he'd get up about 11:00 or so—just in time to make it to Mass and then teach his classes.[17]

Cathy also remembers driving up to Maine for vacation, which she and Tim did on a number of occasions. On one of these summer trips, Warren brought over his mother and introduced her to his great friends, Tim and Cathy. "She was the most poised, gracious, refined lady you would ever meet," remembers Cathy:

> We had tea. She was elderly but an incredible conversa-tionalist and sharp as a tack. She was such a contrast to Warren! You could see, though, where the intelligence and the art of writing came from. After she died, we went and visited the home in Maine. When we were there, they were doing scenes from Dunnybrook [the play] and I think the niece [Carrie] was acting one of the parts. I had read the book and began crying hysterically because I had loved the book. But Warren was so pleased that we could go up there and share all of that with him.[18]

What struck Cathy as well was the incredible moral sense of War-ren's mother and the solid ideas of good, bad, and duty. "I am always amazed," she says. "Where do people get this when they don't have God? But they somehow had it from the history and the land and the community. He grew up in that."[19] Both Tim and Cathy agree that Warren's childhood deeply nurtured one of his outstanding charac-teristics: a tremendous love of the good.

> Warren had an intense love for the good. He *loved* the good. He was so idealistic, and whenever he found the ideal in

---

17. Cathy O'Donnell, interview by author.
18. Ibid.
19. Ibid.

259

the real, it just moved him in the most profound and deepest way possible. This is one of the great attributes that he
had. He loved goodness wherever he saw it: in family relationships, in courage, in friendship, in acts and events of
history. That's why his imagination was so struck by these
dramatic events that took place in history.[20]

The last entries Warren recorded in his "Brief Summary of a Life
History" were for the years 1988 and 1989. Next to the year 1988, he
writes: "Peaceful year as chairman of the history department, residence Manassas, second big European trip as adult, completion of the
Seventy Years of the Communist Revolution." And for 1989: "Year of the
great counter-revolution against communism, formation of the Washington group, residence Manassas, beginning of writing of *Isabel of
Spain* and collected short stories *The Tarrant Chronicles.*"

These short synopses contain what would make up the bulk of
Warren's activities for the latter part of his life. Besides his teaching and
work at the college, Warren wrote voluminously, continued his life-
long fight against the tyranny of communism, and traveled extensively.
All told, Warren's poor typewriter was pounded upon night after night
producing four massive unpublished novels, a fictional series known as
The Tarrant Chronicles, and thirteen historical works including his *History of Christendom* which he laid out in six volumes. As has been stated,
his approach to understanding history is that men, not movements,
make history. Using his free will, man either cooperates with or rejects
the grace offered by God, making decisions which determine his being
and weaving the tapestry of history. On the inside jacket of his *The Rise
and Fall of the Communist Revolution,* he writes: "Though this is the history
of an ideological movement in action, the author firmly believes that
men, not ideologies or economics, make history. Therefore the narrative concentrates on its actors—on the heroism, compromise, or cow-
ardice with which men and nations faced this ultimate challenge." That
God took a man from a family with a long tradition of story-telling,

---

20. Timothy O'Donnell, interview by author.

who was raised with an incredible sense of right and wrong, duty, and a sense of duty and purpose—bestowed upon him a tremendous love of the truth, and baptized him with a Christian understanding, indeed makes for a master story-teller. One could make the case that he is the flower on the vine of his family's "gift for yarning."

Warren never gave up fighting against what he considered to be the greatest external threat to the freedom of the West and the greatest evil of the twentieth century: atheistic communism. In 1985, he founded a newsletter called "The Freedom Fighter," which kept readers updated on anti-communist efforts throughout the world. It covered resistance leaders Jonas Savimbi in Angola, Ahmad Shah Massoud in Afghanistan, and the freedom fighters of Nicaragua, among others. He would also found an association, called the Nike group, dedicated to defeating communism. As he tells it:

> I brought together what we called the Nike group of Americans to aim at total victory over communism. It included Andy Eiva and an assortment of unique personalities whose dedication matched his. One was Margaret Calhoun, a Southern belle known to her friends as "Ducky," who had made herself an expert on movements to fight communism in Africa, specifically in Angola and Mozambique. Another was Herbert Romerstein, who had been a communist once like Whittaker Chambers and had become a world authority on the communist revolution. Another was Carl Linden, a tall slender man who had been an analyst of communist propaganda with me in the Central Intelligence Agency. We met in apartments and stayed up late. We never forgot that, in the immortal words of General Douglas MacArthur, *there is no substitute for victory.* Above all, we always knew that there were thousands more who shared our commitment and would not rest until communism was destroyed.[21]

---

21. Dr. Warren Carroll, "Andrew Eiva and the End of the Communist Empire" (lecture, Christendom College, Front Royal, VA, February 23, 2010). An au-

One of what Warren calls "his most cherished memories of a lifetime" occurred in conjunction with Andrew Eiva, a U.S.-born Lithuanian who played a major role in bringing down communist power in that country and who was part of the Nike group. In 1983, Andy had founded his own group, called the Federation for American Afghan Action, to secure American aid for the Afghan freedom fighters. No armchair soldier, Andy was a graduate of West Point and a Green Beret specializing in Soviet weapons, tactics, and languages. He was a self-taught expert on covert CIA operations, especially in Afghanistan, and had spent time in that country training guerilla fighters and organizing a program to encourage large Soviet defections there. Returning to the United States, he spent his time demanding and working to obtain grass-roots support for legislation giving effective aid to the Afghan guerillas.[22] Warren would later report that:

> Our government neither knew nor apparently cared what he was doing. He was not on active duty, but was doing all this on his own. His Washington apartment, which I often visited, was strewn with clothes and scraps of food. My brother-in-law Pete Westhoff gave him his old bicycle to get around in, since Andy could not afford a car. Andy had almost no money, except the little he could raise by mail appeals on behalf of the Afghans.[23]

In 1990, Andy's focus shifted from Afghanistan back to his beloved Lithuania. Having been swallowed up by Stalin's Russia in 1940 with the rest of eastern Europe, by the beginning of 1990, the Lithuanians were rising up on a wave of freedom demonstrations sweeping

---

dio recording of this lecture may be accessed at https://media.christendom. edu/2010/02/andrew-eiva-and-the-end-of-the-communist-empire/

22. "Remarks of Andrew Eiva to the Republican Platform Committee's National Security Subcommittee," Federation for American Afghan Action, 13 August 1984, personal papers of Laura S. Gossin.

23. Carroll, "Andrew Eiva and the End of the Communist Empire."

across communist eastern Europe. Following a rally for independence by a quarter of a million people in the city of Vilnius, Lithuania formally declared its independence from the Soviet Union on March 11. Mikhail Gorbachev, general secretary of the Communist Party of the Soviet Union, dismissed this declaration as null and void. Tensions mounted throughout the rest of that year, and on January 8, 1991, the two sides drew battle lines in and around a large, new parliament building in Vilnius which was occupied by the Lithuanians. Warren continues the story:

> About thirty [pro-Soviet] demonstrators penetrated the building, but were met by fifteen members of the Lithuanian national karate team, who threw them out. About 100 Soviet armored vehicles entered Vilnius that day. At eleven o'clock that evening, a plane landed at Vilnius airport containing about fifty members of the elite Alpha group of Soviet special forces. About fifty thousand Lithuanians now stood guard at the parliament building, protecting it with their bodies alone, since none of them were armed. Others inside had a few weapons, pathetically inadequate for their task. On the morning of January 11, an inventory of their arms showed five shotguns, three .22-caliber single-shot bolt-action rifles, and one rusty pistol.[24]

Over the next number of days, Soviet tanks and troops attacked Lithuanian strongholds while freedom-loving Lithuanians poured into the capital from surrounding areas. On the morning of January 13, Soviet tanks surrounded the now seventy thousand Lithuanians defending the parliament building. There was only one trained officer in the building, who quickly took command of the defense of the building, instructing the defenders to make thousands of Molotov cocktails, which had proven effective against Soviet tanks. Mass was said in front of the building, and the defenders began singing Catho-

---

24. Ibid.

lic hymns. The officer spoke to the crowd as tensions reached a fever pitch, telling them that "their presence in such numbers was already a great moral victory over communism."[25] But the Soviet troop commanders, biting at the bit to attack "while their men were still ready and willing," never received such orders.[26] The tide had turned, and putting down a resistance movement by bulldozing over its people was no longer going to be tolerated. The Soviets were in a precarious position and, by the end of the month, withdrew the extra troops sent in to put down the demonstrators. "In effect," writes Warren, "this amounted to a recognition of their independence."[27]

Avidly following the unfolding of these events, which were being reported on by the U.S. news media, Warren called his friend Andy to ask him what he knew about the situation. "Andy was my best source," he says, "because he followed and advised anti-communist armed resistance groups all over the world, from Lithuania to Africa and Afghanistan. What did he know about the confrontation in Vilnius? Andy told me on the telephone, electrifyingly, 'I was there, *and I was in command*!'" The "only trained officer" in the parliament building was none other than Warren's friend Andrew Eiva. It wasn't often that Warren's "one man who can make a difference" was his own friend and acquaintance and in this case, became for him "one of my most cherished memories of a lifetime." "Men make history, and on that day in Vilnius at the parliament building—January 8, 1991—Andy Eiva made history."[28]

Having devoted so much of his time and energy to the defeat of communism, Warren chronicles its final crumbling, spanning the critical year of 1991, first month by month and then hour by hour, in his *The Rise and Fall of the Communist Revolution*. And it is worth quoting the final paragraphs in full:

---

25. Dr. Warren H. Carroll, *The Rise and Fall of the Communist Revolution* (Front Royal, VA: Christendom Press, 1989), 759.

26. Ibid., 760.

27. Ibid., 762.

28. Carroll, "Andrew Eiva and the End of the Communist Empire."

Gorbachev was beaten; after his last appeal for a Union-wide referendum on the Commonwealth of Independent States was completely ignored, he had no choice but to agree to the complete dissolution of the Soviet Union. Yeltsin and his officials occupied the Kremlin on December 19; Gorbachev formally resigned his now vanished office of president of the Soviet Union on December 25, the day of the official transfer of all power from the Soviet Union to the Russian republic in the Kremlin, solemnized by a flag change in the early evening.

That change took place at 7:35 p.m. It was the stuff of dreams for some, who had imagined how it might happen on some far-off glorious day, but had never expected it so soon. Floodlit against the darkness, the red flag with the hammer and sickle whipped and crackled in the Arctic wind. For seventy-four years it had flown over the Kremlin, a vivid and terrible symbol of the ultimate revolution for which the Kremlin was headquarters.

Now its day was done. The world watched on television. The cameras focused. The tricolor of pre-revolutionary Russia was made ready for raising. As the bloody banner of man-made apocalypse came fluttering down the Kremlin flagpole under the radiant stars of Christmas night, the communist revolution in the west was dead.[29]

Warren must have felt such rejoicing in his soul![30] But his rejoicing

---

29. Carroll, *The Rise and Fall of the Communist Revolution*, 778.
30. In 2005, Warren was approached by Marcel Guarnizo, the brother of a Christendom alumna, who was organizing a group to bring the Catholic Church in Russia back to life. Marcel was asking for Warren's help for his fledgling organization named Aid to the church in Russia. Warren was thrilled to offer his assistance, promptly writing a check for $100 which doubled what the group had in the bank at the time. The group eventually raised millions, built a seminary in Russia, and set up educational opportunities in eastern Europe to train young men who had no formal education. Warren became a board member, and when he became unable to drive, a limousine was sent to pick him up for meetings. When Warren

was not to be kept hidden as he was also in hot demand as a speaker, both in the field of all things communist and, interestingly, in the field of all things Christopher Columbus, as the world approached the 500th anniversary of his voyages. In their Christmas letter of 1991, Anne states:

> In October, Warren's latest book was published, *Isabel of Spain: The Catholic Queen*. This is the only book he has written which is based almost entirely on primary sources; he spent many long days and nights studying Spanish documents in order to write the book. There is also extensive material on Christopher Columbus, and the book was timed to come out near Columbus Day.
>
> With the five hundredth anniversary of Columbus' first voyage coming up, Warren has been in demand as a speaker on Columbus. He's not quite politically correct because he insists that Columbus really did discover America and that this discovery was a good thing. The native Americas really were better off being exposed to western civilization and Christianity rather than being left to eat each other (Caribbean cannibals) or cut each other's hearts out (Aztecs).
>
> Warren is also in demand as a speaker on the fall of communism. Whenever some major event happens in what used to be the Soviet Union, one or more radio stations call him to get his sage comments. If a call for a speaking engagement comes in, I ask him if it's for Columbus or communism. It's almost always one or the other.[31]

At the dawning of the decade of the 1990s, Warren and Anne, having spent the 1980s in a rented apartment in Manassas, bought a townhouse about a fifteen-minute walk from Anne's Seton School.[32]

---

was unable to leave his house after his first stroke, the meeting was brought to him! He was very proud of the role he played in this effort.

31. Anne and Warren Carroll to dear friends, Advent letter 1991, Maine Women Writers Collection.

32. Warren and Anne had sold their Haymarket house in 1979, moving into a one-

They had always lived very simply, not being at all extravagant in their lifestyle but making do happily and contentedly with just those things necessary. The same decade brought more changes to the Carroll family including the death of Anne's father in 1995 and Warren's mother in 1999 (at age ninety-four). Anne and Warren's Christmas letter of 1997 mentions the celebration of the college's twentieth anniversary, at which "Warren even wore a tux, although reluctantly."[33] Although unable to attend this gala event at which Cardinal Schotte of the Vatican was in attendance, Warren's old friend and mentor Mrs. Marie Donahue sent a fitting tribute:

> I was delighted to learn that you are honoring Dr. Warren H. Carroll at a tribute dinner on the twentieth anniversary of his founding of Christendom College and regret that I will be unable to attend. Warren was a student in my English classes at Berwick Academy, the most brilliant boy I ever had the privilege to work with. He read omnivorously and wrote with originality, grace, and power.... But it was Warren's character that I admired and appreciated most— his integrity, his concern for his fellow students, his desire to be of service. Most dramatic proof of these qualities is his founding of Christendom College and his writing the history of Christendom, a scholarly, thoroughly researched, eminently readable account of our heritage.... May God bless and reward Warren for living his faith so exemplarily and sharing his knowledge and beliefs so generously.[34]

Warren had kept up his friendship with his high school English teacher for fifty years! Added to his evident qualities of integrity and humility was that of loyalty.

---

bedroom apartment in Manassas.

33. Anne and Warren Carroll to dear friends, Advent letter 1997, Maine Women Writers Collection.

34. Marie Donahue to John Ciskanik, St. Patrick's Day, 1998, Maine Women Writers Collection.

In March of 1998, Warren celebrated his sixty-sixth birthday. Enjoying decent health up to this point, things took a downward turn for him shortly after this celebration. In the fall, Warren suffered a TIA—a pre-stroke, not a complete blockage but a partial blockage of blood to the brain. In the middle of teaching a class, his speech all of a sudden became garbled which was so unlike him that the students and faculty knew something was wrong and arranged to have him driven home. Warren hated hospitals; he hated emergency rooms; he didn't want to go anywhere but home. Phoning his doctor, Anne was told, "Take him in," which she did. "He was in the hospital maybe two days," she says. "He recovered and was back to normal, but from then on, he would have these little periods when he would start to black out. But he could tell they were coming on, so he would just wait until the 'episode' passed. He even continued to drive, but would pull over to the side of the road waiting for it to pass. And then he'd go on."[35] This event launched the final phase of Warren's life, in which God would mercifully grant him both the time to complete his work, and the opportunity to purify his soul through suffering.

Throughout the next year, Warren worked furiously on volume four of his history entitled *The Cleaving of Christendom*. "The thought was crossing his mind that maybe he was not going to live much longer," says Anne. "He even said it to me. And he definitely wanted to finish that book! So he was working on it every spare minute—researching and writing."[36] "He is grateful to God," read their Christmas letter of that year, "for each day of health and continued ability to work."[37] And his premonition was correct. On September 1, 1999, the phone rang at Seton School. The call was for Anne:

> I got a call—it was Warren on the phone and he said, "I think this might be the crisis." I was thinking, the crisis of

---

35. Anne Carroll, interview with author.

36. Ibid.

37. Anne and Warren Carroll to dear friends, Advent letter 1998, Maine Women Writers Collection.

Christendom [the title of volume six of Warren's history] or the crisis with Warren? He had gone to CVS and had blacked out—smashed onto the floor. CVS had called 911 and the EMTs came. He came to and said, "No! I want to go back home!" So they made him sign a paper saying that he refused to go to the hospital. Then we called the doctor and he said, "We have to admit him." So we did, and he was fussing about that. That was on a Wednesday. The next day was Thursday. On Friday he had a major stroke. It was like a deep sleep. You could get him to say something, like somebody would shout at him, "What's your name?" and he'd say, "Carroll—C-A-R-R-O-L-L!" And then they would say, "Well, what's your first name?" And he'd say, "Warren—W-A-R-R-E-N." And then he'd go back to sleep again. He couldn't really answer questions. It was like a reflex—if you asked him his name it would pop out, but he mostly was just sound asleep.

Warren spent about ten days in the Prince William Hospital, followed by about seven weeks in a nursing home where he did rehabilitation. This time period would function as a preparation, for both Warren and Anne, for his second major stroke, still eleven years in the future. And it required major adjustments for them both. To begin with, Warren absolutely *hated* to be without his beloved Anne. And this included both the days and the nights. As a result, Anne spent every minute in which she was not teaching at Warren's bedside. She did not spend the nights during Warren's stay in the hospital and even went home on the first night after he was moved to the nursing home. But when she returned the next day, she was told that all Warren would say was, "Where's my wife, get my wife over here—I've got to have my wife!" And from that day on—she spent the nights in the nursing home—on a little mat on the floor. When the Seton community found out what was going on, two lovely women insisted on giving Anne a bit of relief by staying with Warren for two nights a week.[38] "But even

---

38. These angels of mercy were Mrs. Jane Pennefather and Mrs. Hope Shaw.

then," says Anne, "he wanted *me*! He would settle for someone else as long as he knew I was coming but about 4:00 in the morning he would start saying, 'Call Anne and get her over here.'"[39] Anne continues her account:

> He had some delusions. At one point, he thought he was commanding the Pacific fleet in World War II, but they gave him some medicine and he stopped having them. They were kind of funny. . . . He did rehab but he was a terrible patient! That's one reason I had to stay there, otherwise all the nurses and nurses aids would have quit. He was terrible! He didn't want to do what they told him to do. Pete Grimberg came over one day and brought the Pilgrim Virgin [a traveling statue of Our Lady of Fatima] and put it in his room. And he had been refusing to walk. They had these parallel bars and you're supposed to hold on and walk, and he would just walk a couple of steps and stop. But the day after Pete brought the statue, he walked twenty feet! So he always said, "Pete Grimberg and the Pilgrim Virgin are what started me on my rehab."[40]

While subjecting Warren and Anne to the purifying fire of suffering, however, God showed His love and mercy in other ways. The first was that the nursing home was only a short distance from Seton School, so close that Anne could walk there on her lunch hour. And secondly, Warren had delivered his completed manuscript for volume four of his *History of Christendom* for publication—just one day before the stroke occurred. In Anne's words, "[The latest volume] was all done. And then God said, 'O.K, now.'"[41]

Obviously, Warren was forced to relinquish his classes at the college for the remainder of not only the semester, but the entire school

---

39. Anne Carroll, interview by author.
40. Ibid.
41. Ibid.

year of 1999–2000. He refused, however, to cancel a trip he had planned in March. The year 2000 had been declared a Jubilee Year by Pope John Paul II, and the college had planned a pilgrimage to the Holy Land and Rome in honor of this Jubilee. Knowing Warren's precarious condition, Anne suggested his instead coming with her on the Seton School pilgrimage planned for June, but he was adamant, declaring, "I want to go with Tim and Cathy [O'Donnell]!"[42] And so off he went, with some friends from California along to keep an eye on him. "He once got separated from the group in Manger Square in Bethlehem, and he just sat down and waited. And in about an hour, Cathy showed up and said, 'There you are!'"[43]

Settling into a post-stroke life, Warren began teaching again in the fall of 2000. Although his teaching never quite reached its pre-stroke caliber, he was able to teach one class that year and added a second one for the 2001–2002 academic year. In the spring a class on his hero, John Paul the Great, was the last class the seventy-year-old would teach to his beloved students at Christendom College. He retired as head of the history department, and in his own words, "passed the torch to its current president, my best friend, Timothy O'Donnell, who has proved the ideal successor."[44] Anne describes Warren's retirement in her Christmas letter of 2002:

> In May, Warren taught his last regular class at C.C., retiring from teaching after twenty-five years. He gave up classroom teaching so that he could devote all of his energies to working on his *History of Christendom*. He has no regrets about retiring because his successors in the history department are fine young men who are well qualified to carry on the Christendom tradition of teaching Christ-centered history. He still goes out to the college occasionally for special occasions. . . . The rest of the time he is at

---

42. Ibid.
43. Ibid.
44. Carroll, *A History of Christendom*, vol. 6, *The Crisis of Christendom*, 810.

home researching and writing. . . . Warren's other main
pastime is planning trips.[45]

And plan trips he did! Ever since those "far-reaching car trips"
of his youth, Warren had had an urge to travel. He was forced to put
some of his adventures on hold during the stressful days of founding
the college, but now that those days were behind him, there was literally no place on the globe he did not want to see with his own eyes.
Arranged around Anne's teaching schedule, the older but still *very*
adventurous couple used every school vacation to travel. Christmas
of 2000 was spent in Peru, Christmas of 2001 on Easter Island, and
Christmas of 2002 in the Philippines! There were also annual trips
during the Easter and summer vacations. They took a cruise to Alaska
and one to Norway, and they saw a tango show in Buenos Aires. In
Malta, they heard there was an historical movie about the country
playing at a theater in downtown Valletta, so they decided to go—
only to find out that that movie was not shown on Saturdays, and it was
Saturday. "Well, what *are* you showing?" they asked. "The Lion, the
Witch, and the Wardrobe," was the answer. "So we went to that, and
Warren loved it!" says Anne.[46]

Not all of their trips involved crossing oceans. Warren had purchased a new car in 2001, which they used to visit Anne's family in Colorado. They also made their way back to Warren's old stomping grounds
in Maine for different events, including the wedding of the daughter of
Warren's niece Carrie, Warren's fiftieth college reunion, and his sixtieth
high school reunion. On one visit to Maine, Warren and Anne took a
walk in the woods, to the place where Warren had proposed. Even at age
seventy, Warren remained a romantic. Eventually, Warren and Anne
would each visit every state in the U.S., most of them together.

In every place, of every corner of the world to which they traveled, their priority was always the same: the Mass. For their cruises,

---

45. Anne and Warren Carroll to dear friends, Christmas letter 2002, Maine Women
Writers Collection.
46. Anne Carroll, interview by author.

they chose Holland America—because that particular cruise line hired priests to say daily Mass. "We didn't want to go on any other one because we wanted to have daily Mass," says Anne.[47] While visiting the Philippines, they inquired from the locals about the best means of getting transportation to Mass, only to be directed to what Anne describes as a moped. "You pay the driver and hop on the back. We got Warren on, and off he went to Mass on a moped!" On Easter Island, Anne remembers that the Christmas Eve Mass was said in the native language of Rapanui in which saying "Amen" took about eighteen syllables!

> They sang—they had the most magnificent voices. The priest gave his homily part in Rapanui, part in Spanish, and part in English, and it was great—about how we have to witness to Christ and how the Incarnation was the most important thing that ever happened. And they have this custom [at Christmastime] where they bring all these gifts up at the offertory procession—pineapples and all kinds of things. The pineapples were great—the skinned goat on a spit was a little more problematic. The next morning, we went back to the two morning Masses. They invited us to their barbecue (that's what the goat was for), but we couldn't go. But it was so beautiful, and the people were so kind and sweet and friendly and just went out of their way to make us feel welcomed. We both agreed it was one of the best experiences we ever had. . . . We were so glad [for the] experience![48]

But the story that is the most telling of where Warren and Anne's priorities really lay, was of their visit to Buenos Aires. Warren was quite eager to see the Tierra del Fuego, an archipelago created where the Straits of Magellan carve off the southernmost tip of the continent

---

47. Ibid.
48. Ibid.

of South America. There is a highway reaching down to the Strait, but then one must board a boat to reach the archipelago itself. As Anne describes the situation, "We got as far as the end of the highway, down to the tip of Argentina. We wanted to get a cruise but couldn't get one to match our schedule. The only one would put us on the ship for both Christmas Eve and Christmas Day and there would be no Mass. And we decided, no, Mass comes first."[49] So they passed up that last leg of their anticipated trip—for Our Lord.

In 2003, the Carrolls made their final move, from the townhouse they owned in the Irongate section of Manassas to a quaint little house directly across the street from Seton School. "We weren't eager to move because moving is an ordeal," says Anne:

> But because having a house so close to school would make it easy for Warren to be with me all day, and because the Seton community pitched in to take care of all the details—fixing up and selling our townhouse, fixing up the new house, moving everything to the new house, arranging the mortgage and other purchase details of the new house—we agreed to move. It was a beautiful experience to see how so many people stepped forward to make it possible for us to have this new home.
>
> I am still very happy to be here, and the Seton community still helps out when our house is in need of anything—from landscaping to stopping the basement floods, from power washing to putting up a TV antenna so Warren could watch the World Series, to replacing dead appliances—to anything else you can think of.[50]

This move set in motion a daily routine for them which would not change much during Warren's remaining years and would also enable Warren to be with Anne as much as possible. After attending

---

49. Ibid.
50. Anne Carroll, correspondence with author, 20 March 2017.

the 7:00 a.m. Mass at All Saints Church every morning, they would return home, where Anne would fix Warren some breakfast. Then they crossed the street to the school in time for Rosary at 8:00. For the remainder of the school day, Warren delighted in sitting in Anne's classroom, correcting her when he felt it necessary. Seton graduate Kieran DuFrain remembers these classes:

> He would come in and sit in his chair in Mrs. Carroll's classroom—right next to her desk, and would invariably have a Tom Clancy novel with him, he loved Tom Clancy, or whatever book of history he was reading at the time. He would perch his cane in front of him, and it would be about head level as he would sit bent over. And Mrs. Carroll would be teaching and have some random date that she couldn't remember and she would look over and say, "Warren . . . ?" And he would raise his head [and in his gravelly voice] grumble out, "1761!" and then pick up reading in his book where he had left off.
>
> When we were studying the October Revolution and Mrs. Carroll got to Rasputin, she would teach all of his infiltration into the Romanov family and so forth and then she'd get to the assassination. She would stop in class and pick up Warren's book *1917* and say, "And now, I can't tell it any better than this!" And she'd read from the chapter on his assassination. And Dr. Carroll would get this little school-boy look on his face and just stare up at her as she read—with this look and his eyes would never leave her face. He was madly in love with her.
>
> When he really got the biggest smiles on his face— anytime she came to something that they disagreed on in history and she would say, "Now Dr. Carroll doesn't agree with this," and he would interject, "*No, I don't!*" They didn't disagree about much.
>
> Anytime she got to Gettysburg, he would get really excited because of Joshua Chamberlain. "Those good ole

Maine boys!" He was very proud of Chamberlain and Maine.[51]

Kieran and Warren developed a special friendship over the next number of years, due in large part, speculates Kieran, to the fact that he had read Whittaker Chambers' *Witness* on Warren's recommendation. "He was a crotchety old man sitting in Mrs. Carroll's class, and I wasn't afraid to go talk to him," Kieran says:

> When I was a senior, . . . I had some good schools that I had gotten into and that I had scholarships for. And I was trying to decide which one I was going to go to. He [Warren] was sitting in one of those old blue chairs that they put in the lobby for him, and I got the other one and pulled it up. I said, "Dr. Carroll, I gotta make a choice." And he said, "mmmnnnggg, rrruuuuurrrr . . ." and I said, "Well I have all these offers from colleges ,and I gotta decide which one to go to." He said, "Well, which one is Christendom!" And I said, "I didn't apply there." And he looked at me and said, "What's important?" I didn't answer. He said, "Go to Christendom." I literally went to Christendom because Dr. Carroll told me to! I got a wife and three kids out of the deal. When I told him I was marrying a girl from Christendom, he was so happy. That's half the reason he founded the school! For all the Catholic marriages.[52]

Another Seton student who developed a special and close relationship with Warren in his later years was Eileen Bartolozzi:

> I started Seton in 2001 and graduated in 2007. I was a fairly precocious student and asked a lot of questions. The

---

51. Kieran DuFrain, interview by author, 6 February 2016.
52. Ibid.

only time in my Seton career when I was totally speech-
less was with Dr. Carroll. He would sit in on the classes,
yelling out, "QUESTION ON THE RIGHT! QUESTION ON
THE LEFT!" [his way of letting Anne know someone had
a question]. And by my junior or senior year, I was on my
eight or nine millionth question, and all of a sudden I hear,
"QUESTION FROM EILEEN!" And I didn't know what to
say. He had called me *by name!* I knew I had asked too
many questions.

Then I went off to William and Mary for college.
But I was home for a Seton basketball game (my brother
was playing), and I was having a really hard time at
school, so I went to the chapel to pray and to think about
what God wanted from me. What does He expect from
me and how am I supposed to maneuver in this big bad
world where all these people want to tell me I'm wrong,
that my faith is wrong, and that I'm foolish? And I had
trouble seeing value in my life at that point. I was just
floundering around. Dr. Carroll just happened to be in
the chapel when I was there, and for whatever reason, I
felt compelled to talk to him. He was obviously near the
end of his life and a little forgetful, a little stodgy, a little
curmudgeonly. But I felt totally compelled to talk to him
and I thought, "Oh my gosh, I'm interrupting him while
he's praying in the chapel—this is so obnoxious!" But
I came up and whispered, "Um, hi, Dr. Carroll. I don't
know if you remember me, but I'm Eileen Bartolozzi."
And he shouts, "YOU'RE EILEEN BARTOLOZZI!" And I
[said], "*Oh!* You *do* remember me." And we proceeded to
talk for the next hour or hour and a half.

We had one of the most profound conversations of
my life. I don't remember the details. He shared his story,
where he grew up, his leaving faith in general, his pursuit
of academia as king. Different times in his life, he shared
that he was suicidal because that was something that I
was thinking about. And we had this conversation about

what it is like in an irreligious academic setting, how faith translates to more than [what we learn as young children]. I think sometimes at Seton, you're in an environment that is so rigorously and assertively Catholic—which is great. But at the same time, sometimes when you're a kid, you think you're checking boxes. "O.K., I said the Rosary, check." But it's a little bit less about your relationship with Christ sometimes, and [you do it] because this is just what we do. And then what happens when you leave that? Then you ask, well, why *do* you go to Mass?—and things like that. Of course we had all of the knowledge from Mrs. Carroll and all of the arguments for the faith, but . . . then we need to cultivate that relationship with Christ. So he and I talked about that . . . and we talked about a million things!

From that time on, every time I was home from college, I would just go see him. We'd hang out and just chat. My mom would bring dinner to the Carrolls on Tuesdays, and she would tell him about my life away at school.

He was just really a great sounding board. And sometimes the conversations were just totally non-sensical, admittedly, I don't think he was always totally with it when we were talking.

He became this important grandfatherly figure to me. He always tried to get me to transfer to Christendom College, of course. That was one of our regular conversations, and I would say, "Dr. Carroll, I'm not going to Christendom. I appreciate it, but I'm doing well where I am."[53]

Both of these stories illustrate quite well Warren's character in his old age. Under a gruff exterior there was such a tender heart; but it took some courage and some patience to find it. "The kids at Seton in those days got to know a different side of him," muses Anne. "Not the

---

53. Eileen Bartolozzi, interview by author, 25 September 2016.

intellectual side, but the human side."[54] And because they knew him, not as an intellectual giant, but as an elderly, suffering man who didn't hesitate to bop them with his cane as he attempted to clear a path for himself through a very crowded hallway, they could interact naturally with him in such ways as singing "Make Way for Prince Ali" as he navigated his way through the school.[55]

Another person who came to know the Carrolls quite well and was invaluable in Warren's last years was Ruth McCaa. Living across the street from them and two doors down from the school, Ruth, who had done substitute teaching in the public school system, began tutoring Seton students in 2002. One day, shortly after she began working with Seton students and having some questions regarding curriculum, she walked across the street to consult Mrs. Carroll:

> Dr. Carroll couldn't get up to answer the door. I think that was very frustrating for him. And I knocked on the door, and he yelled out, "*Who is it? Who* is at the door!" And the windows were open, and he had this very gruff voice and was kind of loud. So I sort of said through the window, "I was looking for Mrs. Carroll." And he said "Well she's *not here*—she's *at the school! Why* do you people have to bother us!" Clearly he was stressed. I was sobbing and disturbed and thought, "Oh, what have I done!" But it was not long after that that I found out what a dearly affectionate man he is, and he had his moments that were difficult for him. Clearly, if he could have come to the door, he would have, and he was struggling to get to the door but wasn't able to. And the frustration that that must have involved. That scared me, and I didn't go back anytime soon. But after a while, I got to know him at the school itself and got to interact with him and understand his illness and how it affected him and what he was dealing with. He's a very courageous man, very courageous. And loyal to a tee.

---

54. Anne Carroll, interview with author.
55. "Make Way for Prince Ali" is the title of a song from the Disney movie *Aladdin*.

My goodness, once he knew me, there was nothing he wouldn't have done. He introduced me to Tim O'Donnell as his "good friend, Mrs. McCaa, who is Scottish." And they got into the Scottish people and the Irish people. He was always so gracious towards me.

I got to know him mostly through the school because he went to Anne's classes and would sit in on them. Not very long into my tutoring, I started going to Mrs. Carroll's summer-school classes—she taught almost everything, so I went to learn more about the classes and the curriculum. I said, "I'll pay—as a student, [if you will] let me sit in on your classes." Then I made a deal with her. I said, "I love sitting in on your classes, I so enjoy them, if you are ever sick and can't go to class, I will substitute for you for free." She never missed teaching, but she called on me later on when Dr. Carroll was ill and she was visiting him. I also went to her classes during the school year, so I got to know Dr. Carroll from sitting in class with him, and also in the teachers' lounge afterwards. We would sit and chat there. During class, . . . she would be lecturing, and he would sit in the front of the room, and if a student would raise his hand and she didn't notice him, he would say, "Question on the right!" And I would be mortified when he said, "Mrs. McCaa has a question!" I would try to only raise my hand if another student didn't understand either. He wanted to get to my questions because I think he knew my questions might be more complicated, especially in apologetics or religion classes, [so he would shout out], "*Mrs. McCaa has a question!*"[56]

In July of 2006, Warren suffered a further blow to his health. Anne came home from teaching a summer-school class to find Warren complaining that he felt pressure on his chest. Not knowing what exactly

---

56. Ruth McCaa, interview by author, 18 January 2016.

to do, she called the doctor, who advised her to "keep an eye on it." A friend came over with Mexican food and poured Warren a glass of wine to help him feel better. Still feeling poorly, however, he got up to go lie down—but just collapsed on the bed, whereupon Anne phoned 911. "He was unconscious," remembers Anne, "but he came back to consciousness when the EMTs came and demanded, 'Am I going to have to wait a long time in the emergency room?'" He was taken to the emergency room and airlifted the next morning to the cardiovascular unit at Inova Hospital, where it was confirmed that he had had a heart attack. Stents were put in owing to multiple blood clots.[57]

God was not quite ready yet to call him home, though, and by the start of the school year, he was back in his designated chair in Anne's classroom. To accommodate his new level of mobility, Anne moved her classroom to the first floor. "He would still take walks," she says. "He would go down the block—to the funeral home and sit on their porch. Then down to the insurance agency. And when he was feeling pretty good, he'd go around to the Manassas Medical Center and sit on *their* porch. Then he'd come back and say a few Rosaries. He would always tell people, 'You need to walk, you need to walk.'"[58]

And this bent-over, white-headed man with his cane—who slowly paced the few blocks from his wife's classroom to the different businesses, where he sat on their porches and said his Rosaries—was still the determined boy who had replied so long ago, when questioned whether he planned to be a teacher like his father or a writer like his mother, "I intend to do both!" He knew his calling, and refused to relinquish his responsibility to the end. Soon after his retirement, the college had asked him if he would come back and give monthly lectures, which he heartily agreed to do. "He spent a lot of time working on those lectures," remembers Anne. "They meant a lot to him. They kept him going. He gave about six a year and had them planned 'till about the year 2020. Some he would take from his books, but some

---

57. Anne Carroll, interview by author.
58. Ibid.

were original."[59] Since Anne could not attend most of these lectures because of her rigorous teaching schedule, the college would send a van out to pick him up. He would give his lecture and then have dinner at the college. Christendom student Andrew Bodoh made this van run several times:

> As a 2007 graduate, I was among one of the first classes not to know Dr. Carroll as a professor, but I had the pleasure of driving him between his home and the college for several of his monthly lectures at Christendom. It was always such a pleasure to spend time with him. I remember in particular one conversation. I told him I was writing my thesis on a history of the pro-life movement, and I had read about the early involvement of *Triumph* magazine, even before Roe v. Wade. I asked him about one of the early anti-abortion protests *Triumph* sponsored, one of the first in the nation, and he was so excited I knew about it. "I was there! I was there!" he said as he told me the story. I realized he was a man who knew both the importance of writing history and of making history.[60]

While many of the younger junior-high and high-school students at Seton may not have had the time to discover both the tenderness and brilliance behind the mask of old age, the students at Christendom certainly did:

> I never had Dr. Carroll as a professor, but I still had him as a teacher. My junior year saw Dr. Carroll's return to campus to give monthly lectures. I sat in the overcrowded Chapel Crypt with what seemed like most of campus, absorbing like sponges Dr. Carroll's account of Malta and its staunch defense against attackers, be they Turks or Na-

---

59. Ibid.
60. Andrew Bodoh, alumni tributes, 2011, on file at Christendom College.

zis. He mentioned how he had hoped to write a history of Malta, even in his youth, but he never had a chance. He mentioned that he still wanted to write it, but that he was getting old and was unsure if he would be able to write the volume. He then charged the history majors in the room to do what he might not have time left to do. It was a jarring thought, a world without Dr. Carroll. I had just begun to know him, barely, in reading his works for school. I would know him a little better over the next year, but nowhere near the intimacy that others could claim. At the same time, Dr. Carroll made you feel like you were important, that he knew you well. This was all in the first moment of meeting him.

One of the features of Dr. Carroll's lectures was his attendance at dinner immediately following the talk. He would sit at a table near the entrance and students would come and talk with him. Some would sit with him, conversing on anything. He would linger and talk and sign books when he was finished eating. His reaction to signing books wasn't an irritated "Who-do-I-make-this-out-to?" attitude. He would ask the person if they had read the book, did they like it, etc. He livened up when he signed his favorite book (*The Guillotine and the Cross*) and even made a sort of joke when I asked him to sign a copy of *Seventy Years of the Communist Revolution* (the commie rev book that was outdated). "You do know this is out of date," he said, smiling a little.[61]

Ruth often attended these lectures. "I saw him one day where he had fallen in the road," She says:

He should not have gone, and yet he went that night to give that lecture. I was really concerned, but nothing was going to stop him. . . . He would insist on standing—al-

---

61. Matthew Rose, alumni tributes, 2011.

ways very professional. Neither did he try to sugarcoat anything—he was very clear minded in analyzing things according to the truth. The humility that was involved in that. The importance of the job he was doing was his focus. The fact that he couldn't maybe speak as clearly, or look great—at the end, none of that stopped him from trying to give his lectures or read the Easter Proclamation. There were many examples where he would overlook his limitations and go on despite them.[62]

And his writing? Volume five of his *History of Christendom*, entitled *The Revolution Against Christendom*, was published in 2005. And he was working on volume six. Says Anne, "His mind wasn't as well-organized. He would write a chapter, and it wouldn't be chronological, and he'd have to rewrite some things. So he couldn't think as clearly, but there were still flashes of brilliance in it. You can't turn that off—strokes or no strokes."[63]

Two stories attest to the razor-sharp memory which Warren possessed even into his later years. The first is related by Anne's brother Pete. "One time I was reading a poem, and it had the word 'Ouse' in it, and Warren was sitting in his chair. He had already had one of his strokes. And I said, 'Ouse, do you know what that is?' I looked at my sister, 'Do you think it is a misprint?' And she said, 'It has to be.' And Warren looked over and said, 'Ouse is a river in England.' And I said, 'How do you *know* that!' 'I read it once,' he said."[64]

The second story is from Sharon Hickson, a professor at Christendom, and shows that it was not just historical and geographical facts which were imprinted on the index cards of Warren's rolodex mind:

> One evening he came over to our house for dinner, and we were talking about historical, Catholic stuff as usual.

---

62. Ruth McCaa, interview by author.

63. Anne Carroll, interview by author.

64. Pete Westhoff, interview by author.

And somehow something came up about sports. And he wound up telling us how much he loved baseball. It was very moving. All through high school he was the water boy, and finally during the last game, they let him play. But then it came out that he was a fanatic Boston Red Sox fan. And so am I. My uncle was a manager for them, and my dad knew a lot of the players. So Warren starts reeling off these statistics of the games, and he knew the bottom of the fourth inning played in which world series and who did what, and he knew every single player of every single Red Sox team, especially during the championships, and he could describe particular plays! And we thought, "Wow, this is Warren Carroll!"[65]

Although his health continued to deteriorate, Warren's enthusiasm for life was still strong. He was planning a trip to New Zealand for the summer of 2011! But at the same time, he might have had an idea that his time on earth was running out. He had written in his notebook, where he kept track of the lectures he was giving at the college, that he wanted "The Watchwords of Christendom College—Truth Exists, the Incarnation Happened" to be his last lecture. Originally scheduled for the fall of 2010, he moved it up, for some reason, to April. With that lecture behind him, he had scheduled a lecture on Christopher Columbus for October 24. But he never delivered it. The day before he was scheduled to make the hour-long trip to the college, he suffered his second major stroke, the main effect of which was to deprive him of most of his ability to speak.[66] Anne describes the immediate aftermath:

He was in the hospital and then in rehabilitation, and he hated every minute of it. Everybody talked me out of

---

65. Sharon Hickson, interview by author.

66. He had delivered a lecture on the Portuguese Age of Exploration in September, so the April lecture on the watchwords of the college turned out to be his penultimate lecture. Anne delivered his prepared lecture on Columbus in November of 2011 *in memoriam.*

spending the nights there. So I agreed, but with hindsight, I wish I hadn't agreed. I think that's what God wanted me to do, but it was hard. Every night I had to wait until he went to sleep—otherwise he wouldn't let me go. He would wake up in the middle of the night and start calling for me. I came back in the mornings, and I tried to come during my free period, and then I came after school. I did nothing else. I was either in church, at the school, with Warren, or in my bed sleeping. He gave the rehab people lots of trouble. He hated being away from me and from home.[67]

Thankfully, Anne was not alone in shoring up Warren's spirits during this time. Among his visitors were Tim and Cathy O'Donnell, Kieran DuFrain, and Ruth McCaa, who, each in their own way, brought a drink of cool water to relieve the heat of Warren's final battle. "When he first got ill," says Cathy, "I was pregnant with my youngest."

But it meant the world to him for us to visit. When we would see him after the stroke, when he couldn't speak anymore, it was so, so difficult. The thought that this man, for whom words were everything and who enjoyed conversation so much, couldn't even talk. He would try to talk and couldn't get his meaning across, and he was so frustrated. But he could pray, he could say the Hail Mary. Tim would come and play Irish songs for him, and he could sing along with some of the verses.[68]

Tim agrees:

The music was his gift to me—that I could actually play music, and he would enjoy it. But I made him laugh when he couldn't really speak at all, and I said, "Warren, you're ful-

---

67. Anne Carroll, interview by author.
68. Cathy O'Donnell, interview by author.

filling the Gospel mandate—let your yes be yes and your
no be no and everything else is from the devil." And he just
went "AAAAARRRRR" [chuckling in the Warren Carroll
way]. Because he could say, "No, no, no," or "Yes, yes, yes."[69]

Kieran, who was by then a graduate from Christendom and teaching at Seton School, read to Warren while he lay there in his hospital
bed. He read one of Warren's favorite books, *The Ballad of the White Horse*
by G. K. Chesterton—the story of King Alfred's heroic battle against
the Danes in 878. "We got through the entire book," Kieran delightedly
declares. He also thinks that some of Warren's favorite lines probably
carried great meaning for him at that particular time in his life:

> There is a line in there, I think from book two. Albert has
> a vision of Our Lady, and she's telling him that he's going
> to win. But she says he still needs to fight. And the line is:
> "I tell you naught for your comfort, / Yea, naught for your
> desire, / Save that the sky grows darker yet / And the sea
> rises higher. / Night shall be thrice night over you, / And
> heaven an iron cope. / Do you have joy without a cause, /
> Yea, faith without a hope?"[70] And that sums up everything
> he did.[71]

Ruth visited often over that seven-week period and remembers
some of Warren's funnier moments:

> When he couldn't speak in the hospital bed, he wanted us
> to pray for this person, and we couldn't figure out who it
> was. We went through the alphabet but still couldn't fig-
> ure it out. He would say, "My good friend," and we would
> get that part but not the name. So Anne went through the

---

69. Timothy O'Donnell, interview by author.
70. These lines are in Book I, 254–261.
71. Kieran DuFrain, interview by author.

list of all his friends. As it turns out, it was Christopher Columbus! He had written about him and had such an admiration for him.[72]

Warren was released on December 17, and settled back into his daily routine. "He came back and was sitting in his chair in my classroom," says Anne:

> I was giving a lecture on a presidential election and I said, "This election was in 1898," and he shouts, "1896!" And of course he was right. So he couldn't always talk, but he could say some things. This was a purification for him, and he knew it. When Brendan McGuire [a young history professor at Christendom] came down with cancer, Warren said he would offer his sufferings for Brendan. We couldn't go anywhere then. I had to cancel the reservations to New Zealand. He could talk a little bit. He could say things that he knew by memory, like his prayers. He could read a little bit—he'd get tired after a while. But he often could not get his thoughts out into words. Usually, he could say enough that after a while, I could figure it out. But it was frustrating—it was painful for him. He wanted to finish his book. He'd say, "*Chapters!*" and that meant we went to the computer, we'd call up a chapter, and we'd work on it.[73]

The last months of Warren's life are best told in the small vignettes pulled from the memory of friend and neighbor Ruth McCaa, who became invaluable to the Carrolls—a blessing for both them and herself. What follows is an unedited account, in her words, of his last months:

---

72. Ruth McCaa, interview by author.
73. Anne Carroll, interview by author.

So I also went out with Dr. Carroll to St. Patrick's Day celebrations at Christendom College. He always read the Easter Proclamation. That was another sad thing. The third year I went, he still wanted to go, but he couldn't read it any longer. It was so difficult for him. He was so gracious and said what a great job the other fellow did—I don't remember who read it. It was hard for him to sit up. I was in charge of searching for a pillow. I think this was the last St. Patrick's day before he died.

Sometimes with Mrs. Carroll and sometimes without her, we would go to the Catholic culture talks.[74] Often they had speakers that Warren was interested in. I would see them online and say, "Why don't we go to this or that one?" Sometimes Anne could come but often she had grading to do so Catherine Craig and I would load him up in the car and take him. He always loved those things. Even the book club—he just loved it![75] Anne would have to leave to grade papers and he would say, "Well, I will be the last person to leave!"

And he was always such a wealth of knowledge. Even towards the end, when you would think that he was not consciously aware of the lecture that Anne was giving, he would always bring a book. The man never went anywhere without a book in his hand. I was wondering, "How can he be reading—he can't even hold the book!" Even when I knew that his cognitive skills were declining, it didn't matter. The comfort of holding the book—just holding it! And he knew the stories—he didn't have to read them—he had them memorized

He never wanted to be out of [Anne's] sight. To see the two of them together was just a testimony to what a Catholic marriage should be. Towards the end, he would

---

74. The Institute of Catholic Culture.

75. Ruth began a small book club at her home to read Dr. Carroll's smaller books. He participated, reading selections from his own books. "Even *he* would tear up at these readings," reports Ruth.

be there in class and his feet would start to hurt—I guess lack of circulation or something, but they would ache. And he would moan. And she would stop the lecture, lift his feet, take his shoes off, massage them a little bit, put his shoes back on, right in the middle of class. The kids were amazed. It was a wonderful thing to see.

When he was in the wheelchair, they hired someone to push him to the school in the chair. And the helper would say, "Let's go to the teachers' lounge and get you some lunch." And I would go with him and help. I would fix his tea—it had to be just right—not too hot, not too cold. He would want to eat that lunch so quickly so he could get back into the classroom with Anne. The whole idea was to give her a class where she wouldn't have to be worried about what he was doing and give him a little break. But he would fuss so much at the man. He would be saying, "Now, Dr. Carroll, your wife is a lovely woman, she just needs some time, we're not going to bother her." And he would reply, "No, no, no," he was just so agitated and just wanted to be with her. When he really wanted to be understood, you could see the tremendous effort [it took] for him to get something out. So I would go back into the classroom and tell Anne, "You know he doesn't want to stay in the teachers' lounge—he just wants to be back in here." She looked at me and said, "Well, he's in charge." And that was their marriage. What he wants to do is what we do. This was the last year or so.

He knew that she was struggling—she injured her back, probably from getting him in and out of bed, and getting him dressed, and in and out of chairs—God knows how she did that. It took three or four nurses to do what she was doing—bathing him, dressing him . . . So when she hurt her back, we decided they needed a new mattress because it was old and yucky. I was shopping around to get a good price, and he was struggling to say things, but he managed to get out, "Money is no object." He was worried about her back. Another time he was worried that she didn't have this pillow behind her back in the car. He was fussing, and we couldn't figure out why. But it was, "Where is her pillow?" When it was vitally important to him he could get things out. Her health and comfort were very important to him.

When he would have a bad night, sometimes the next day Anne would be completely exhausted. But she would give her lectures and do a great job. And I would be wheeling him back home for a nap or something, and he would look at me and say, "Isn't she magnificent! Especially since she didn't get to sleep at all last night because I was awake." He recognized the sacrifice involved there. I told her that after he died, and I think it meant a lot to her. We were anxious for her as well. It was physically and emotionally taxing on her.

He would go to daily Mass until he was falling over. Sometimes I would sit behind them on purpose because he would start to fall, and I could push him back up. Anne would be praying and didn't notice all the time. Then Anne would go, and I would stay with him.

He died in July 2011, but he went to her summer-school classes that summer right up until he died. He was still going to daily Mass at the beginning of the summer. Other people would sit with him during the day if I had something I had to do. We would still wheel him to the classroom until he couldn't [go] anymore. At that point it was a quandary. Anne decided to hold her summer-school classes in her living room. He would sit in this chair—a lift chair. The students would all be in chairs in their tiny living room. Then he would get too uncomfortable. He was always uncomfortable at this point. He would want to go to the bed to rest—but he didn't want to leave her. He needed water all the time. I had once given him seltzer water and he liked it, so that was his new thing. When he was in the bedroom and he wanted Anne to come in, he would call for water. He did need water, but he didn't need it every five minutes! So we would hear from the bedroom, "Seltzer water, seltzer water!" He knew this was a way to get her into the room. So I said to Anne, "I'll bring in the water and maybe when he sees that it isn't getting you in the room, he'll stop calling." So I did, and it worked, but then when he saw that calling for water wasn't going to work, he said he wasn't tired anymore and wanted to get back into his chair! Finally, when he couldn't stay in his chair, she would pull her chair into the hallway and teach from the hallway. Even when I watched him when she went to morning Mass—within minutes he was calling for her. "Anne, Anne, where is she?" He would continually ask for the time, even though she had only left a few minutes ago. Sometimes he was happier when twenty minutes had passed, and she was closer to coming home.

The day before he died, or no more than two days before, I had gone to the farmers' market and they had fresh peaches there. And I bought one for him and he was very pleased.[76]

July 6, 2011, was Warren and Anne's forty-fourth wedding anniversary. Beginning on their first anniversary, when they had dined at a Chinese restaurant, they had celebrated every subsequent anniversary by finding a different place to eat, often one serving a particular ethnic cuisine. This year, however, they had not planned a restaurant, which was providential because that evening, Warren began to shake uncontrollably. Anne called 911 and Warren was taken to the hospital where he was put in intensive care. Since the doctors really didn't know what was wrong with him and he was hungry, they allowed him to have a turkey sandwich. "So that was our forty-fourth anniversary dinner," says Anne. After twelve nights spent in the hospital, shuffled back and forth between a regular hospital room and the intensive care

---

76. Ruth McCaa, interview by author.

unit, Warren went home. The doctors still had no explanation for the episodes of shaking.[77] Extremely weak, he had to be taken home in an ambulance because he did not have the strength even to get into Anne's car.

The next day, a Sunday, was July 17. Anne returned from Mass to find Warren coughing badly, needing to clear his throat. "Can't you clear your throat?" she asked, and he replied, "No."

> Then it got quiet and I thought, "Oh, good, he's asleep," because he had had a terrible night. He hadn't slept. I thought, "Thank you, God." So I fell asleep. I woke up and he was still, I thought, asleep. The phone rang, so I answered it, and after that I fell asleep again. When I woke up, he was still asleep, and I thought, "Something isn't right." I didn't know what to do. I wasn't thinking clearly. I called Ruth and asked her to come over. She said, "He doesn't look so good." So we called 911. They got here, but said he had been dead for about two hours already. People can't believe that I didn't realize he was dead. But I didn't, or maybe I didn't want to believe it.
>
> His heart just stopped beating. I think his heart just gave out. He had a pacemaker. Fortunately Ruth was there to hold my hand. Pretty soon, lots of people started coming—it had gotten out on Facebook. I called Pete and Tim. Susie Jackson, who had just graduated, worked for the rescue squad and she was at All Saints. She looked at her beeper and saw the address and so she started sending out the word. Pretty soon all sorts of people were here.
>
> It was a pretty peaceful death. It was God's providence that I was asleep because if I had been awake, I would have called 911. But God didn't want him revived. He wanted him to die peacefully, not with them pounding

---

77. A second episode had occurred after the sixth day, when he was being sent home. As they were checking out, Warren began shaking again and became very disoriented, so they put him back in intensive care.

on his chest and doing all this other stuff. And I would have felt I had to. And I think God was being merciful to both of us. I'm not sorry that it happened the way it did.

And thinking about it afterward, after something has happened—you've been taking care of somebody and each day is just "each day." You've lived through that day. But after it's over and you look back, you realize how much he suffered. And so I realized it was time for him to go. God said, "You've done your job on earth. It's time to go." I miss him more than any words could ever say, but it was God's will.[78]

---

78. Anne Carroll, interview with author.

Epilogue

The twentieth century was accursed, with more martyr-
doms than any other, shrouded by its rejection of truth. It
was the century of my birth, and my mission was to overcome it and to help Christ save souls through my teaching
and writing. . . . When death comes for me, I will be able to
present to my Lord a life of service and triumph in fealty
to Him. Above all, I will be able to give Him Christendom
College and all its graduates, and all those they reach and
influence.[1]

–Dr. Warren H. Carroll

THE DEEP NIGHT'S BLACK darkness of July 26, 2011, lightened to a
pale gray; the sun yawned and stretched from its bed below the horizon and began slowly sneaking towards the tops of the trees lining
a horseshoe-shaped curve of the beautiful and placid Shenandoah
River; a cloudless day had dawned. Approximately an hour east of
this tranquil awakening, the body of a man began its journey through
the rites and ceremonies which forge a Catholic funeral. People from
all over poured into All Saints' Catholic Church in Manassas. Father
Bob Cilinski gave a homily in which he remembered Dr. Warren
Carroll as "a man on a mission with a message of hope." Delivering

---

1. Carroll, *A History of Christendom*, vol. 6, *The Crisis of Christendom*, 810.

the eulogy, Warren's best friend, Tim O'Donnell, recounted:

> Answering the question, "Why did God want Chris-
> tendom College to grow and flourish?" Dr. Carroll re-
> sponded, "Because Christendom is educating young men
> and women who will bring what our great and holy Pope
> John Paul II calls 'the new springtime of the church.'" And
> he continued, "In the face of scandals and despair, believe
> in that springtime! It's coming—and nothing can stop it!
> For proof, look at our history. Our graduates will be lead-
> ing the new springtime!"

Warren had made his last demand for "seltzer water!" rested his
eyes for the last time on his cherished Anne, and filled his lungs with
their last draught of oxygen on July 17—the Feast of the Carmelite
Martyrs of Compiègne. And we will take the time here—to sit by his
feet and, in the spirit of his great, great, great Uncle Columby, listen to
him yarn one last time. In his book *The Guillotine and the Cross*, Warren
describes the final hours of this community of Carmelite nuns as they
made their own journey to death, condemned by the atheistic horror
that was the French Revolution:

> On July 17, the sixteen sisters were brought before Fou-
> quier-Tinville. All cases were now being disposed of
> within twenty-four hours as Robespierre had wished;
> theirs was no exception. They were charged with hav-
> ing received arms for the émigrés; their prioress, Sister
> Teresa, answered by holding up a crucifix. "Here are the
> only arms that we have ever had in our house." They were
> charged with possessing an altar-cloth with designs hon-
> oring the old monarchy (perhaps the fleur-de-lis) and
> were asked to deny any attachment to the royal family. Sis-
> ter Teresa responded: "If that is a crime, we are all guilty
> of it; you can never tear out of our hearts the attachment
> for Louis XVI and his family. Your laws cannot prohibit

feeling; they cannot extend their empire to the affections of the soul; God alone has the right to judge them." They were charged with corresponding with priests forced to leave the country because they would not take the constitutional oath; they freely admitted this. Finally they were charged with the catchall indictment by which any serious Catholic in France could be guillotined during the Terror: "fanaticism." Sister Henriette, who had been Gabrielle de Croissy, challenged Fouquier-Tinville to his face: "Citizen, it is your duty to respond to the request of one condemned; I call upon you to answer us and to tell us just what you mean by the word 'fanatic.'" "I mean," snapped the public prosecutor of the Terror, "your attachment to your childish beliefs and your silly religious practices." "Let us rejoice, my dear Mother and Sisters, in the joy of the Lord," said Sister Henriette, "that we shall die for our holy religion, our faith, our confidence in the Holy Roman Catholic Church.

That same day they went to the guillotine. The journey in the carts took more than an hour. All the way the Carmelite sisters sang—the "Miserere," "Salve Regina," and "Te Deum." Beholding them, a total silence fell on the raucous, brutal crowd, most of them cheapened and hardened by day after day of the spectacle of public slaughter. At the foot of the towering killing machine, their eyes raised to Heaven, the sisters sang "Veni Creator Spiritus." One by one, they renewed their religious vows. They pardoned their executioners. One observer cried out: "Look at them and see if they do not have the air of angels! By my faith, if these women did not all go straight to Paradise, then no one is there!"

Sister Teresa, their prioress, requested and obtained permission to go last under the knife. The youngest, Sister Constance, went first. She climbed the steps of the guillotine "with the air of a queen going to receive her crown," singing "Laudate Dominum omnes gentes:" "all peoples praise the Lord." She placed her head in the position for death without allowing the executioner to touch her. Each sister followed her example, those remaining singing likewise with each, until only the prioress was left, holding in her hand a small figure of the Blessed Virgin Mary. The killing of each martyr required about two minutes. It was about eight o'clock in the evening, still bright at midsummer. During the whole time the profound silence of the crowd about the guillotine endured unbroken.

Two years before when the horror began, the Carmelite community at Compiègne had offered itself as a holocaust, that peace might be restored to France and the church. The return of full peace was still twenty-one years in the future. But the Reign of Terror had only ten days left to run. Years of war, oppression, and persecution were yet to come, but the mass official killing in the public squares of Paris was about to end. The Cross had vanquished the guillotine.[2]

My friends—we too are members of a community; the Christendom community. You may be a former student, parent of a student, professor, nephew of a professor, or the neighbor of a cousin of someone whose daughter is considering attending the school when she turns eighteen in seven years. You are reading this book for a reason. Whatever your attachment to the Christendom community is or isn't, you can be a part of the new springtime of the church and, therefore, a part of Dr. Carroll's vision. However, as we have just finished reading, this new springtime may require a period of offering in order to be implemented. It may involve an offering of your life—or mine. It is possible that this period has already passed. Dr. Carroll's remarks at the head of this epilogue state that such a period has occurred. Is it over? We do not know. But if there is anything that we can learn from the life of Dr. Warren Hasty Carroll, it is that anyone's life can

---

2. Warren H. Carroll, *The Guillotine and the Cross* (Manassas, VA: Trinity Communications, 1986), 178–179.

and does make a difference. Your life makes a difference. Dr. Carroll's vision was very much an apostolic vision with himself as the dad, and we, his children and grandchildren, employing our own particular gifts in our own particular life circumstances to expand that vision, which itself is part of the larger vision of the Catholic Church.[3] What is that larger vision? Holiness.

One of Dr. Carroll's most beloved heroes, Pope St. John Paul the Great, spoke often of the universal call to holiness and connected it with the new springtime in the church. The response that is needed is an openness to the action of the Holy Spirit. Dr. Carroll had this openness and allowed the Holy Spirit to direct his life. In God's providence, this direction for Dr. Carroll involved the gargantuan task of starting a college! Pope St. John Paul called his work "great." We too can hear this word bestowed upon our own lives if we do what he did. Are we called to found colleges? Maybe—but most likely not. What we are called to do is to become saints in whatever way is meant for us as individuals. For St. John Paul II used that same word—great—when he wrote in his poem *Material*: "The greatness of work is *inside* man."[4] (the emphasis is my own). This great work that we can and must do is *inside* of us—in the realm of being—and its name is holiness.

"Dare to be great!" is a challenge from Christendom to its students. I think that this is an attitude that people felt in the presence of Dr. Carroll. He was *daring* us to become holy in whatever way God was calling us. I wonder if he thought of the road to holiness that his heroes trod as he fought his own battles in his final years—as he fought the battle for patience and resignation when he, a great lover of words, could utter only a few disjointed phrases; as he fought the battle of self-surrender when things did not go as he had desired in the

---

3. Although Warren and Anne had no biological children of their own, Warren leaves behind him an entire legacy of people who consider themselves his "children." These children now have their own children and so it continues. On February 10, 2011, however, Warren acquired a namesake when Kieran DuFrain and his wife Lauren gave their first son the name of Warren in Dr. Carroll's honor.

4. Pope John Paul II, *The Place Within: The Poetry of Pope John Paul II*, ed. Jerzy Peterkiewicz (New York, NY: Random House, 1979), 63.

establishment of the college; as he fought the battle of humility and love when he felt betrayed by those he trusted. Did he recall the physical deeds of his great heroes and internalize them as spiritual battles and deeds? We would like to think that he did.

In June of 1988, Warren had written to his mother, "We finally saw Covadonga where Pelayo made his great stand."[5] Pelayo's "great stand" launched a 770-year war which would eventually return Spain to its Catholic heritage, that same heritage in which Warren had immersed himself so enthusiastically during his time at El Escorial. Christendom College is itself Warren's "great stand," by which he flung down his gauntlet, facing the extensive rot in higher education head on and refusing to give up on America's young people. Will it take 770 years to accomplish its mission? Let's hope not. But as we each try our best in whatever way is laid out for us to fight the good fight, let us keep Dr. Carroll's pronouncement on the epic war, launched by Pelayo's refusal to give up the fight, in our minds and hearts:

> Regain the land—yes, all the land! The goal of the Reconquest!
> That was Alfonso's goal for them, his great campaign a test
> That showed it someday could be done, if they kept the quest
> Before their eyes for always, and kept the foe hard pressed.[6]

Dr. Timothy O'Donnell came to the end of his eulogy:

> Thank you, Warren, for the gift of your friendship, for your witness to the faith, your tender love for Anne. Thank you for your vision, your tenacity of purpose, your

---

5. Warren Carroll to Gladys Carroll, 17 June 1988, Box 7-B2, Folder 6, Archive Collection, Caroline Jones.

6. Carroll, *A History of Christendom*, vol. 6, *The Crisis of Christendom*, 840–841

love of the good. And for all those whose lives you have touched and inspired through your teaching, your works, the founding of Christendom College, and your staunch unwavering loyalty to the Apostolic See and the person of the Holy Father.

The crowd of funeral-goers made their way back to their cars, driving the hour west to Christendom College where a small plot of ground was prepared to receive the body of its founder. As a final fare-well, Tim's voice rang out a cappella over that horseshoe-shaped curve in the Shenandoah River as the sun smiled down on the little scene unfolding below her warm eyes, to the notes of "Bonnie Charlie:"

Will ye no come back again?
Will ye no come back again?
Better lo'ed ye canna be,
Will ye no come back again?

The spirit of Bonnie Prince Charlie is a spirit shared by Warren. It is a fighting spirit—the spirit of the church militant. Let us go forth from Warren's story, then, in apostolic hope, with courage and deter-mination, to become part of that army of saints he loved and admired so much and thereby to *restore all things in Christ*!

Index

Chronological List of Works

YEAR OF PUBLICATION IS given except for unpublished works:

Mission to the Stars (first space novel; unpublished), 1956

Song of the Morning Stars (unpublished), 1960

First *The Tarrant Chronicles* stories, 1963

Banner in the Sky (unpublished), date unknown

1917: Red Banners, White Mantle, 1981

Our Lady of Guadalupe and the Conquest of Darkness, 1983

A History of Christendom, Vol. I: The Founding of Christendom (begun 1969, resumed 1975), 1985

The Guillotine and the Cross, 1986

A History of Christendom, Vol. II: The Building of Christendom (begun 1982), 1987

Follow the Eagle (unpublished), 1985–1987

Seventy Years of the Communist Revolution (begun 1987), 1989

Isabel of Spain: The Catholic Queen (begun 1989), 1991

A History of Christendom, Vol. III: The Glory of Christendom, 1993

The Rise and Fall of the Communist Revolution, 1995

The Last Crusade, 1996

A History of Christendom, Vol. IV: The Cleaving of Christendom, 2000

The Tarrant Chronicles: The Book of Victor Tarrant, 2002

A History of Christendom, Vol. V: The Revolution against Christendom, 2005

A History of Christendom, Vol. VI: The Crisis of Christendom, 2013
(posthumously)